Atlantic Liners of the Cunard Line

To George and Elise,

Happy Anniversary # 42, 5/31/91
and Bon Voyage, 9/11/91!

Love,

Lisa, Rob, and George

Atlantic Liners of the Cunard Line

From 1884 to the present day

Neil McCart

PSL

Patrick Stephens Limited

To Caroline and Louise, fellow shiplovers.

First published in 1990

British Library Cataloguing in Publication Data

McCart, Neil
   Atlantic liners of the Cunard line from 1884 to the present day.
   1. North Atlantic Ocean. Passenger transport. Shipping. Liners, history
   I. Title
   387.2'432'091631

   ISBN 1-85260-065-9

Front endpaper Lusitania *on her full power trials, 1907.* (University of Liverpool)
Title page Queen Mary *leaves Southampton for the last time.* (F. R. Sherlock)
Rear endpaper Mauretania *in her 1962 green cruising livery.* (E. H. Cole)

Patrick Stephens Limited is part of the Thorsons Publishing Group, Wellingborough, Northamptonshire NN8 2RQ, England.

Printed in Great Britain by Butler & Tanner, Frome, Somerset
Typesetting by MJL Limited, Hitchin, Hertfordshire

10 9 8 7 6 5 4 3 2 1

Patrick Stephens Limited, part of Thorsons, a division of the Collins Publishing Group, has published authoritative, quality books for enthusiasts for more than twenty years. During that time the company has established a reputation as one of the world's leading publishers of books on aviation, maritime, military, model-making, motor cycling, motoring, motor racing, railway and railway modelling subjects. Readers or authors with suggestions for books they would like to see published are invited to write to: The Editorial Director, Patrick Stephens Limited, Thorsons Publishing Group, Wellingborough, Northants, NN8 2RQ.

Contents

Acknowledgements   6
Foreword   8
Introduction   10
1   A History of the Cunard Line   11
2   Umbria and Etruria, 1884   14
3   Campania and Lucania, 1893   22
4   Ivernia and Saxonia, 1900   31
5   Pannonia and Slavonia, 1903   38
6   Carpathia, 1903   42
7   Caronia and Carmania, 1905   46
8   Lusitania, 1907   55
9   Mauretania, 1907   69
10   The 'A' Class of 1911
    Ascania, Ausonia and Albania   86
11   Franconia and Laconia, 1911   89
12   The 'A' Class of 1913-17
    Andania, Alaunia and Aurania   93
13   Aquitania, 1914   97
14   Berengaria, 1920   110
15   Albania, 1921   123
16   Scythia, 1921   125

17   Samaria, 1922   129
18   Laconia, 1922   133
19   Tyrrhenia/Lancastria, 1922   138
20   The 'A' Class of 1922
    Andania, Antonia and Ausonia   144
21   Franconia, 1923   152
22   The 'A' Class of 1925
    Aurania, Alaunia and Ascania   157
23   Carinthia, 1925   165
24   Queen Mary, 1936   169
25   Mauretania, 1939   184
26   Queen Elizabeth, 1940   191
27   Media and Parthia, 1947-48   205
28   Caronia, 1949   208
29   The 1950s Quartet
    Saxonia, Ivernia, Carinthia   214
    and Sylvania
30   Queen Elizabeth 2, 1969   223
Bibliography   235
Index   237

Acknowledgements

The author gratefully acknowledges the help given by the following individuals and organisations in the preparation of this book.

Mr Paul J. Kemp & Dr Conrad Wood, Imperial War Museum

Mr D. Ashby, Naval Historical Library, Ministry of Defence

Major A.E. Van Jaarsveldt, South African Defence Force

Helen Heynes, PR Dept, Cunard Line Ltd

S.C. Bailey, Department of Transport

Mr Michael Cook MA & Mrs Andrea Owen, University of Liverpool

Ho Yuen-tung, Hong Kong Government Information Services

Staff of the University of Baltimore, Steamship Historical Society of America Collection

Staff of the Public Record Office, Kew, London

Staff of the British Newspaper Library, Colindale, London

Roger Beecham and the staff of Cheltenham Reference Library

Richard Kerlin, PR Department and Bill M. Winberg, Archives Administrator, Wrather Port Properties, Long Beach, California

Kathleen Campbell, HMT *Lancastria* Association

Sylvie Gervais, Public Archives of Canada

Rolf Finck, Hapag Lloyd AG, Hamburg, West Germany

James Doyle, Cobh Information Service

R.R. Aspinall, Librarian, PLA & Museum in Docklands Project London

Mr E.H. Cole

Mr J. Keith Byass

Adrian Vicary, Maritime Photo Library

Mr A. Duncan

Mrs L.M. Streeter, Skyfotos Ltd

Mr Monty Beckett, Southampton

Mr Ron Forrest, Wright & Logan, Portsmouth

Mr R.G. Todd, National Maritime Museum

Mr Michael Cassar, Malta

Mr Robert Pabst, Cape Town, South Africa

Judy Young, *South China Morning Post*

Jane Holloway, *Daily Telegraph*

Mr Everett E. Viez, Boynton Beach, Florida, California

Non Morgan, *Financial Times*

Mr James L. Shaw, Oregon, USA

Mr F. Roger Sherlock, Southampton

Mr F. Tom Grover, Brighton

Mr Ralf Witthohn, West Germany

Dr Arnold Kludas, West Germany

Marc Stirrup, Photo Graphic (Inc Stewart Bale)

Mr A.H.E. Townshend, Portsmouth

Mrs J. Dinwoodie, Norwich

Mr L.A. Sklenar, Exeter

John Lindop, Cheshire

Mr Steve R. Ovett, Brighton

F.H. Austin, Peterborough

D.G. Perkins, Crawley, Sussex

Peter Jackson, Chester

G. Strickland, Peterborough

C.E. Collyer, Watford

C.A. Turner, Loughton, Essex

E.A. Chappell, Bracknell, Berks

C.G. Thompson, Dereham, Norfolk

Mr Campbell Finley, Mull, Argyll

C.G. Baker, Gillingham, Kent

Theodore W. Scull, New York, USA

S.B. Harnett, Whitstable, Kent

D.T. Hall, County Archivist, Lancashire County Council

Mr J. Dakres, Preston, Lancashire
Mr Allin Martin, Swindon Village, Cheltenham
Mr Donald A. Reynolds, Portsmouth
D.H.G Lovelock, Southampton
Mr Norman Blundell, Portsmouth
Mrs D. Larkin, Eastleigh, Hampshire
Mr Ivan Morris, Southampton
Mr Wayne Morris, Adelaide, Australia
E. Bowers, Southampton
John Tether, Enfield, Middlesex
Charles Nash, Cobh
Billy Lee, Douglas, Cork
John Farrell, Southampton
Fred J. Dennis, Southampton

Timothy Cadogan, Cork County Library
Mrs P. O'Neill, Cork
Mr Andrew Burns, Records Analyst, British Steel Corporation
Clifford Parsons, World Ship Society
Mr Des Venables, Gwynedd, Wales
Elaine Hart, *Illustrated London News*
Dr I.L. Buxton, University of Newcastle upon Tyne
Derek H. Deere, Marine Publications International Ltd
The Editor, *Navy News*
The Editor, *Southern Evening Echo*
The Editor, *The News*, Portsmouth
Finally, my wife Freda and daughter Caroline for their invaluable help.

Foreword

by Sir Nigel Broackes,
Chairman of Trafalgar House

One hundred and fifty years ago Samuel Cunard's first transatlantic steamship set off from Liverpool bound for Halifax and Boston. Since that ship was the first to operate a transatlantic timetable — with a scheduled time of departure and a scheduled time of arrival — it is also fair to say that the *Britannia* was the very first 'Atlantic liner', not just of Cunard but of any line.

Samuel Cunard had hit on a good idea in what was, in effect, a maritime continuation of the railways. Business — underwritten by the Royal Mail contract — prospered; and as it prospered, competition grew and the number of liners multiplied.

But Cunard was a wise man. He put his emphasis on safety and reliability and let others put the emphasis on speed and novelty. Having made the original innovation, he deliberately held back in the sphere of marble bathrooms, *fin-de-siècle* ballrooms and steam-operated shoe brushes; in those things he followed at a safe distance, only venturing into new developments when competitors had suffered the teething problems.

Such caution and concern for safety paid business dividends. Cunard's record of never having been responsible for the loss of a single passenger — a record which still holds today —

became in those early days a major, if largely unremarked, incentive to travel with the Line.

Over the last century and a half, Cunard has owned and operated over 200 passenger ships, most of them Atlantic liners, and including some of the most famous names. *Mauretania, Aquitania, Queen Mary* and *Queen Elizabeth* are all ships which even now are spoken of with awe and respect.

Cunard liners were, and remain, inseparable from the mainstream of Britain's maritime history: they have played their part in wars, have provided the epitome of glamour in the 'thirties and 'forties, have employed tens of thousands of people and have carried millions of others countless millions of miles.

They still do so. For while Cunard operated the first true Atlantic liner, it now operates the last — the *QE2*, the flagship of the British merchant marine.

The *QE2* came into service in 1969 on a wave of British gloom about her commercial prospects; the contemporary wisdom was that she would lose money throughout whatever career she might have.

The predictions were wrong. And I'm pleased to say that Trafalgar House, which acquired Cunard in 1971, was the prime force in confounding the pessimists. The new vision which we provided wrenched Cunard away from attitudes which sufficed when a transatlantic sea crossing was 'the only way to cross', and pointed the Company towards entirely new marketing strategies based principally on the concept of cruising; and transatlantic crossings, which by the mid-'sixties seemed certain candidates for extinction, have become a prime sector of our business as the *QE2* has been projected — quite rightly — as a destination in her own right.

Indeed, so successful is the *QE2* that two years ago we undertook the biggest re-engining programme in maritime history, by replacing her steam boilers and turbines with diesel-electric motors in order to ensure that she would sail well into the next century! The *QE2* is currently the greatest success story in British shipping — and we intend that she, as the last of the true Atlantic liners, will continue to be so.

Through her, and other vessels in the fleet, Cunard has a bright future. It is no longer a future dependent on shipping as a necessary means of transport, but a future supported by a booming but highly competitive leisure industry. Cunard's continuing commitment to quality and style — with which its name is now synonymous — is as guaranteed to underpin that future against competitors as prudence and caution have underpinned it for the last 150 years.

Introduction

Just over 100 years ago, in 1885, the crack Cunard liners *Umbria* and *Etruria* could carry 1,350 passengers across the Atlantic in one voyage, and such a voyage, barring breakdowns, would have taken seven days. Today three Boeing 747 aircraft carry approximately that number from London to New York in about 6-6½ hours, so the liners are now redundant, except for the leisure industry. However, in the years of the liner's heyday, the Cunard Line led the world with their ships which were household names on both sides of the Atlantic.

Cunard had a safety record second to none, but it suffered wartime tragedies which remain some of the world's most terrible maritime disasters. The *Lusitania* in 1915 is a legend, whereas the sinking of the *Lancastria* in June 1940 is not so well known, even though it is believed that as many as 4,000 people may have lost their lives. Although the name Cunard is synonymous with the Atlantic ferry both in peacetime and wartime, Cunard passenger ships were to be found the world over. In the years before the Second World War the *Franconia* and the *Laconia* were noted for their world cruises, and in their later years even such Atlantic giants as the first *Mauretania*, *Aquitania*, *Queen Mary* and *Queen Elizabeth* also made cruises, with varying degrees of success.

During the two world wars, and indeed in the South African War of 1899-1902, the ships of the Cunard Line served their country with distinction. In the First World War *HMS Carmania* fought a spirited action in the best traditions of the Royal Navy, and the aircraft carrier *HMS Campania*, another ex-Cunarder, laid the foundations for today's Fleet Air Arm. In the Second World War, the contribution of the two *Queens* is legendary and their fast trooping voyages helped to shorten the war in Europe. In more recent times, the *QE2* made her contribution during the Falklands conflict.

The 1960s were painful years for Cunard, with the company slowly coming to terms with air travel. Today the *QE2* is a successful cruise liner, and even her few transatlantic voyages are sold as holidays, but the years of planning and building were difficult and at times it seemed that the ship would become a millstone around the company's neck. Happily this did not happen, and today the *QE2* is the pride of the British Merchant Marine.

This book tells the story of the Atlantic liners large and small which sailed under the Cunard houseflag during the last 100 years, when they reigned supreme on the Atlantic Ocean. It is a salute to the company which, despite intense competition from home and abroad, was the world leader in travel between the Old and New Worlds.

1

A History of the Cunard Line

The first steamship to cross the Atlantic was the *Savannah*, a 320-ton wooden sailing ship fitted with collapsible paddle wheels and an auxiliary engine. She left her home port of Savannah in Georgia on 24 May 1819 and arrived in Liverpool after a voyage of 27 days on 20 June. However, her engine was used for only about 80 hours of the voyage, and for the remainder she was under sail. In spite of this transatlantic crossing being advertised in local newspapers, there were no passengers on board and very little cargo. It seems that the *Savannah* was ahead of her time and little interest was shown in her steam engine. She ended her career as a sailing vessel and was wrecked off Fire Island Light, New York, in 1821.

It was another 14 years before the next steamship crossed the Atlantic, the vessel this time being the Canadian paddle steamer *Royal William* operated by the Quebec & Halifax S N Co, amongst whose shareholders were Samuel Cunard and his two brothers Henry and Joseph. The *Royal William* had been employed on a coastal service out of Quebec, but financial problems had forced her owners to offer the ship for sale. It was decided to sell her in London, and so on 17 August 1833 *Royal William* left Pictou, Nova Scotia, for England. This time there were seven passengers on board, and after an eventful voyage she arrived in London on 12 September, the crossing taking 26 days. These first two steamship voyages across the Atlantic were quite

definitely 'one-off' affairs, but it was soon to become the only way to cross the Atlantic, and would remain so until the early 1950s when air travel began to take over from the ocean grey-hounds.

Samuel Cunard was born in Halifax, Nova Scotia, on 21 November 1787, the son of a German emigrant who had crossed into Canada after the American Declaration of Independence in 1776. By 1838 Samuel and his brothers owned some 40 sailing ships and, when the Admiralty asked for tenders for a North Atlantic mail service, Samuel Cunard was determined to win it. Cunard's tender allowed for fortnightly sailings between Liverpool and Halifax, Nova Scotia, by 300 hp ships, with feeder services to Boston and Quebec. The service was to start on 1 May 1840, just one year after acceptance of the tender. However, Samuel Cunard had one major problem — he had no suitable ships.

In the event, it was 15 May 1840 before the first Cunard steamship, the 648 gross ton *Unicorn* with Samuel Cunard on board, sailed from Liverpool. She arrived in Halifax 17 days later on 1 June, and thereafter took her place in the feeder service to Quebec. It was almost another two months before the *Britannia* inaugurated the North Atlantic mail service from Liverpool on 4 July 1840 (the 64th anniversary of the American Declaration of Independence) *Britannia* arrived in Halifax 11 days later, and on 19 July she arrived in Boston to a tremendous welcome.

The full title of the owning company, which was incorporated in 1839, was the British and North American Steam Packet Company — quite a mouthful — but fortunately it very soon became known as the Cunard Line.

For the next six years the Cunard Line had a monopoly of the transatlantic steamship service, but in 1845, with the passing of an Act in Congress, the American Ocean Steam Navigation Company's ship *Washington* inaugurated a New York–Southampton–Bremen service carrying the US mails. Although this company did not last long, it heralded the emergence of some fierce competition for the biggest and fastest ships on the route. To counter this competition Cunard offered a weekly service across the Atlantic during the summer months and a fortnightly service in the winter. However, the most important development was the transfer from Halifax to New York as the major terminal port in the New World.

By 1852 another American company, the Collins Line, was running four vessels on the North Atlantic, all of which were superior to anything Cunard owned, and this time Cunard rose up to meet the competition by operating a year-round weekly service, dropping Halifax altogether as a port of call and building two ships, the *Arabia* and *Persia*, which were bigger and more luxurious than the Collins vessels.

In 1854, with the outbreak of war in the Crimea, Cunard's fortunes dropped, for with the Admiralty requisitioning 14 of its ships, the Collins Line was left to monopolize the North Atlantic. This might have spelled the demise of Cunard had not disaster befallen its rival, when on 27 September 1854 the steamer *Arctic* was lost off Cape Race after colliding with a small French vessel. Out of the 391 passengers on board there were only 45 survivors, and among those lost were Mrs Collins, the wife of the owner, and their two children.

This tragic accident brought the travelling public back to Cunard, which had a good safety record; by February 1856, with a piece treaty having been signed in Paris, the company could look forward to the return of its ships. Five years later

saw the first moves in the American Civil War, and this badly affected Cunard's emigrant traffic to the New World. However, the company was able to weather this loss in revenue by the increase in demand for war supplies. In April 1865, Sir Samuel Cunard died and later that year the American Civil War ended.

By now Cunard's main competitor for the North Atlantic trade was the Liverpool-based Inman Line, but in September 1869 the Oceanic Steam Navigation Company was incorporated. This new company was always referred to as the White Star Line and within 65 years Cunard and this new company would be irrevocably merged. However, in 1872 Cunard had once again to answer the challenge of superior ships and it was 1881 before the *Servia* (1) was able to outshine the White Star ships.

In 1893 the record-breaking Cunard vessels *Campania* and *Lucania* entered service and this marked the start of a fierce race for supremacy on the North Atlantic between British and German companies. In 1897, Norddeutscher Lloyd introduced its 'superliner' *Kaiser Wilhelm der Grosse*. She was a ship of 14,349 gross tons, with four tall funnels, and a style and image which was to symbolize size and power on the North Atlantic for 40 years. For ten of those years the German ships dominated the Atlantic service, but in 1907 the magnificent duo *Lusitania* and *Mauretania* wrested back once more the size and speed records for Cunard. The former ship will always be remembered for her tragic sinking off Ireland in May 1915, and the latter as the vessel which dominated the North Atlantic for 22 years.

During the First World War Cunard's ships were once again requisitioned for government service as troopships and armed merchant cruisers. By the time hostilities came to an end in November 1918, Cunard had lost 22 of its ships, half of these being passenger vessels. The company put in hand a huge building programme, and in addition were allocated as war reparations the German liner *Imperator*, which was re-named *Berengaria*.

For ten years after the end of the war Cunard's

Mauretania held the transatlantic records, but in 1929 German ships again swept Cunard's best off the seas. However, once more Cunard found the answer in two giant vessels which were to replace the ageing trio of *Mauretania*, *Aquitania* and *Berengaria*. But although the keel of hull 534 was laid down on the Clyde in December 1930, in the following year the economic depression caused work to be stopped.

With the German ships *Bremen* and *Europa* raking in the best of the profits on the North Atlantic, the fortunes of Cunard were at an all-time low. However, in October 1932 negotiations between Cunard, White Star and the British government resulted in a rescue package. The Chancellor of the Exchequer, Mr Neville Chamberlain, had always wanted a strong British company for the Atlantic, and the offer of a £9½ million low-interest loan brought about an agreed merger between the Atlantic giants. Cunard was the senior partner in the new Cunard White Star Ltd, and for the White Star it was the beginning of the end. Of the £9½ million loan, £3 million was to complete hull 534, £1½ million was to be working capital and £5 million was for the building of the second giant vessel.

Work was re-started on hull 534, which became the *Queen Mary*, and the second giant was, of course, the *Queen Elizabeth*. However, before the two could sail together across the Atlantic the Second World War intervened. Once again Cunard's ships were requisitioned by the government, but this time the losses through enemy action were not as heavy as before, even though that of *Lancastria* off St Nazaire in June 1940 remains one of the world's worst maritime disasters. In addition, four ships were purchased by the Admiralty for service as naval depot ships.

In 1949 the White Star Line disappeared, although its remaining ships kept the black-topped buff funnels. By now the age of the transatlantic liner was fast coming to an end, as air travel started to dominate the Atlantic crossing. Work was under way to develop the Boeing 707, a 500 mph airliner with a passenger capacity of 130. Despite the fact that all commercial indications were against it, Cunard nevertheless built four ships for its Canadian service. By 1956 the number of passengers travelling by air overtook sea travellers for the first time. Even this depressing fact did not have an immediate effect on the Cunard board. Plans were in hand for the Q3, a 75,000 ton ship which was to succeed the two *Queens* on the North Atlantic. However, in 1961 this idea was dropped and three years later the contract for a smaller vessel was placed. She was to be capable of passing through both the Suez and Panama Canals, and her primary role was to be that of a cruise-ship. At last Cunard had broken free from the North Atlantic with its new liner, which was, of course, the *QE2*.

In the early 1970s Cunard took delivery of its first purpose-built cruise-ships, and as part of the Trafalgar House group of companies its post-war fortunes have revived and gone from strength to strength. Cunard's two latest acquisitions, the former Norwegian American Line's *Sagafjord* and *Vistafjord*, make it one of the world's largest cruising fleets, a far cry from the days when Samuel Cunard struggled to make his proposed transatlantic service a reality.

2
Umbria and *Etruria*, 1884

It is fitting that the story of Cunard passenger ships over the last 100 years should begin with the *Umbria* and *Etruria* of 1884, for these were the last Cunarders to be fitted for auxiliary sail, and the last of the company's major vessels to be built with single screws. Thus they marked the end of an era, for although steam propulsion at sea reigned supreme, the days of the square-rigged sailing-ships could only now be remembered with nostalgia by many seafarers. By today's standards the two ships do not appear at all impressive, but in 1884 they were record-breakers and the largest liners then in service.

Umbria and *Etruria* were built for the prestigious Liverpool–New York service, and the order for the two vessels went to John Elder & Company of Glasgow. Finance was raised by the issue of £250,000 worth of debentures, and by a part exchange deal with the builders, whereby two old Cunarders *Parthia* and *Batavia* were handed over for re-sale. Surprisingly, both vessels, which in 1884 were already 14 years old, survived for longer than either *Umbria* or *Etruria*. The *Parthia*, re-named *Straits Maru*, was finally broken up in 1952.

While *Umbria* and *Etruria* were on the stocks, Admiralty officials kept in touch with the builders in order that the ships could be designed with easy conversion to auxiliary cruisers should they be required in time of war. *Umbria* was the first of the pair to be launched, and she was christened by the Honourable Mrs Hope on Wednesday 25 June 1884. The event received wide coverage in the press, the main point being that *Umbria* was then the largest ship in the world except for the *Great Eastern*, which was then 25 years old and redundant.* Just over 12 weeks later, her sister ship *Etruria* was launched, and by the end of the year the fitting out of both vessels had been completed.

Both *Umbria* and *Etruria* were very similar in appearance, their main distinguishing feature being two enormous funnels which gave an impression of great power. They were also fitted with three steel masts which could be fully rigged with an extensive spread of canvas. Both ships had a gross tonnage of 7,718, with an overall length of 519 feet (159.7 m) and a breadth of 57 ft 2 in (17.6 m). They were powered by a set of triple, three-crank compound engines, which drove a single screw and gave a service speed of 19 knots. The steam was provided by nine double-ended boilers which could consume some 320 tons of coal a day. They were also the

* In June 1884 the *Great Eastern* had already been laid up at Milford Haven for some years, and in April of that year it had been announced that plans were in hand to fit her out as a coal hulk at Gibraltar. She was to have her paddle engines and boilers removed and numerous side ports cut in her hull, as well as having hydraulic cranes fitted on the upper deck. The Admiralty was in favour of this plan, as the arrival of *Great Eastern* at Gibraltar would have dispensed with a multitude of smaller hulks at the port. However, the plan came to nothing and two years later she was turned into an exhibition ship.

first Cunard ships to be equipped with refrigeration machinery, but it was their single screws which brought them most publicity during their careers.

Each of the two ships had accommodation for 550 first and 800 second class passengers, although in late 1892 this was altered to accommodate 500 first, 160 second and 800 steerage passengers. The first class public rooms, with their ornately carved furniture and heavy velvet curtains, together with the clutter of bric-à-brac, epitomized the luxury of the upper class Victorian home. These rooms, together with the first class passenger cabins, were situated on the promenade, upper, saloon and main decks. The ladies' boudoir was forward on the promenade deck, just aft of the main foyer, and immediately below on the upper deck was the music room. Also on this deck was the smoking room, which of course in those days was 'for gentlemen only'. Immediately below on the saloon deck were the dining saloons for both first and second class passengers, amidships and right aft respectively. There was also a smoking room for the second class gentlemen in the after deck-house situated on the upper deck, and by the standards of the day the second class accommodation was spacious and comfortable.

By early October 1884 *Umbria* had completed her trials and on the 4th of that month she sailed for Liverpool to prepare for her maiden voyage across to New York which she actually undertook on 1 November, commanded by Captain Theodore Cook. He was Cunard's senior captain and had served his apprenticeship in square-rigged sailing-ships, a training which it was said produced the finest seamen. This particular voyage broke no records and shortly afterwards political troubles brought her North Atlantic service temporarily to a halt. In early 1884 Russia had seemed intent on moving its armies south into Afghanistan, and Britain, with its huge Indian Empire to protect, was very sensitive to any frontier changes in Central Asia. By the New Year of 1885 the crisis had come to a head with both powers facing up to each other and the British declaring that 'any southerly

Top *The* Umbria *in the River Mersey dressed overall for Queen Victoria's 70th birthday, 24 May 1889.* (University of Liverpool)

Above *The two enormous funnels of the* Etruria *gave the impression of great power.* (University of Liverpool)

moves by Russian forces would have to be regarded as a declaration of war on England'. As part of its preparations for what was thought to be an inevitable conflict, the British government chartered several passenger liners for service as armed merchant cruisers (AMCs), amongst which were both *Umbria* and *Etruria*.

Etruria had been completed in March 1885 and on the 26th of that month had arrived in the Clyde from Liverpool. Immediately upon tying up alongside Sandon Dock those on board found that she and *Umbria* were both on charter to the Admiralty. However, within days a settlement of the dispute was reached and *Etruria* was released from government service, but, as a precautionary measure, the Admiralty retained *Umbria* for six months. She was fitted with

The Etruria *at sea with sails rigged. The sisters* Umbria *and* Etruria *were the last Cunarders to be fitted for auxiliary sail and the last to be built with single screws.* (National Maritime Museum)

5 inch guns and, in the words of Vice-Admiral Fitzgerald, speaking of both the *Umbria* and *Oregon*, 'if occasion had arisen to tell their capabilities, the *Umbria* and *Oregon* would have shown themselves to be powerful auxiliaries to our iron-clad navy'.

In the meantime, on 25 April 1885, commanded by Captain McMicken, *Etruria* sailed on her maiden Atlantic crossing from Liverpool, calling at Queenstown the following day. Then, with her next westbound crossing she won the Blue Riband for Cunard. On 20 September 1885 she was involved in a collision in Lower New York Bay with the 4,276 gross ton cargo ship *Canada*, owned by the National Steamship Company of Limerick. *Etruria* was outward bound and at anchor waiting for dense fog to lift when the *Canada* collided with her starboard side. Fortunately, although the other vessel scraped alongside *Etruria* carrying away a portion of her rigging, there were no casualties and no further damage was caused. Also in that September *Umbria* resumed her service with Cunard and for the next few years the two ships maintained the Atlantic service without major incident.

On 12 April 1890 *Umbria* left New York carrying 334 saloon, 80 second class and 241 steerage passengers. Five days after leaving the port, when she was in mid-Atlantic in a position 43°N/39°W, she came across the Norwegian barque *Magdalena* waterlogged and drifting helplessly after suffering a collision with an iceberg. Captain Gunderson of the *Magdalena* and his eight-man crew were very lucky to have been spotted and, after setting fire to their derelict ship, the men were taken on board *Umbria* and four days later were landed at Liverpool.

For the rest of that decade the two ships ran trouble-free across the Atlantic, although in September 1889 the Inman Line's vessel *City of Paris* took the speed record from them. Then towards the end of 1892 the *Umbria* was involved in a drama on the Atlantic which highlighted a weakness which was to dog the two vessels for the remainder of their careers. She sailed from Liverpool on Saturday 17 December that year and, after an overnight passage down the Irish Sea, she called at Queenstown at lunchtime the following day. When she left that port at a few minutes after 2 pm on Sunday 18 December, she had on board 400 passengers, 130 of whom were in the first class, and a large amount of mail. She was commanded by Captain M'Kay and she was due to dock at New York on Christmas Day. However, in those days before radio communications, any problems only became apparent after the vessels became days overdue at their port of destination. So it was with *Umbria* when, on 28 December, she had still not reached New York. Newspapers on both sides of the Atlantic began to speculate on what the cause of the delay could be and, although they were confident in *Umbria*'s seagoing qualities, there was obviously deep concern for the safety of those on board. On the following day, 29 December, the Wilson steamship *Galileo* arrived in New York from Hull and she brought the first news of the missing *Umbria*. It seems that on Christmas Day the *Galileo*'s lookouts had sighted the other ship in a position 42° 52'N/58° 55'W, apparently disabled. *Galileo*'s master saw that she exhibited three red lights, indicating that she was unmanageable, but she did not require assistance. The weather at the time was foul with severe north-westerly gales and blinding showers of hail and snow. However, as she did not request any help and she was lying easily in the water, despite the gales *Galileo* continued her voyage.

A few hours later another steamer, the *Monrovian*, arrived in New York, and she too reported sighting *Umbria* on 21 December, steaming westwards and apparently in good condition. On 30 December the steamship *Manhanset* arrived in New York from Bristol and her master, Captain Duck, reported that he had sighted *Umbria* at 1.30 pm on 26 December, when she was hove to and carrying out repairs to her shaft. In an interview to reporters he said: 'The weather was very hazy and it was impossible to see any distance ahead when we sighted *Umbria*. I should say we were within two miles of her before we saw her. I altered my course two points in order to pass sufficiently close to signal. It was necessary to be very careful as the sea was heavy and a strong gale was blowing. The *Umbria* was drifting with the sea, lying easily. She had then no canvas up. Her three sea anchors were out in the form of a triangle, made out of spars lashed together and fastened to the ship by a heavy chain cable. I should say that the *Umbria* was drifting eastwards at the rate of a mile an hour. Many of the passengers, who were on decks, were muffled up. I spoke to the ship and asked if aid was needed. The reply was "non". We remained by the *Umbria* from 1.30 pm to 3.30 pm. Shortly after leaving her we passed a Cunarder from Boston, bound eastwards. She would, I think, pass close to the Umbria.'

The Cunarder referred to by Captain Duck was the *Gallia*, commanded by Captain Ferguson, and she arrived on the scene at just after 3.30 pm on 26 December. Her part in the drama was to raise a controversy which would last for some months.

By now preparations were being made in New York to amount a rescue mission, with the Moran Towing Company making available their largest tug, should they be asked to help search for the *Umbria*. In fact, the *Umbria*'s troubles had started at 5.25 pm on Friday 23 December 1892, when she was in a position 42° 48'N/57° 17'W, and her propeller shaft fractured at the thrust block. The main engines were stopped immediately and the ship drifted helplessly in gale force winds and a heavy sea while Mr Tomlinson, her Chief Engineer, worked with his staff to improvize repairs and get her under way again.

The first knowledge that passengers had of the accident was at 7.30 pm, when Captain M'Kay went to the first class smoke room to inform the gentlemen who were assembled there. He told one passenger, Mr Henry J. Harper, that he 'would accept a tow from any vessel large enough that came within hailing distance'. To quote a contemporary report: 'There was very little commotion among the ladies when they were informed, they were just as calm as the men'. It seems that most passengers went to bed as normal despite the fact that their ship was at the mercy of the seas, and at just after dawn the next day they were woken by the sound of a gun and the deep roar of the ship's whistle. Captain M'Kay had sighted a ship travelling east and succeeded in attracting her attention. She was the Hamburg Amerika vessel *Bohemia*, and by 8.15 am she was within hailing distance and agreed to tow the stricken vessel to New York. After she had helped to strengthen the *Umbria*'s hawsers the tow began, and everything went well until mid-afternoon when a severe storm blew up, and after dusk the two ships could not even see each other's lights. At about 10 pm the towing line parted and in the thick blizzard conditions the two ships lost each other and once again *Umbria* was drifting helplessly. Next morning, when daylight came, there was no sign of the *Bohemia*.

On Sunday 25 December, an above average attendance was noted at Divine Service, and it was at dusk on that day that *Galileo* came upon the scene. She was unable to assist owing to lack of coal. During the afternoon of Monday 26 December, the *Manhanset* was sighted and, hardly had she departed on her way, when the *Gallia* arrived. According to some witnesses, the following signals were exchanged. *Umbria* to *Gal-*

lia: 'Disabled — stand by'. Reply: 'Can not stand by, carrying mails'. *Umbria*: 'We hold you responsible'. It seems that *Gallia* then dipped her ensign and continued her voyage to Queenstown. According to Mr Henry Harper, a distinguished US passenger who seems to have been close to Captain M'Kay, the captain told him that he had signalled *Gallia* twice asking her to stay.

Meanwhile, down below, the Chief Engineer was faced with the huge task of repairing the awkward break in the shaft with the vessel rolling and pitching in heavy seas. What is more, the only equipment available were drills, hammers and cold chisels. In the event he drilled three keyways out of the solid steel and fitted steel collars by means of 5 inch diameter bolts. This task was completed by Tuesday 27 December, and at 4 am that day a trial was undertaken, but one of the bolts broke after two hours. However, by 8 pm that day a successful repair was achieved and the engines were running at slow-ahead.

Fortunately this silenced the grumblings amongst the passengers, who had been kept well informed all through the emergency by notices which had been posted throughout the ship. *Umbria* finally arrived alongside her berth in the Cunard company's dock in New York at 11 am on Saturday 31 December 1892 and her arrival was witnessed by thousands of New Yorkers who gathered to cheer her in. The crowds were so thick that it took the police some time to clear a space for the gangway.

Once the excitement of her arrival had subsided the recriminations began, as accusations ranging from neglect to sabotage made the news headlines on both sides of the Atlantic. First of all Captain Jones of the *Galileo* was accused of refusing to tow the *Umbria*, which he strenuously denied. Then a story circulated that the towing hawsers of the *Bohemia* had been deliberately cut on board that ship. Again, this was vehemently denied by the master of the German vessel. There was no evidence to substantiate either of these accusations, and the facts indicated that both captains had acted correctly.

The third charge was directed at Captain Ferguson of the *Gallia*, and this was the strangest tale to emerge from the whole saga. The *Gallia* arrived in Queenstown on New Years Day 1893, and waiting for her was the world's press. When he was shown the allegations that he had deliberately ignored *Umbria*'s request for assistance, Captain Ferguson refused to be interviewed and the same thing happened when *Gallia* finally arrived at Liverpool. However, a statement from Cunard said that although the *Umbria* had requested assistance, Captain Ferguson decided that she was in no danger and so continued on his voyage. On the following day Cunard invited the press to interview Captain M'Kay at their New York office where the *Umbria*'s master read out a prepared statement which ran thus: 'It has turned out to be as I supposed, the *Gallia* knew we were in no danger, and was therefore perfectly justified in proceeding on her voyage. I have no criticisms to make on the conduct of Captain Ferguson'. It all appeared to be a peacemaking exercise by the company, for numerous witnesses on board *Umbria* testified to Captain M'Kay's disgust at his fellow Cunard master refusing to assist.

After undergoing temporary repairs in New York, *Umbria* left the port for Liverpool on 26 January 1893. She had on board a full cargo, but no passengers, as the company 'did not want to risk a large number of passengers on board'. The weather was fine for the voyage and the vessel maintained a speed of 13 knots for most of the transatlantic crossing. She finally arrived in the Mersey on Saturday 4 February 1893, and as she steamed up river a large number of people gathered to watch her progress. *Umbria* was towed into the Albert Dock, Birkenhead, and after discharging her cargo she entered the graving dock where she was fitted with a new 20-foot shaft which had been cast to replace the broken section. It was 1 April that year before *Umbria* sailed again for Queenstown and New York.

Just over three years later the *Umbria* was involved in another mishap; this time it was in New York harbour and fortunately the damage was minimal. *Umbria* left her pier at the foot of Clarkson Street in the North River at 9 am on Saturday 28 June 1896. Just over an hour later, in the ship channel near the turn into Gedney Channel, two miles from Sandy Hook, she hit the laden wreck of the coal barge *Andrew Jackson*. The former crack American clipper had been sunk by the British steamship *Vedra* just a month earlier, and *Umbria* stuck fast on the sunken hulk. All day she remained thus until, with a combination of a flood tide and the services of seven tugs, she was pulled free, to the cheers of a large group of passengers who were travelling to Henley to see a Yale crew row in the regatta. After she was freed, the *Umbria* steamed outside the bar and dropped anchor in order that divers could examine the hull. Finally at 10 pm that evening she left New York, headed into the Atlantic and set course for Queenstown.

Just over three years later, on 12 October 1899, the Boer War broke out in South Africa. The Admiralty hastily mustered 600,000 tons of shipping as transports for soldiers, horses and guns, and on Friday 22 December that year, *Umbria* was chartered for service as a troop transport. She had arrived in the Mersey from New York on Saturday 16 December 1899 and had been due to sail again a week later, but instead work commenced to prepare her for trooping duties. She made her first sailing from Southampton in this role when she left the Empress Dock on Thursday 11 January 1900. She had on board men of the Warwickshire, Derbyshire and Durham Militia, and they disembarked at Cape Town on the evening of Monday 29 January. From Cape Town *Umbria* went round to Port Elizabeth and East London to unload cargo in those ports. On 21 February she left Cape Town for Southampton with ten officers and 215 men of the Seaforth Highlanders who had been wounded during the debacle at Magersfontein on 11 December 1899. She arrived in Southampton on Tuesday 14 March, and the seriously wounded men were taken to Netley Hospital.

Meanwhile *Etruria*, which so far had had a trouble-free career, was also experiencing problems with her propeller shaft. She had left Liverpool on 6 January 1900 and arrived in New York one week later on the 13th. Whilst in New York, engineers examined the propeller shaft and found cracks which were not there when she left Liverpool. To guard against the possibility of an accident on the homeward voyage, Cunard cancelled her sailing and despatched a new propeller shaft to be fitted in New York. She finally left New York on 17 February and her next sailing from Liverpool was on 3 March, exactly a month after she had been scheduled to sail.

Etruria remained on the North Atlantic throughout 1900, while *Umbria* carried troops to South Africa from Southampton where the docks were now always full of troop transports, with sometimes up to six sailings a day. Her second sailing in this role was on 25 March 1900, when she left with 119 officers and 2,108 men of artillery companies of Militia and Infantry drafts of the line. She arrived in Cape Town on 16 April, three weeks after leaving England. From there *Umbria* sailed into completely new waters when she went as far north as Lourenco Marques. On 18 May, when Mafeking was relieved, she was in Port Natal (now Durban) for the celebrations. She left Cape Town for the last time on Thursday 7 June with over 600 wounded men on board, and arrived in Southampton 19 days later on 26 June. By now the urgent need for transports had eased and *Umbria* was released by the Admiralty and returned to Cunard. After a refit she resumed her sailings to New York on Saturday 21 July.

Both *Umbria* and *Etruria* remained on the Liverpool–New York run without incident until the beginning of 1902. On Saturday 22 February *Etruria* left New York. She was due in Queenstown on 1 March, and on 26 February she radioed the westbound *Umbria* to pass on a message from a passenger. However, that evening her propeller shaft fractured, which left her drifting helplessly. She tried in vain to raise the *Umbria* again but, in the days before the *Titanic* disaster, radio operators did not work 24 hour shifts. Rockets were sent up and fortunately these were seen by the Leyland ship *William Cliff*, which was alongside her in less than an hour. She stood by *Etruria* during the night whilst the engineers attempted to make good temporary repairs. Sails were raised and the Cunarder set course for the Azores, which were about 500 miles to the south-east. The following day the *William Cliff* took *Etruria* in tow, and a painfully slow voyage to Horta in the Azores followed. *Etruria* anchored off Horta at 6 pm on Sunday 9 March and Cunard made arrangements to transfer her passengers to another ship and make temporary repairs to the broken propeller shaft.

Fortunately the company was able to charter the elderly Royal Mail liner *Elbe*, which left Southampton for Horta on 10 March. Five days later, with all *Etruria*'s passengers and mails on board, *Elbe* left the Azores and arrived back in Southampton on the evening of 19 March. As for the *Etruria*, it was the summer of 1902 before she was in service once again. However, later that same year after a particularly rough Atlantic crossing in early October, an inspection of her propeller shaft showed serious cracks, and her sailing, which was scheduled for 4 October, was cancelled and a new shaft was sent out from England. It was 4 pm on Saturday 1 November before *Etruria* left New York and she arrived in Liverpool eight days later. It had not been a good year for the ship, but she was able to resume her scheduled service on 15 November that year.

In early 1903 *Etruria* was again in the news when, on 28 February, whilst leaving New York for Liverpool, she ran aground at the entrance to the Gedrey Channel. Fortunately she was resting easily on sand and mud, and after she had been refloated later that day no damage was found.

Just three months later *Umbria* was making headlines around the world in a story which would not sound unfamiliar today. At noon on Saturday 9 May 1903 in New York, shortly before she was due to sail, a letter was received at police headquarters stating that a bomb had been put on the steamship pier to be loaded aboard the *Umbria*. The letter went on to say that the Mafia Society was aiming to destroy British ships sailing from New York, and originally it had been intended to put the bomb

on the White Star liner *Oceanic*, but as there were a large number of women and children aboard, they had decided on the *Umbria*.

Immediately the New York police cordoned off the pier and arranged to delay the vessel's sailing. The bomb was discovered in a plain wooden box 3 feet long by 2 feet wide, placed near the first class gangway. One of the police officers put a rope round the box and lowered it into the sea. When it was raised the box was found to contain 100 lb of dynamite with a crude but effective fuse and timing mechanism. There is no doubt that had it been taken on board and exploded it would have caused severe damage. Witnesses testified to the fact that the box had been placed there by two men of 'Italian' appearance, and the police eventually traced the manufacturer of the bomb to a lodging house in Chicago. Happily *Umbria* sailed after only a short delay and arrived in Liverpool on Saturday 16 May without further incident.

Later that year, at 2.30 pm on 10 October, *Etruria* was only four hours out of New York when she was struck by a freak wave. Apparently the wave, which was about 50 feet high, hit the port side of the ship carrying away part of the forebridge and smashing the guardrail stanchions. A number of first class passengers, who were sitting in deck chairs by the bridge at the time, received the full force of the water and a Canadian passenger was fatally injured. Several other passengers were hurt but fortunately there were no other deaths.

In January 1907, two of *Etruria*'s seamen were killed while they were trying to secure the lashings of the starboard anchor during a rough westbound crossing.

By this time both *Umbria* and *Etruria* were well past their prime and technical progress had well and truly overtaken them. Later that year the *Lusitania* and *Mauretania* were due to enter service, so the days of the elderly sisters, which had entered service 23 years previously, were numbered.

In August 1908 *Etruria* prepared to make her last Atlantic crossing. At 5 pm on Wednesday 26 August she left the dock at Liverpool and was moving stern first to anchor opposite Princes landing stage where passengers would embark, when unfortunately a hopper crossing the Mersey got too close and was violently rammed by the liner. *Etruria*'s rudder and propeller were driven deep into the hopper almost cutting it in two; however, being stuck fast on the propeller prevented the hopper from sinking. *Etruria* then drifted helplessly in the river and the hopper was crushed against the landing stage. Unfortunately the accident seriously damaged *Etruria*'s propeller, rudder and steering gear and it was obvious that her sailing would have to be cancelled. Cunard officials met the passengers, about 600 saloon and second class, and organized hotels for them in Liverpool. They were able to sail on board *Umbria* on Friday 28 August.

Etruria was taken into dock and temporary repairs were made, but she did not sail the Atlantic again, being laid up instead in reserve at Birkenhead. *Umbria* too was laid up on her return from New York on 18 October 1908, and it seemed to be the end of the line for both ships. In October 1909 Cunard announced that *Etruria* had been sold to the shipbreakers Thomas W. Ward for £16,750, although it was some months before she reached the final graveyard. She eventually arrived at Preston in Lancashire on Sunday 10 April 1910, having been towed from Birkenhead by the tug *Black Cock*.

However, for *Umbria* there was to be a short reprieve, for the *Lucania* had been seriously damaged by fire and the *Campania* was to undergo a refit. *Lucania* had been due to make several crossings during the time *Campania* was laid up so *Umbria* was brought back into service in her place. She left Liverpool on the first of three crossings on Christmas Day 1909, arriving in New York at midnight on 2 January 1910. She was commanded by Captain R.C. Warr, who was in fact appointed to the position of Commodore of the Cunard Line on New Years Eve 1909, which meant a double celebration for him.

Umbria left Liverpool for her final westbound crossing on Saturday 12 February 1910 and her last sailing from New York began at 6 pm on Wednesday 23 February. She arrived in the Mersey for the last time on Friday 4 March and as soon as her passengers were disembarked work began de-storing the ship and stripping her of her fittings. Within days of her arrival in the Mersey, *Umbria* was sold to the Forth Shipbreaking Company for £20,000. There is no doubt that the two Victorian Cunarders had been considered, in their day, two giants of the North Atlantic.

Technical data	
Gross tonnage	7,718
Net tonnage	3,286 (*Umbria*), 3,258 (*Etruria*)
Length overall	501 ft 6 in (154.3 m)
Breadth	57 ft 2 in (17.6 m)
Both ships single screw, powered by a compound engine; 14,500 IHP, 19 knots.	

3
Campania and *Lucania*, 1893

The entry into service of these two Cunarders in 1893 really started the great international race for supremacy on the North Atlantic, for it was at about this time that Germany set about building up her mercantile and naval fleets to equal those of the British. In England Queen Victoria had been on the throne for 56 years and the country felt secure behind the mighty Royal Navy. However, Germany was becoming more and more influential in European politics, and although the *Campania* and *Lucania* held the North Atlantic speed records for four years, from 1897 onwards German liners swept all opposition from the seas for the next ten years.

The two Cunarders were designed as record-breakers to compete directly with the White Star liners *Majestic* and *Teutonic*, and the two Inman ships *City of New York* and *City of Paris*. *Campania* and *Lucania* were only 72 feet (22.15m) shorter than the *Great Eastern* had been and for a few years they had the distinction of being the largest ships in the world. Of the two sisters perhaps *Campania* is the best remembered, for she became one of the Royal Navy's pioneers in naval aviation.

Both ships were built on the Clyde at Govan, the contract going to the Fairfield Shipbuilding Company of Glasgow (which was in fact the old John Elder and Company) in August 1891. Both ships had a gross tonnage of 12,950 which by today's standards is not great, but in 1892 they were enormous vessels. As an example, the rud-

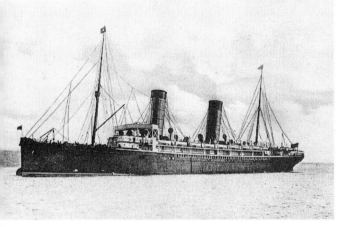

Top left RMS Lucania *anchored in the Mersey.* (Author's collection)

Left RMS Campania *in the Mersey.* (Author's collection)

ders for the two ships were formed of single steel plates, and they were so wide that no British company possessed the necessary machinery to build them. In the event the work had to be done by Krupp of Essen. The launch of the two ships also presented considerable problems. With an overall length of 620 feet (190.75m), and the River Clyde at Govan being so narrow, it was decided to launch them stern first and obliquely downstream.

The first of the two sisters to take to the water was the *Campania*. She was launched at 1.45 pm on Thursday 8 September 1892 by Lady Burns, the wife of Sir John Burns of Wemyss Castle and Chairman of the Cunard Line. Among the 300 official guests at the ceremony was Mr Bruce Ismay of the White Star Line and a representative of Harland & Wolff Ltd. It was also a big day for Clydesiders, with thousands of people crowding both banks of the river. Despite the fact that one of Harland & Wolff's directors was at the ceremony, it did not stop a rather acrimonious exchange of letters between Sir Edward Harland and Mr John Inglis of Fairfields which were published in *The Times*. Sir Edward spoke of 'Cunard's crowing effort' with the *Campania* being 'almost a facsimile of White Star's *Majestic* and *Teutonic*, not only in the model and general arrangements of superstructure, but also in the mode of construction'. He went on to say that 'the owners and builders of the White Star may feel quite flattered by the spirit of imitation'. The letter was an indication of the fierce competition between the two companies. After her launching, *Campania* was towed to a specially prepared jetty close to the launching way where she was to be completed for sea.

Five months later, on the afternoon of Thursday 2 February 1893, the second of the two sisters was launched. *Lucania* was christened by the Countess of Egerton and, despite the bitterly cold weather, a crowd of about 80,000 spectators turned out to witness the event. This time Sir William G. Pearce MP, the Chairman of Fairfields, who had been away in Europe at the time of *Campania*'s launch, presided over dinner that evening to celebrate what had been a successful day.

As *Lucania* lay in the fitting-out berth in the last week of March 1893, *Campania* left the Clyde bound for Liverpool. However, she did not sail directly there but went instead round the north and west coast of Ireland, and at 6 pm on Friday 31 March she was sighted off Roches Point in Ireland. She did not communicate with Queenstown, but proceeded straight to Liverpool and entered the Mersey the following morning completely decked out with bunting.

By mid-morning *Campania* had anchored opposite the north end of the Princes landing stage in Liverpool. After drydocking at Birkenhead she sailed north again for the Clyde and on 10 April 1893 she started her trials off Skelmorlie. These were a complete success — in fact, the ship achieved almost 23 knots which was well in excess of the contract requirement. There were several VIPs on board including Sir William Pearce for the builders and Sir John Burns for Cunard. A notable engineer of the day, Lord Kelvin, was on board simply for the novelty of being on the world's fastest ship. On Saturday 15 April, five days after starting her trials, *Campania* was handed over to Cunard and a large party was held on board to celebrate the event before the vessel left once again for the River Mersey.

Campania sailed on her maiden voyage from Liverpool on Saturday 22 April 1893. Five days later, on Thursday 27 April, she encountered strong head winds and heavy seas, and on the following two days she was slowed down somewhat by dense fog. However, she arrived off Sandy Hook at 5.24 pm on Saturday 29 April some six days and eight hours after leaving Liverpool. The new vessel attracted great attention in New York and on the Wednesday following her arrival Cunard opened her to the public which attracted great crowds.

Exactly a week after her arrival at 11.05 am on Saturday 6 May, *Campania* left New York. Half an hour earlier the *Paris* (ex-*City of Paris*) had left the port, but 109 miles east of Sandy Hook *Campania* steamed past her. She made the passage from New York to Queenstown in five days, 17 hours and 27 minutes, which beat the *Paris*'s record. This was despite the fact that *Campania* stopped for two hours during the voyage in order to remedy a steering gear defect. She arrived off the Mersey the following evening, her first round voyage having been a great success. In June 1893 she made a record voyage from Liverpool to New York of five days, 13 hours and 29 minutes, thus gaining the Blue Riband for Cunard.

In the following month, on 31 July, *Lucania* left the Clyde for Birkenhead and drydocking at Laird's yard prior to her trials. However, once in drydock it was found that some of her hull plating was damaged and repairs were undertaken. This hitch in the timetable meant either delaying her maiden voyage or cancelling her full speed trials on the Clyde. The latter solution was decided upon, so *Lucania* left Liverpool on her maiden voyage to New York on the evening of Saturday 2 September 1893 and made a record voyage westward, taking the Blue Riband from her sister. For the time being the two Cunarders dominated the scene but, like the race for naval supremacy, the battle for the largest and fastest passenger ship on the North Atlantic was to be between Britain and Germany.

In the meantime, however, *Campania* and *Lucania* not only swept all before them with the speed records, but they also set new standards of luxury for transatlantic passengers. Both ships had accommodation for 600 first, 400 second

RMS Lucania *in the Mersey. (Author's collection)*

and 1,000 third class passengers. Those travelling in the first class had cabins ranging from the usual staterooms to luxurious *en suite* apartments all of which were amidships on the upper deck. Most of the first class public rooms were on the shade deck. The drawing room surrounded the well above the first class dining saloon in the centre of the ship. This room was panelled with satinwood and cedar, and the furniture was upholstered in brocade. Forward of this was the library in the shape of a horseshoe with a bookcase at the after end, and writing tables arranged around the room below the portholes. The bulkheads were finished with ambayna wood in rosewood styles.

Aft of the drawing room on the same deck was the gentlemen's drawing room, panelled in carved oak with a carved overmantle and seats covered with light brown pigskin; rising from the domed ceiling were highly decorated skylights. The first class dining saloon, which was directly beneath the drawing room, seated 430 passengers at one sitting and extended across the whole width of the ship. The ceiling was panelled in white and gold with bulkheads of dark Spanish mahogany. The whole room was lit by electricity, a novelty in those days, the lamps being contained in 5 inch diameter cut glass globes.

To propel the new ships at the record-breaking speeds of up to 22 knots, they were fitted with two sets of triple expansion engines, each in separate rooms placed on either side of a dividing centre-line bulkhead which was fitted with watertight doors. The steam at 165 psi was supplied by 12 coal-fired double-ended boilers, each boiler having four furnaces in each end. The two vessels were the first twin screw steamers built for Cunard, and with their straight stem, elliptical stern, two pole masts and two enormous funnels, they were an imposing sight. Indeed, the size of the funnels was the cause of much comment in the contemporary press with statements like: 'Some idea of the magnitude of the funnels can be gained by the fact that a mail coach could be driven through them'. In fact, the funnels were built to a height of 130 feet (40m) from the keel and with an external diameter of 21 feet (6.5m). It was the start of the myth which equated the size of a ship's funnel with her power. Altogether the cost to Cunard for the two ships was £1,300,000, and they were set to dominate the North Atlantic.

During 1893 and 1894 *Campania* and *Lucania* gained the speed records for both the eastbound and westbound crossings between Liverpool and New York and for the next four years they remained unchallenged until, in May 1898, the Norddeutscher Lloyd ship *Kaiser Wilhelm der Grosse* took all the Atlantic records and the Blue Riband. The *Kaiser* was a powerful-looking ship with four funnels. Henceforth power on the Atlantic would be judged, not only by the size of funnels, but also by the number.

On 21 July 1900, seven years after entering service, *Campania* was involved in a serious collision at sea. She was homeward bound from New York when at noon on Friday 20 July, some 207 miles west of Queenstown, she ran into thick fog. Speed was reduced and the vessel moved very slowly towards the coast. Just before dusk that day she almost collided with a schooner, but fortunately the fog lifted at Roches Point outside Queenstown. However, Captain Walker, the master of *Campania*, decided to remain some four miles offshore and tenders came out to the ship. After a stop of just over 1½ hours, *Campania* got under way again at 2.38 am on Saturday 21 July. Unfortunately she ran straight into the fog again, which had thickened, and 30 miles north-east of Tuskar Light a sailing ship came across her bows.

The *Embleton*, a Liverpool-registered barque, was bound from her home port for Wellington in New Zealand. She was commanded by a Norwegian, Captain Nilssen, and she was owned by Messrs Iredale and Porter of Liverpool. *Embleton* had left the Mersey on the evening of Thursday 19 July, being towed as far as Holyhead. During the following 36 hours she made little progress in very light winds and at 8 am on the morning of Saturday 21 July she was close hauled on a port tack under easy sail: fore and main top sails and top gallant sails, flying jib, main stay sail and spanker. The starboard watch had gone below for breakfast and the port watch had just taken over, when they heard the whistle of what appeared to be a large steamer. The *Embleton*, as was common on sailing-ships, answered with a trumpet. The steamer's whistle was heard several times and the sailing-ship held its course. At 8.25 am the second mate on the *Embleton* heard 'the rush of the steamers bows'. He put his head down the skylight and shouted to Captain Nilssen: 'I think the steamer is getting too close'. However, before the master could get on deck *Campania* sliced clean through the *Embleton* just abaft of the mainmast on the starboard side.

The forward half of the sailing ship sank instantly, and the after part swung round and damaged *Campania*'s starboard side leaving the surface of the sea littered with wreckage. On board the *Campania* one of the passengers who witnessed the incident said: 'The bugle had just sounded for breakfast, a few minutes after 8.30 am. My cabin was aft on the promenade deck. Even there the revs of the screw were, at that hour, scarcely perceptible. There came a sudden grinding crash, then a second. Then the throb of the reversed engines and the shiver of the steamer struggling with two conflicting forces; then silence, then the cries and the quick rush of men along the deck. I looked over the side and saw what was left of the sailing ship floating past. I could see no heads on the water.'

The first class dining saloon of SS Lucania. *(National Maritime Museum)*

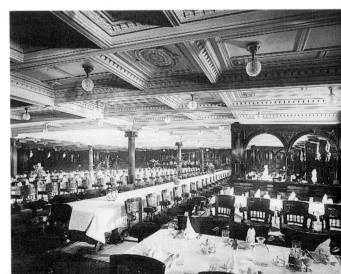

Campania's boat was lowered immediately and after searching for an hour it returned with seven survivors. Of *Embleton*'s 18 crew members, 11 perished, most of whom were trapped in the forward half. No one on board *Campania* was injured but the ship itself was damaged. Her forward plating was buckled, the forepeak flooded, the starboard rails forward were ripped off, her fore-topmast was broken and the steel rigging torn and twisted. During the remainder of the voyage to Liverpool, *Campania*'s passengers and crew collected £700 for the relatives of *Embleton*'s dead. She reached the Mersey without further incident, and a week later, at 7 pm on Saturday 28 July she left once again for New York.

Five years later *Campania* was once again in the news. She sailed from Liverpool on Saturday 7 October 1905 for her usual crossing to New York via Queenstown, and three days later was in mid-Atlantic making full headway on what was a fresh, blustery day. Many of the passengers were on deck and the steerage decks in particular were full of merrymakers. Suddenly the ship lurched to port and scooped up an enormous sea. The wave came on board amidships on the port side and swept across the steerage deck. The ship's side was buried so deeply that passengers on the deck above were submerged to their waists as the immense volume of water rolled aft, then surged forward. All the cabin passengers on the upper deck managed to cling to supports, and they were saved. However, on the steerage deck the guardrails were smashed and five passengers were swept overboard and lost, others being dashed against the rails. As well as the five passengers who were lost, 29 others were injured. Ten of these suffered serious injuries such as broken limbs and ribs, the remainder being cut and bruised.

It was the first time for 60 years that Cunard had lost any passengers through accident. There were tales of heroism though, such as that of Stewardess Cotes who rushed into the huge wave in order to rescue two children who were being carried towards the broken rail. Happily all three of them lived to tell the tale. Two days later on

13 October *Campania* arrived in New York.

With the entry into service of the *Lusitania* and *Mauretania* in 1907, both *Campania* and *Lucania* spent some time each year laid up at Liverpool. In early 1909 *Lucania* made only one round voyage to New York before being laid up in the Huskisson Dock at Liverpool. Then, at just after 7 pm on Saturday 14 August 1909, a warm summer's evening, fire was discovered. With only a caretaker on board little could be done to deal with it, and by the time the Liverpool fire brigade attended, the first class saloon was an inferno and the fire was burning out of control. Despite the fact that two fire engines were pumping some 2,000 gallons of water a minute onto the blazing ship, the flames gradually worked their way forward, consuming the ornate woodwork. By this time the heat was intense and the flames, which were shooting high into the air, attracted thousands of people on the Cheshire side of the Mersey, whilst the dock itself was besieged by the large crowd which had gathered from all parts of the city.

By the early hours of the morning, with great quantities of water still being poured into her, the inevitable happened — *Lucania* took on a list which was made worse by water entering through the coaling ports. At about 3 am on Sunday 15 August, she heeled right over and her funnels crashed into the cranes and quayside sheds. Six firemen who were on a gangway were thrown into the water, but were fortunately all rescued. Several tugs were attached to the vessel by wire hawsers and together they pulled her upright and into the middle of the dock, where she settled firmly in the mud. The fire brigade managed to get their hoses back on board and continued to fight the fire, but it was not until noon that the blaze was extinguished and the fire brigade were able to relinquish their task.

Lucania was seriously damaged. Everything forward of her funnels was completely gutted and all the deck plates had been twisted into fantastic shapes by the intense heat. The flames had been checked by her engine-room bulkhead, and subsequently the after part of the ship was still intact. Although she had settled on the dock bottom in 30 feet of water, the upper portion of the vessel was above the waterline. *Lucania* had been due to make her next voyage to New York in October 1909, and it was thought at first that she could be refitted in time for this.

Five days after the fire, *Lucania* was refloated and a full survey was carried out in the midships and forward sections. In the event it was decided that the damage was too great to make repairs a viable proposition, so she was sold to Thomas W. Ward, the shipbreakers as she lay, and soon afterwards she steamed down to Swansea under her own power to be broken up.

For the next five years *Campania* carried on the transatlantic service. On Saturday 14 April 1914 she made her 250th crossing between Liverpool and New York. It was to be her final peacetime voyage for the Cunard company, and she arrived back in Liverpool on Thursday 13 May. Ten days later she left Glasgow for New York via Londonderry, but this time she was chartered to the Anchor Line, with her funnels painted in Anchor black. Single first class fares started at £15 per person and she proved popular on the two voyages she made for the company; the second of these, from Glasgow to New York, commenced on 20 June 1914, but three weeks later she was back with Cunard and laid up at Stobcross Quay, Glasgow. It appeared that her career was over.

While she lay alongside the quay at Glasgow at about midnight on 19 July 1914, fire broke out in the bread store on board. For a time it appeared that the blaze might get a hold, but fortunately the crew and the city firemen were able to extinguish it.

There is no doubt that the outbreak of war on 4 August 1914 saved *Campania* from the scrapyard; following the requisitioning of Cunard ships as troop transports or armed merchant cruisers, she made three more Atlantic voyages. She sailed from Liverpool and for two months she was the only Cunard vessel on the route. By the end of September 1914, however, it was clear that the *Lusitania* and *Mauretania* could maintain the Liverpool–New York route, so at the end of the third voyage which had started

in Liverpool on 26 September, *Campania* was again withdrawn from service and put up for sale as scrap. Once again the timing was fortuitous, for the Admiralty was looking for a ship which could be converted reasonably easily to carry seaplanes for what was to be the beginnings of the Fleet Air Arm.

On the outbreak of war, the Royal Navy had only one ship which had been converted to carry seaplanes; this was HMS *Ark Royal*, a vessel which had been converted from a collier whilst on the stocks. Between 1914 and 1917, eight cross-Channel steamers, the *Empress*, *Engadine*, *Riviera*, *Ben-My Chree*, *Manxman*, *Vindex*, *Pegasus* and *Nairana*, were all taken over by the Admiralty and converted to carry seaplanes. However, all of them, including the *Ark Royal*, suffered from a major handicap, which was that the vessels had to come to a standstill for the seaplanes, which were carried in the holds, to be lowered into the water for take-off and subsequently brought inboard again. *Campania* was to change this and provide a major step forward for the Royal Navy.

Thus, instead of being sold to shipbreakers, *Campania*, was bought by the Admiralty in October 1914 and sent to Cammel Laird's Birkenhead for the conversion work to be carried out. She was by far the biggest vessel to undergo conversion for this purpose, and the Fairey 'Campania' seaplane was especially designed to operate from her decks. Six months after work started, on 17 April 1915, the seaplane carrier HMS *Campania* commissioned at Birkenhead, commanded by Captain Scham RN. *Campania* now looked very different from the record-breaking transatlantic liner of 22 years previously. Her long low superstructure had proved ideal for conversion. From her stem aft to her bridge deck was a wooden flight deck 160 feet (48.8m) long. Between decks she could accommodate ten aircraft, and these could be brought up to the flight deck by an internal lift. The wings of *Campania*'s aircraft were detachable rather than of the folding type, and this enabled a larger number to be carried as the wings could be stowed above the body of the aircraft. To enable the Fairey

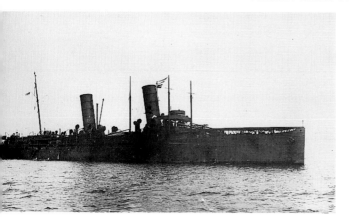

*HMS Campania in 1915 with her 160-foot flight deck.
(Imperial War Museum)*

'Campania' to take off, the aircraft was placed on a wheeled trolley for the run along the flight deck, and once airborne it had a speed of 80 mph with a ceiling of 2,000 feet and an endurance of three hours.

HMS *Campania* left Birkenhead on 30 April 1915 and five days later she arrived in Scapa Flow to join the Grand Fleet. This rather incongruous-looking 'ugly duckling', which joined the magnificent battleships and battle-cruisers commanded by Sir John Jellicoe, was obviously a very interesting novelty, for the day after her arrival the C in C and Vice-Admiral Sir George Warrener boarded, in order that they could watch her being put through her paces.

Soon after her arrival in Scapa Flow, HMS *Campania* made history for the Royal Navy when for the first time an aircraft took off from her flight deck whilst she was under way, although she still had to stop in order to recover the aircraft. After six months of trials in and out of Scapa Flow with the Grand Fleet it became obvious that *Campania* had two major faults. Her speed was inadequate to enable her to keep station with the rest of the fleet, a handicap which could not be remedied, and her flight deck was not considered long enough. The latter could be put right, so on 1 December 1915 she arrived once again at Cammel Laird's dock in Birkenhead for another major refit.

Towards the end of the alteration, on 9 March

1916, there was a fire in the drying room on board. Fortunately once again it was extinguished quickly and damage was minimal. The incident did not delay the refit and on 5 April HMS *Campania* was towed stern first out of the dock. The following day she left the Mersey for trials in Belfast Lough, before departing once again for Scapa Flow to re-join the Grand Fleet. Again her appearance had been altered drastically, with the bridge deck dismantled and the fore funnel divided in order to allow the longer flight deck which was now 220 feet (67m) long.

Soon after her arrival in Scapa Flow the Battle of Jutland took place in the North Sea. HMS *Campania* should have accompanied the battle fleet, but she was delayed in Scapa Flow with engine trouble, not sailing until the early hours of 31 May 1916, the day of the battle. In the event, Admiral Jellicoe did not wish to risk her loss by U-boats and he ordered her back to Scapa Flow. It is interesting to speculate on what might have transpired had the British Admiral had the benefit of HMS *Campania*'s seaplanes to assist with observations of the enemy fleet. HMS *Campania* spent the remainder of 1916 sailing in and out of Scapa Flow, and the hazards of naval aviation at that time can be judged by the large numbers of seaplanes lost. On one

HMS Campania leaving dock at Birkenhead after her refit in the spring of 1916, when her flight deck was extended to 220 feet. (Fleet Air Arm Museum)

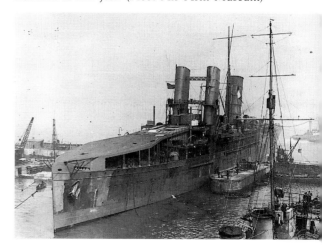

occasion, on 9 September 1916, a Schneider seaplane failed to return from patrol and the two aircraft sent to search for the wreckage also crashed. On 24 November, HMS *Campania* arrived in the Mersey again and this time she tied up alongside the Canada Dock for another refit. It was 25 February 1917 when she sailed once more for Scapa Flow, arriving there two days later, and before long the first seaplane was wrecked on take-off. Then, at 11.25 pm on 17 April, fire broke out in an after storeroom whilst the vessel was at Scapa Flow. It burned for over four hours before the storeroom was flooded and the fire extinguished.

The rest of that year was spent in and out of Scapa Flow and other Scottish ports. She was at Scapa Flow when the battleship *Vanguard* blew up and sank. Ten days later, on 19 July 1917, she was visited by Admiral Sims of the United States Navy, and the following month she lost two more aircraft, although fortunately the pilots were saved. On the afternoon of 3 November 1917, a successful test flight of a 9400 Sopwith two-seater aircraft was carried out. The plane had a passenger on board and fuel for eight hours, and it was airborne after a run of just under 50 feet. It was also found that by taking only six hours' supply of fuel, a radio transmitter and machine gun could also be carried.

In March 1918 she again underwent a refit at Liverpool, and it was not until 4 May that she arrived back at Scapa Flow. By October 1918 she was operating, with other ships of the Grand Fleet, from Burntisland in the Firth of Forth. She spent her last day at sea on 4 November 1918, arriving back in Burntisland Roads late that day and anchoring there. Also at anchor were the battleships *Royal Oak*, *Ramillies* and *Revenge*, together with the battle-cruiser *Glorious* and the aircraft carrier *Furious*.

In the early hours of the morning of 5 November a heavy squall blew up from the west, and at 3.40 am watchkeepers on board *Royal Oak* saw that *Campania* was dragging her anchors. Five minutes later she collided with the stern of *Royal Oak*, causing her to drag her anchors. Both ships then collided with HMS *Glorious* and a gaping hole was torn in *Campania*'s port side at the stern. At 4.45 am it was clear that *Campania* was sinking by the stern. She had cleared both *Royal Oak* and *Glorious* by 5.30 am, and just over three hours later, at 8.35 am, one of her boilers exploded and she sank stern first in a position 8¾ cables and 163° from Burntisland West Passage.

Two days later the following brief announcement appeared in *The Times*: 'The Secretary of the Admiralty announces:- One of HM auxiliaries was sunk as the result of a collision on Novem-

HMS Campania *with a Fairey 'Campania' on her flight deck.* (Fleet Air Arm Museum)

A seaplane taking off from HMS Campania. (Fleet Air Arm Museum)

HMS Campania *sinking by the stern on the morning of 5 November 1918 off Burntisland.* (A. Kludas)

ber 5. There were no casualties.' It was an ignominious end for a ship which had broken all records on the North Atlantic, and had laid the foundations for the modern Fleet Air Arm. However, on 11 November, just four days after the announcement from the Admiralty, the First World War ended. Not many people were interested in *Campania*'s fate at that moment.

Technical data	
Gross tonnage	12,950 (*Campania*), 12,952 (*Lucania*)
Net tonnage	4,974 (*Campania*), 4,975 (*Lucania*)
Length overall	601 feet (184.9m)
Breadth	65 ft 2 in (20.05m)

Both ships twin screw, powered by two sets of triple expansion engines; 30,000 IHP, 23 knots.

4
Ivernia and *Saxonia*, 1900

In the last decade of the nineteenth century plans were in hand to modernize the Cunard fleet, and it was a programme which would be completed with the *Mauretania* and *Lusitania* in 1907. In the last year of the century a number of Cunard ships were on hire to the government, some of which were elderly, and it was clear that once their service with the government was over they would need replacing. Amongst the tonnage required were large intermediate steamers for the Liverpool to Boston route, vessels with ample cargo capacity and accommodation for a large number of passengers. In 1898 orders were placed for two such ships, of 14,000 gross tons, and they were to become the *Ivernia* and *Saxonia*.

The contract for the first of the two sisters went to Swan Hunter at Wallsend on Tyne, and the *Ivernia* was launched on the afternoon of Thursday 21 September 1899. The ceremony took place in the presence of about 20,000 spectators, with the ship being christened by the Countess of Ravensworth. Three months later came the *Saxonia*, which had been built on Clydebank by John Brown & Co Ltd. Her launching ceremony took place on Saturday 16 December 1899, and this time the naming was carried out by the Hon Mrs G.A. Burns, the wife of one of Cunard's directors.

Both ships provided accommodation for 164 first, 200 second and 1,500 third class passengers. Of course, great publicity was given at the time to the fact that the two liners could easily be

Above *The Saxonia at anchor in the River Mersey.* (Author's collection)

Below SS Ivernia *with her long slim funnel, four masts and a clutter of ventilator cowls.* (Photographic — Stewart Bale)

converted to accommodate 2,000 infantry troops, a regiment of cavalry and a battery of artillery. Stalls were also fitted in order that about 800 head of cattle and 80 horses could be carried. Both vessels had four complete steel decks, lower, main, upper and shelter, and also a steel orlop deck from the forward boiler room to the stem. The bridge deck, which was also above the shelter deck, was 280 feet (86.15 m) long, and the space between the orlop and lower decks forward was insulated for carrying chilled beef. The refrigeration machinery was fitted in a deckhouse on the upper deck.

The first class passengers were accommodated amidships, and the standards were a great improvement on previous ships on this route. The main dining saloon was an elaborately decorated space two decks high with a large central dome. The tables were of the long refectory

Above *The elaborately decorated first class dining saloon of SS Saxonia.* (National Maritime Museum)

Left *A second class two-berth cabin, SS Saxonia.* (National Maritime Museum)

Right *The third class dining space, SS Saxonia.* (National Maritime Museum)

style, with a few smaller ones at each side. The second class accommodation was abaft that of the first class and the third class passengers were accommodated on the main deck forward of the engine room, with a covered promenade space at the forward end of the upper deck. Aft of the engine room on the same deck were the cattle stalls, which were designed to comply with US cattle regulations.

Ivernia and *Saxonia* were twin screw ships, powered by two sets of quadruple expansion engines. The steam was provided by nine single-ended, three-furnace, coal-fired boilers which provided steam at 210 psi; the bunker capacity was 1,500 tons. In all, the main propulsion machinery developed 9,500 IHP giving a speed of 16 knots, and was to prove economical and reliable over the years of service.

The *Ivernia* was the first of the pair to be com-

pleted, and on 24 March 1900 she ran her trials in the North Sea, achieving a speed of just over 16½ knots. When the ships entered service they were the largest in the Cunard fleet, and with their large funnels with heavy rims, which towered 75 feet (23m) above the boat deck, they were instantly recognizable. *Ivernia* made her maiden voyage from Liverpool on 14 April 1900, but it was to New York rather than Boston as had been originally intended, for she had to take the place of ships which were on hire to the government as troop transports for the war in South Africa.

Saxonia made her maiden voyage from Liverpool to Boston on 22 May 1900 and, although she was a sister to *Ivernia*, there were several distinct differences in the profiles of the two ships. *Ivernia* had longer bulwark plating at the stem, while *Saxonia* had two derrick posts on the

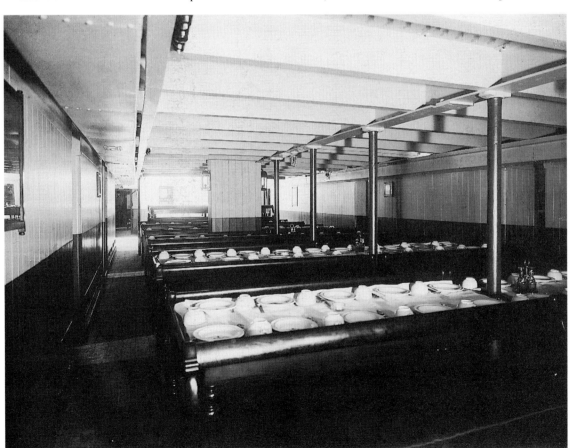

fore deck and an upper bridge deck, as well as a small boat deck beneath the mainmast.

After two round voyages to New York, *Ivernia* reverted to her intended route between Liverpool, Queenstown and Boston, and for the next nine years both ships provided an excellent service for Cunard. In August 1902, *Ivernia* made her fastest Atlantic voyages; she completed her outward journey to Boston in seven days, three hours, 21 minutes, and on the homeward crossing knocked an hour off that time with an average speed of just over 16 knots. Both vessels attained a good reputation for reliability and steadiness at sea. The first mishap to either of the two sisters occurred on Thursday 16 September 1909, when *Saxonia* was homeward bound from Boston. At 3.30 am that morning she was in the Crosby Channel in the River Mersey when a thick fog came down. As she reduced speed, a small tramp steamer came across her bows, and in the manoeuvres that followed she went aground on the Burbo Bank. Tugs were immediately despatched but it was some five hours later, at high tide, that she was pulled free and was able to proceed to the landing stage to disembark her passengers. After an

Looking aft to Saxonia's *navigation bridge.* (National Maritime Museum)

examination by divers it was established that no damage had been done and she was able to continue in service.

Two years later, in May 1911, *Ivernia* was involved in a far more serious incident which left her out of service for five months. She had left Boston for Queenstown and Liverpool on 16 May, 1911, with a crew of 281 and 729 passengers. The voyage had been without incident until 11.40 am on 24 May, when Captain Thomas Potter set a course which would put the Daunts Rock Lightship on his port bow, then, in order to go into Queenstown Harbour, he altered course to pass inside the lightship. Unfortunately *Ivernia* had encountered fog as she approached the Irish coast, and this had not improved as she got closer to Queenstown. The seamen aboard the Daunts Rock Lightship were firing their fog-gun at regular intervals, although this was not heard by Captain Potter. He felt confident of his course, so did not reduce his speed. At 11.49 am, as many of the passengers were on deck looking out for the tender from Queenstown, *Ivernia* struck the submerged Daunts Rock. The collision tore a hole 10 feet wide some 150 feet from the stem in the ship's bottom, and the passengers felt a grating sensation as the bottom of the vessel dragged over the rock.

The engines were immediately put full astern as *Ivernia* listed heavily to starboard. Fortunately the vessel was swung free and she was able to continue towards Queenstown at a very slow speed. The watertight doors were closed, but this measure was unable to prevent serious flooding to the forward compartments. Captain Potter decided to take his ship into the inner harbour at Queenstown, very close to where she usually anchored. Once there, as there seemed to be no immediate danger, he anchored in order that all the passengers could be disembarked by tender, for it was clear that his ship could not continue the voyage to Liverpool. The tender, which had left the deep-water quay at Queenstown, met *Ivernia* just 15 minutes after the accident, and those on board were startled to see the Cunarder down by the head. The passengers were told to make preparations for landing and to get as much baggage ready as they could. Many passengers were having lunch at the time of the accident, but it had soon become clear that all was not well and so the instructions came as no surprise.

With an hour of *Ivernia's* arrival, the first 250 cabin passengers had left the ship, and they were followed by the remainder in a quick succession of tenders. Once they were all landed, the officers and crew of *Ivernia* were able to devote their attention to the salvaging of their ship. As the result of a message to Admiral Coke, who was in command of the Irish Station, the government launch *Hellespont* was soon on the scene with powerful pumps on board. By this time the water was gaining steadily on the ship's pumps and it was hoped that the machinery on board *Hellespont* could change this state of affairs. However, it was soon apparent that the intake of water was still increasing, and during the afternoon it was decided to beach the *Ivernia* on the spitbank. This was accomplished with the aid of tugs and the immediate danger to the vessel was averted. By this time she was so far down by the head that the water level was up as far as her hawse pipe.

Inside the ship, all the cargo in the forward holds, which consisted mainly of sugar, was ruined, as was most of the third class baggage. By Monday 5 June 1911 operations for salving the *Ivernia* had started and soon the divers discovered the full extent of the damage. On the port side they found that the ship's plating had been torn over a length of 40 feet (12.3m), and on the starboard side abreast No 2 hold the damage extended over 30 feet (9.2m). It was on the starboard side that large pieces of timber from an old wreck were found firmly wedged into the fractures. The evidence indicated that *Ivernia* had struck the remains of an American ship, the *Audacious*, a wooden vessel, which had foundered on Daunts Rock many years previously.

In mid-June, *Ivernia's* boilers were lit and steam was raised, and nine days later, on 24 June 1911, she was at last refloated. Soon afterwards she steamed under her own power, accompanied by tugs, to Liverpool where permanent repairs were

made. During her long stay in Queenstown she had been a landmark to the people of the town, and special steamers had been run from Monkstown to connect with the local train from Cork to view the stranded ship. A local vessel, the SS *Avorey*, ran excursions to the *Ivernia* and, according to Mr Charles Nash, the son of a Cunard pilot in the town, 'she was only about 20 minutes rowing away from the shore, and the whole town used to go fishing round her; she seemed to be good bait.'

In July 1911 the Board of Trade held an inquiry into the collision, presided over by a Liverpool stipendiary magistrate and two ship's masters. They delivered their judgement on Saturday 22 July 1911 and it ran thus: 'Having regard to the state of the weather after 11.30 am on 24 May 1911, (a) the vessel should not have continued on the same course, (b) she was navigated at too great a rate of speed, (c) the lead was not used, and it should have been. The SS *Ivernia* struck on or near Daunts Rock, at or about 11.49 am on 24 May, and was seriously damaged thereby, in consequence of the wrongful act and default of the master Thomas Potter, in navigating the vessel at too great a rate of speed in the increasingly thick weather which was experienced after the Old Head of Kinsale had been passed, and in neglecting to verify the actual position of the vessel from time to time by means of the lead.' Captain Potter was severely censured and was ordered to pay £50 costs, but it was felt that, owing to his long service, the painful task of dealing with his master's certficate was not necessary. Soon afterwards, Captain Potter passed through Queenstown again as an emigrant to start a new life in the United States.

For *Ivernia* it was some three months before she returned to service, leaving Liverpool for Boston on 17 October 1911. However, she made only two voyages on this route before she was transferred to the Cunard service from Trieste and Fiume, in the Mediterranean, to New York, together with *Saxonia*. This service had been opened in 1903 by Cunard who very soon found that the transport of the mainly Italian and Hungarian emigrants to the New World was extremely profitable. For the next two years both ships ran through the Mediterranean Sea, calling at Genoa, Naples, Patras and Gibraltar in addition to Trieste and Fiume. In 1913 there were rumours circulating that conditions for emigrants in the Cunard ships operating out of the Mediterranean were well below standard, but as the vessels were inspected on each voyage by a special commission appointed by the Hungarian government, there does not appear to have been any truth in this.

In July 1914, just before the outbreak of war, the two ships were both outward bound from the Mediterranean. *Saxonia* left Gibraltar on 16 July 1914 and arrived in New York ten days later. *Ivernia* left Trieste on the 21st, and she was in Gibraltar when war broke out. On completion of the voyage to New York, *Ivernia* returned to Liverpool where she was taken on hire by the government as a troop transport. *Saxonia* meanwhile left New York during August 1914 and she also returned to Liverpool. For a time she was used as a POW accommodation ship in the Thames, before continuing in the company's service. Between May 1915 and October 1916 she made a dozen round voyages between Liverpool and New York. By now the two sister ships were following different careers, with *Ivernia* making a number of trooping voyages to Canada and the Mediterranean theatre of war.

On 28 December 1916 she left Marseilles with a full complement of over 1,000 troops and a crew of 307. She was bound for Alexandria and was under the command of Captain William Turner, late of the *Lusitania*. On New Year's Eve the destroyer HMS *Rifleman* left Malta to escort her for the final leg of the voyage through the Aegean Sea. At 10.12 am on the following morning they were some 58 miles south-east of Cape Matapan in Greece when *Ivernia* was torpedoed by *UB 47*. The torpedo hit the starboard side abreast the funnel and exploded with terrific force in a boiler room. 22 members of the ship's company were killed instantly by the explosion, and HMS *Rifleman* tried to locate the U-boat. Soon afterwards she went alongside the crippled Cunarder and took off 666 troops and 36 crew

members. More survivors, including Captain Turner, were taken off by accompanying trawlers. A further 85 casualties were incurred when the *Rifleman*, racing to find the U-boat, sank one of *Ivernia's* boats. Within an hour of being torpedoed *Ivernia* sank, and her survivors were landed at Suda Bay in Crete the same day. Altogether there were 120 casualties, with 36 crew members and 84 troops killed in the disaster.

In 1917 *Saxonia* was taken over by the government under the liner requisition scheme, and made numerous voyages between New York and Liverpool carrying troops and cargo. In December 1918, after the Armistice, along with many other ships, she transported US troops from Brest back home to New York. One of her officers recalled this period and how the American soldiers were model passengers, being so happy to be going home. He remembered the terrific welcome they received in New York from 'Mayor Hylan's Welcome Committee', the masses of small boats all sounding their whistles, and the tenders crowded with young women waving and blowing kisses, 'so that the doughboys were quite beside themselves'. At the pier there were long trestle tables laden with doughnuts, ice-cream, cakes and cigarettes. The same young women who had welcomed the soldiers on the tenders were there to serve them, and despite being weighed down with kit such as steel helmets and rifles, they were all given plenty of goodies. In the words of *Saxonia's* third officer, 'It was a happy scene, typical of the spontaneous affection of the American character'. On the return voyage she carried passengers on the company's account, and much-needed cargo. *Saxonia* made her final voyage on government service in early April, and after returning to Liverpool she was refitted for peacetime service once again.

By September 1919 *Saxonia* was ready to join the Cunard fleet once more, and on the 27th of that month she was moored off Tilbury, now to join the London–Cherbourg–Halifax service. For the first voyage her third class accommodation was taken by Canadian troops, and they were conveyed to Tilbury from London's St Pancras station in lorries, while other passengers were embarked in tenders from Old Swan Pier near London Bridge and taken down the Thames to join the ship. *Saxonia* left Tilbury on the afternoon of Monday 29 September 1919, and ahead of her were another five years of unbroken service with Cunard.

By 1924 several new medium-sized ships had been added to the Cunard fleet, and *Saxonia*, with her long, slim funnel, four masts, festoons of ventilator cowls and decks cluttered with lifeboats, was well and truly outdated. In November of that year she was laid up at Tilbury and four months later, in March 1925, she was sold to Dutch shipbreakers for £47,000. She was finally broken up at Hendrik Ido Ambacht, near Rotterdam.

Technical data

Gross tonnage	14,067 (*Ivernia*), 14,281 (*Saxonia*)
Net tonnage	9,058 (*Ivernia*), 9,100 (*Saxonia*)
Length overall	598 ft (184m)
Breadth	64 ft 9 in (19.92m)

Both ships twin screw, powered by two sets of quadruple expansion engines; 10,500 IHP, 16 knots.

5
Pannonia and *Slavonia*, 1903

During the first few years of the twentieth century Cunard was negotiating with the Hungarian government in order to win a contract to operate a service between Fiume, now Rijeka in Yugoslavia but then part of the Austro–Hungarian Empire, and New York. The contract was mainly for the conveying of emigrants to the New World, and in the spring of 1904 the Hungarian Minister of the Interior agreed that the business should be awarded to Cunard.

In anticipation of this new and very important trade Cunard had prepared four ships to run on the route, the first two of which were the *Pannonia* and *Slavonia*. The former was laid down in 1902 by John Brown & Co of Clydebank for Sir Christopher Furness. However, even before the launch the uncompleted hull was purchased by Cunard and completed specifically for the Mediterranean–New York service. She was launched on 5 September 1902, and was ready for sea in early May 1903. After completing her acceptance trials she left for Trieste later that month.

The *Pannonia* was a vessel of 9,851 gross tons with an overall length of 486 feet and a breadth of 59 feet. She had a straight stem, a central bridge deck, a poop deck with a counterstern, a tall slender funnel and four masts. She was a twin screw ship, powered by two sets of triple expansion engines and her four single-ended coal-fired boilers supplied steam and 90 psi. In all, the main propulsion machinery developed

811 NHP and gave the ship a service speed of just over 12 knots. *Pannonia* was essentially an emigrant ship with accommodation for only 90 first and 70 second class passengers. Her third class had dormitory accommodation for 2,066 passengers.

The *Slavonia* was a similar ship to *Pannonia* and had originally a gross tonnage of 8,831. She was built on the River Wear at Sunderland by Sir James Laing & Sons for the British India Line. The keel was laid in early 1902 and she was lauched on 15 November of that year as the *Yamuna*. At that time she was the largest ship to be built on the River Wear, and in order to complete her she had to be moved down river below the bridges for the fitting of her funnel and masts, which was finished in June 1903. *Slavonia* had an overall length of 510 feet (157m), and a profile similar to the *Pannonia*, with a straight stem, a central bridge, a poop deck and a counterstern. She also had a tall, slim funnel centrally placed over the superstructure, but only two masts. Again, like the *Pannonia*, she was a twin screw ship powered by two sets of triple expansion engines and coal fired with six single-ended boilers. These provided steam at 200 psi and, with 929 NHP, the ship had a speed of 12½ knots.

Originally *Yamuna* was intended for the British India Line service between London and Calcutta, calling occasionally at Singapore and other ports around Burma and Malaya as well. She

The British India liner Yamuna, *which became Cunard's* Slavonia. (P&O)

had been designed to carry 40 first class passengers and as was common in ships operating east of Suez, 800 deck passengers. She left London for India in the summer of 1903, and it soon became clear that she was too big for BI's service, which required its ships to call at small, out of the way ports with very shallow waters. The *Yamuna* only stayed with the BI Line for five months before Cunard, which was looking for another ship for its Mediterranean–New York service, offered to buy her. This offer was accepted by the British India Line and the new owners sent the vessel back to Sunderland in order that she could be modified for their very different service.

Her accommodation was altered to carry 70 first, 74 second and 1,900 third class passengers. With the installation of the emigrant dormitories, the ship's gross tonnage was increased to 10,606, and her name was changed to *Slavonia*. She left Sunderland for a positioning voyage to Trieste on 17 March 1904 and thus joined Cunard's new service, which was to give hope to so many emigrants from eastern Europe.

The Pannonia, *with her sister* Slavonia, *was intended for the Mediterranean emigrant service.* (University of Liverpool).

Soon after Cunard's new route opened, in May 1904, the Hungarian government was bombarded with requests from other shipping lines, all eager to compete in the carriage of the Hungarian emigrant traffic. Prominent among these was Albert Ballin of the Hamburg–Amerika Line, who had long felt that the route would have a great future. This competition started a price war on the Atlantic as the various companies attempted to undercut each other. At the time Cunard's third class fare from Trieste or Fiume to New York was £2 10s per adult.

Both *Pannonia* and *Slavonia* sailed successfully on the company's account. On their westbound journeys they were full of emigrants, and on the return voyage from New York they carried rather more first and second class passengers as many people returned to their former homes, some of

An excellent view of the Slavonia — *she was wrecked off the Azores in June 1909.* (Photographic — Stewart Bale)

them now materially wealthier than they had been, to visit relatives. Sometimes the two ships would run cruises from Liverpool to the Mediterranean, and *Slavonia* sailed on one such cruise on 3 March 1909 for 14 days to Cadiz, Tangier, Naples and Trieste, then back to Liverpool. Following this cruise she had one more westbound voyage to make before her career was brought to a very premature end.

The *Slavonia* left New York for Trieste and Fiume at 2 pm on Thursday 3 June 1909, with 110 first and second class passengers and 500 in the steerage. For the next six days the voyage passed uneventfully, but during the evening of Wednesday 9 June she encountered thick fog. At the time the ship was in the vicinity of the Azores, the Portuguese islands situated in mid-Atlantic. At 2.30 am on the next day, the *Slavonia* went aground on rocks two miles south-west of Flores Island, one of the most north-westerly of the archipelago, and her engine room was flooded, thus preventing any efforts to get off the rocks under her own steam. Distress messages were sent out immediately and these were received by the Norddeutscher Lloyd's *Prinzess Irene* and Hamburg–Amerika's *Batavia*. Both ships had left New York two days after *Slavonia* bound for Mediterranean ports, and their greater speeds had put them both between 150 and 160 miles west of *Slavonia*'s position.

In the meantime, however, *Slavonia*'s passengers were mustered on the upper deck; generally discipline was good, although one steerage passenger panicked and jumped overboard, but he was rescued by a crew member. The *Prinzess Irene* was the first to arrive on the scene and the transhipment of the cabin passengers started. The *Batavia* arrived soon afterwards and she took on board all the steerage passengers. By midday all of *Slavonia*'s passengers had been transferred and only her crew remained on board; they were landed at Velos on Sao Jorge Island the next day. It was soon becoming clear that the *Slavonia* was a total wreck, and this was confirmed on 16 June. All the baggage on board was lost together with a general cargo consisting mainly of copper ingots, coffee and machinery, as well as three motor cars. The *Prinzess Irene*, which already had a full complement of her own passengers, landed *Slavonia*'s cabin passengers at Gibraltar on 14 June, and three days later *Batavia* disembarked the steerage passengers at Naples. Some days later the Liverpool salvage steamer *Ranger* attempted to save some of the cargo, but very little was salvaged and the *Slavonia* was soon broken up by the heavy Atlantic seas.

Meanwhile, the *Pannonia* continued in the Mediterranean service. On 25 July 1914 she left Gibraltar for New York and she was there when war broke out ten days later. For the time being the Hungarian trade had finished, and for the next 20 months she ran between London and New York carrying only cabin passengers and cargo. At the end of May 1916 Montreal and Quebec were added to her itinerary, and it was not long before her third class quarters were full of troops all eastbound from Canada to the trenches of France. The *Pannonia* survived the First World War and in the remaining months of 1918 made two voyages between Avonmouth and Portland, Oregon, before returning to Tilbury on 3 January 1919.

Two months later she was back in Trieste to resume her original Mediterranean service. Now, with eastern Europe and the Balkan countries in particular still reeling from the surgery which had split up the old Austro–Hungarian Empire, there were plenty of emigrants wishing to start new lives in the United States. Even her east-bound voyages were full of passengers, travelling home to see the families from which they had been separated during the long years of war. One of *Pannonia*'s officers recalls these happy Balkan people singing and dancing 'gay czandas' on the upper decks at sea. However, politically the region was very unstable with many bitter fanatics who were dissatisfied with the way the war had carved up their countries. Trieste especially was a troubled city, with riots and strikes, and perhaps it was inevitable that some of this trouble should spread to the *Pannonia*. During the summer of 1920 the ship's two Italian doctors, who were carried to comply with Italian

The Pannonia *was sold for scrap in 1922.* (Photographic — Stewart Bale)

emigration regulations, attempted to murder each other.

In September 1921 *Pannonia* made her last voyage from the Mediterranean and then returned to the Liverpool–New York route, where she took the place of vessels undergoing overhaul. By the spring of 1922, with the post-war rebuilding programme well under way and new ships joining the Cunard fleet, *Pannonia* was withdrawn from service and laid up in Hamburg. She lay at the port from April to October 1922, before being sold for scrap. *Pannonia* and *Slavonia* were little-known Cunard liners, far removed from the glamour of the Atlantic giants, but they had performed a useful and profitable service for the company.

Technical data	
Gross tonnage	9,851 (*Pannonia*), 10,606 (*Slavonia*)
Net tonnage	6,210 (*Pannonia*), 6,725 (*Slavonia*)
Length overall	486 ft 5 in (149.6m) (*Pannonia*), 510 ft (156.92m) (*Slavonia*)
Breadth	59 ft 3 in (18.23m) (*Pannonia*), 59 ft 6 in (18.3m) (*Slavonia*)

Both ships twin screw, powered by two sets of triple expansion engines; 811 NHP, 12.5 knots (*Pannonia*), 929 NHP, 13 knots (*Slavonia*).

6
Carpathia, 1903

The *Carpathia* will always be remembered as the Cunarder which made the dramatic rescue dash to pick up the survivors of the ill-fated *Titanic*, and there is no doubt that this was the highlight of her career. At 13,603 gross tons, she was a slightly smaller version of the *Ivernia* and *Saxonia*, but she was designed primarily for the Hungarian emigrant service between Fiume and New York. The contract for her construction went to Messrs C.S. Swan Hunter of Newcastle upon Tyne, and she was launched on 6 August 1902. She should have been ready for service in January 1903, but this was delayed by a series of strikes by the joiners who were employed in fitting her out. It was Wednesday 22 April 1903 before *Carpathia* was completed, and she left the Tyne for her trials which took place *en route* to the Mersey. Present on board for the trip round the north coast of Scotland were Sir William White, the director of naval construction, and a number of Cunard directors. Most of the first day was spent in passing down the river to Tynemouth and in trial manoeuvres off the mouth of the river. On the following day the Orkneys and the Hebrides were seen at their best, and in the early hours of Saturday 25 April *Carpathia* anchored in the Mersey off Liverpool which, at dawn, was overshadowed by a pall of haze and smoke.

The building of *Carpathia*, as with *Pannonia* and *Slavonia*, was seen as a bold bid for the custom of the thousands of east European emigrants to the USA. The ship was described as a 'saloon and third class passenger and cargo steamer', and the inducements offered to the would-be emigrants were reasonably cheap fares (£5 10s for the passage), and accommodation which was far superior to anything offered previously. The ship could accommodate 200 second class and up to 1,700 third class passengers. The striking feature about her was the excellence of the third class accommodation. All the passengers in this class were berthed in two, three or four berth cabins, and they had the use of a large dining saloon. Another innovation was the fact that all the meals were included in the fare, which was quite a saving for the passengers. They also had a large smoking room and social room, together with the use of a covered promenade. For the saloon passengers there were airy and well-fitted cabins, and a spacious dining saloon capable of seating all the passengers in one sitting. There was a good-sized smoking room and a lounge, library and writing room combined. The whole of the saloon accommodation was simple and free from any gaudy decoration.

Carpathia was a twin screw ship, powered by two sets of quadruple expansion engines, the steam being provided by seven coal-fired single-engine boilers. The machinery developed 9,000 IHP and gave the ship a service speed of 14 to 15 knots. So, although she was not fast she was economic to run and, from the emigrants' point of view, a comfortable ship. She also had a dead-

SS Carpathia, a slightly smaller version of the Ivernia *and* Saxonia. (University of Liverpool)

weight carrying capacity for over 12,500 tons of cargo.

It was not surprising to find that the maiden voyage, scheduled for Tuesday 5 May 1903, was heavily booked. She left Liverpool that afternoon commanded by Captain J.C. Barr, an experienced Cunard master. She had aboard 140 saloon passengers and 1,650 in the third class. In fact, all those who tried to book steerage could not be accommodated and about 100 would-be passengers had to be left behind at Queenstown. She had a trouble-free voyage and once in New York the majority of the passengers were full of praise for the excellence of the catering and for the ship's steadiness at sea. *Carpathia* continued on the Liverpool–New York run until late November 1903 when she sailed into the Mediterranean to Trieste and Fiume for the winter season. At the end of her season on the emigrant service, and just prior to leaving Fiume for Liverpool, the ship was inspected by several members of the Hungarian Emigration Commission, together with the King of Sweden and the governor of the city, the visit coinciding with Cunard winning the Hungarian emigrant contract. All of the visitors were particularly impressed with

the extreme cleanliness and good order which characterized the ship.

Carpathia sailed once again from Liverpool to New York on Tuesday 31 May 1904, her first year of service having been a great success. She ran without incident over the following years, and every winter she made a positioning cruise from Liverpool to Naples, calling at the most attractive Mediterranean ports. The passengers travelled back from Italy by the overland route — not a great deal different from todays' 'fly-cruises'. By 1909 *Carpathia* was spending all year on the Mediterranean service, and she only returned to Liverpool at the end of each year for an annual overhaul.

At 4.30 pm on 10 February 1912, *Carpathia* left Liverpool commanded by Captain A.H. Rostron RD RNR for her positioning cruise, which took her to Gibraltar, Algiers, Malta, Alexandria, Constantinople and Phaleron Bay (Pireaus). She disembarked her passengers at Trieste on 4 March and then started her season on the service from this port to New York. She left Trieste on the afternoon of 6 March and on her voyage to the USA she called at Fiume, Messina, Palermo, Naples and Gibraltar, arriving in New York at 9 am on the 29th — four days before the *Titanic* was delivered to her owners, the White Star Line. After a 13-day stopover in

New York, *Carpathia* left at 12.03 pm on Thursday 11 April 1912, at exactly the same time as the *Titanic* was making her call at Queenstown before setting out on that fateful voyage into the North Atlantic.

At 11.40 pm on Sunday 14 April 1912, the *Titanic* struck an iceberg in a position 41° 46′N/50° 14′W and, at 12.15 am the following morning, just over half an hour after the collision, when it became clear that his ship was

sinking, Captain Edward J. Smith ordered distress signals to be transmitted. *Carpathia* had been at sea for just over 84 hours, and the air temperature was rising as she set south-easterly courses from New York towards Gibraltar. Her passengers were settling down to their fourth night at sea, and her radio operator Harold Cottam was about to go off duty for the night, for in those days there were no 24-hour radio watches. Suddenly Cottam received the *Titanic*'s distress call; he informed Captain Rostron and the *Carpathia* set a north-westerly course at full speed to cover the 58 miles between herself and the *Titanic*'s last-known position.

The engineers, firemen and greasers did a magnificent job, working their vessel up to a speed of 17 knots, well above what was thought to be her best. Captain Rostron organized his crew to take on board survivors, and it is not difficult to imagine the *Carpathia* shuddering and vibrating as she surged along on her errand of mercy. After dashing through the ice field she arrived at the spot where *Titanic* had sunk at just before 4 am that morning. It is now legendary how *Carpathia* rescued the 703 survivors of the mighty *Titanic*, 1,503 people having perished in those icy waters.

By 9 am that morning *Carpathia* had embarked the survivors and had also taken on board the *Titanic*'s lifeboats. Soon after this the Leyland vessel *Californian* arrived on the scene, having spent the night only 10 to 15 miles from the scene with her radio closed down. Captain Rostron decided that, as he did not have enough food on board to make the Azores, he would return to New York, and at 9.10 pm on Thursday 18 April *Carpathia* was secured alongside pier 54 in the city. Thousands of people witnessed her arrival, for the world was just learning the full horror of the *Titanic* tragedy. Amidst all the controversy and publicity which raged over the next months, the roles of Captain Rostron, his crew and *Carpathia* in the saga were

A lifeboat filled with Titanic *survivors who are about to climb aboard the* Carpathia. *(Illustrated London News)*

beyond reproach. Perhaps the personalities who come to the fore amongst *Carpathia*'s crew besides Captain Rostron himself were her Chief Officer, Thomas W. Hankinson, Chief Engineer Alexander B. Johnstone, Chief Steward Evan H. Hughes, Purser Ernest G.F. Brown and, of course, Harold Cottam the wireless operator and doctors McGee, Leuyel and Risicati. To add to their credit, Cunard declined any recompense for *Carpathia*'s mercy dash, stating that they 'consider it a privilege that *Carpathia* and her crew were the means of picking up the *Titanic*'s survivors'.

Over the next 12 months the honours and awards for Captain Rostron flooded in, but it was business as usual for the *Carpathia*, and two days after she arrived in New York with *Titanic*'s survivors, she left once again for Gibraltar, Naples, Trieste and Fiume, which she reached on 8 May 1912. She made five further voyages to New York from the Mediterranean, the last of them arriving on 5 December 1912. Seven days later she left the port for Boston, Queenstown and Liverpool where she arrived on the last day of the year for her annual overhaul.

Once work was completed, *Carpathia* cruised out to the Mediterranean to position once again for the emigrant service to New York. Fortunately that year passed without incident and, on 4 August 1914, when war broke out, she was in Fiume. She sailed at once for New York, then made one more voyage to the Mediterranean. When she left New York on 5 September 1914, she incurred the wrath of the Italian government for failing to obtain an emigrant licence from the Italian consul-general, which the Italian government required of belligerent ships carrying their nationals. Despite the efforts of the British embassy to mitigate, Cunard was fined 111,500 lire.

For the last months of 1914 *Carpathia*'s terminal port in the Mediterranean was transferred to Piraeus, but in 1915, with the flow of emigrants drying up, she was switched to the Liverpool, New York and Boston run, which she faithfully maintained until her end in July 1918. At just after midnight on 17 July, *Carpathia* was 170 miles north-west of Bishops Rock on her first evening out of Liverpool and bound for Boston, when she was hit by a torpedo fired by *U 55*. Five of her crew, all in the engine room, were killed by the explosion which followed, but fortunately the remaining crew members and her 57 passengers got away safely in the ship's lifeboats. The Azalea-type sloop HMS *Snowdrop* was close to hand and her gunners sighted and engaged the submarine which submerged quickly. At 12.40 am that day, the *Carpathia* sank in a position 49° 25'N/10° 25'W, and all that remained was for the *Snowdrop* to take on board the survivors and return them to Liverpool, from where they had set sail the day before. It was a sad end for a ship which, only six years previously, had made one of the most dramatic rescues in maritime history.

Technical data	
Gross tonnage	13,603
Net tonnage	8,660
Length overall	540 ft (166.15m)
Breadth	64 ft 3 in (19.76m)

Twin screw, powered by two sets of quadruple expansion engines; 9,000 IHP, 15 knots.

7
Caronia and *Carmania*, 1905

When the *Caronia* and *Carmania* first entered service in 1905 they were the largest ships in the Cunard fleet, but this was only for a short time as they were soon overshadowed by the *Lusitania* and *Mauretania*. However, this did not detract from the impression of power that they conveyed throughout their careers. The two sisters were also something of an experiment for the Cunard company, which was eager to compare the steam turbine with conventional reciprocating engines. Therefore it was decided that when new tonnage was built, two almost identical ships would be constructed. One would be powered by quadruple expansion engines, the other would have Parsons steam turbines, in order that the two propulsion systems could be tested under identical conditions.

The contract for the building of the two 21,000 gross ton vessels went to John Brown & Co Ltd at Clydebank, and the first of the pair to be launched was the *Caronia*. The ceremony took place on Tuesday 13 July 1904, when Mrs J. Choate, the wife of the United States Ambassador in London, sent her down the slipway into the River Clyde. At the luncheon which followed the launch, Mr Choate made a speech on behalf of his wife which seems as appropriate today as it was 84 years ago. He started by saying that not only was the *Caronia* the noblest, but she was the largest vessel 'that had ever kissed British waters'. He went on to say that he hoped that the American and British flags which adorned the ship would never be further apart, and that they were emblems of peace, unity and friendship between the two nations, of which he had long been an advocate. He finished by complimenting the Cunard company in being the organization which had done more than any to promote friendship between the two great nations and 'in fact the Cunard company had made the Atlantic a comfortable ferry'.

In fact, the *Caronia* was going to be a very comfortable ferry, especially for those travelling first class. She had a gross tonnage of 19,687 and she was a twin screw ship powered in the traditional manner of the early years of this century by two sets of quadruple expansion engines,

The *Caronia of 1905*. (Author's collection)

which gave her a service speed of 18 knots. The steam was supplied by eight double-ended and five single-ended coal-fired boilers. They generated steam at 200 psi and were worked on a forced draught system.

By 21 January 1905 *Caronia* had been completed and she was opened to the press in the builders' yard at Clydebank; shortly afterwards she sailed for the Mersey and drydocking. Just ten days later she was ready to leave for her trials on the Clyde, and a large number of guests embarked for the voyage. At Skelmorlie she ran over the measured mile at 19½ knots, which was well above her service speed.

The first class passengers had the whole or partial use of five of the eight decks, the topmost of which was the boat deck, with a spacious promenade and a lounge which was open to both the ladies and gentlemen — quite a revolution in the social world of Edwardian Britain, and an idea which had become popular in hotels. Below the boat deck on the upper promenade deck was the drawing room, with an attached writing room, the smoking room and a number of *en suite* state rooms. Beneath this was the promenade deck and a large number of the first class cabins, most of which were single berth. Further aft were the second class smoking room and drawing room. Lower still was the saloon deck with mainly first and second class cabins and the dining saloons for both of these classes. The first class saloon was a beautiful room, with the deckhead open to a round gallery in the centre. It was supported by carved wooden pillars and these, together with the deckhead and panelled sides of the room, were painted in white enamel picked out with gold. The carpets and upholstery were rose coloured and the main source of light came from the pink shaded lamps on the many tables which, when they were covered with clean linen, gleaming cutlery and glass, and decorated with fresh flowers, looked magnificent.

Below again was the upper deck, which on the starboard side had a range of cabins which could be converted from first to second class as required. Beneath the upper deck was the main deck which was given over entirely to the third class accommodation, whose cabins were either two, four or six berth rooms. The steerage accommodation was on the lower deck and it was arranged so that bulkheads could be erected between the berths, and the whole area could be converted into third class cabins as on the deck above. One innovation which was fitted in both ships was the 'Stone–Lloyd' apparatus for closing all watertight doors simultaneously from the bridge by means of hydraulic controls.

The Caronia *in the River Thames.* (Museum in Docklands)

The Caronia *docking at Tilbury.* (Museum in Docklands)

CUNARD R.M.S."CARMANIA"

An excellent painting of the Carmania. (Author's collection)

This description of the accommodation on board the *Caronia* will also serve for the *Carmania*, as the internal layout of the two vessels was very similar.

Caronia, commanded by Captain R.C. Warr, left Liverpool on her maiden voyage to New York on Saturday 25 February 1905, sailing via Queenstown. She arrived in New York nine days later, early in the morning of 6 March. It was an uneventful voyage, with no records attempted and no pressure put on the main propulsion machinery, and she averaged 16.13 knots for the crossing.

A few days earlier, on Tuesday 21 February, the *Carmania* had been launched at Clydebank. This time the naming ceremony was performed by Lady Blythswood, the wife of a former aide to Queen Victoria, and although the event caused quite a stir in the press, a great deal of attention was given to the fact that *Carmania* was a forerunner for the 'big turbine ship of 760 feet to be built for Cunard'. This was of course the *Lusitania*. Later that year, in mid-November, the *Carmania* underwent her speed trials on the Clyde and, despite the fact that she had not been docked for hull cleaning, she achieved a speed of 21 knots, well above the contract requirement. Once her trials were completed and the invited

guests disembarked, the ship left for Liverpool which she reached on Wednesday 22 November 1905. Ten days later, on Saturday 2 December, she too left Liverpool on her maiden voyage to New York via Queenstown. In spite of very severe weather all the way across the Atlantic, *Carmania* arrived off New York on 10 December; she was unable to embark a pilot that evening because of the inclement conditions, so she did not go alongside until the following day.

Several engineering experts had taken passage in *Carmania* for the maiden voyage, and all were eager to see how the turbines performed. She was a triple screw vessel powered by three direct-acting Parsons steam turbines. The centre shaft was driven by the high-pressure turbine and the side shafts by separate low-pressure turbines, with the astern turbines forming the after end of the LP turbines. Although *Carmania*'s machinery took up the same space as *Caronia*'s, there was a weight saving of 5 per cent with the former, whose boilers and steam supply were identical to that of her older sister, and she was coal fired. In spite of the rough weather the new machinery worked very smoothly and all the experts were very enthusiastic about it.

On 17 May 1905, *Caronia*, on her third round voyage to New York, had her first mishap. She was leaving the harbour when she ran aground off Sandy Hook and despite the efforts of seven tugs her bows remained stuck fast in the sandy bottom. She remained this way until 8 am the following day when she was refloated on the high tide, with the aid of the tugs. After anchoring and being inspected by divers, it was ascertained that there was no damage and she was able to resume her voyage, arriving at Liverpool on 27 May. Her master said that the accident was due to a schooner running across *Caronia*'s bows, and he had to choose between ramming the schooner, colliding with the *Kaiser Wilhelm II* or going off his course, which in fact he decided to do.

For the next few years both ships ran without incident, and on 4 September 1909 *Caronia* was the second Cunard vessel to call at Fishguard on her homeward voyage; within 20 minutes of dropping anchor she had landed all her passengers for London and the Continent. In September 1911 the *Carmania* was delayed in Halifax NS with damage to her turbine blades, but fortunately this was repaired in two days and she was able to sail for New York.

However, at 5 pm on Sunday 2 June 1910, she was lying in the Huskisson Dock at Liverpool when fire broke out in her coal bunkers. It was soon evident that the blaze was extremely serious and great volumes of smoke were pouring from the upper decks and superstructure. Three fire brigades attended very quickly and vast quantities of water were pumped into the ship. Despite this it was some three hours before the fire was extinguished, and upon examination the following day it was found that serious damage had been caused to both the first and second class dining saloons, and to passenger cabins and other public rooms. Fortunately no damage was done to the hull or machinery, and repairs were started at once. The *Carmania* had arrived in the Mersey on Sunday 26 May, and she was due to sail again for New York on 4 June. This voyage had to be cancelled and it was Tuesday 27 August 1912 before she was again able to take her place in the Cunard express service.

At noon on Saturday 4 October 1913, *Carmania* left New York for Liverpool and steamed eastwards into foul Atlantic weather with gale force winds and mountainous seas which, at that

The Caronia *at sea.* (University of Liverpool)

time of year, was not unusual. However, at about 8 am on 9 October, *Carmania* received an SOS from the 3,602 gross ton emigrant ship *Volturno*, which was on fire in Mid-Atlantic in a position 48° 30′N/34° 57′W. *Carmania* was about 78 miles away and Captain James Barr set course for the stricken ship. The *Volturno* was owned by the Canadian Northern Steamship Company Ltd, and she had been chartered to the Uranian Steamship Company since 4 April 1910. She had been employed between Rotterdam and the New World, carrying both emigrants and cargo, and it was in this capacity that *Volturno* had left Rotterdam for Halifax NS on Thursday 2 October 1913, carrying 24 first class passengers, 540 steerage passengers and a crew of 93. Part of her cargo consisted of barrels of barium oxide and, after steaming through severe gales for seven days, one of the barrels broke loose and started a serious fire in her forward hold.

Captain Barr made for *Volturno*'s position at 16½ knots which, in the severe weather, was all that could be managed. He had lines put round *Carmania* and got out ladders, and told both the purser and doctor to prepare to receive survivors. He also picked two good boat crews and made six boats ready for lowering. Just over four hours after receiving the SOS, *Carmania* arrived off *Volturno* which was visible for miles because of a huge pall of black smoke. Captain Barr got his ship to leeward of the *Volturno* and lowered a boat which was commanded by *Carmania's* Chief Officer with a volunteer crew. However, in the extremely rough sea it was not long before all the oars but three were washed away and the waves were threatening to swamp the boat. There was no chance of it getting anywhere near the *Volturno* and it was two hours before it could be recovered safely by *Carmania*. Life-rafts were thrown over the side, but these were immediately swept away by the furious seas.

Captain Barr then tried to manoeuvre his ship so that *Carmania's* stem was within 100 feet of *Volturno's* stern, but it was not possible to get lines on board because of the gales. By then other vessels had arrived on the scene and Captain Barr signalled to them that as his ship was hard to manoeuvre he would keep out of the way and not hamper other vessels. All that night *Carmania* stood by along with a growing number of smaller vessels, and during the night she picked up a boat's crew from the *Minneapolis*, who had been away from their ship for five hours. By the next morning the gale had moderated and it was possible to start transferring passengers to the rescue ships. In the event, 103 passengers from the *Volturno* and 30 crew members were lost; *Carmania* took on board only one survivor, and he was landed at Fishguard on 13 October. Six days later, at 8 pm on Saturday 10 October 1913, *Caronia* passed the hulk of the *Volturno* in mid-Atlantic and reported her still burning fiercely. A further four days later, Captain Rostron of the *Carpathia* sighted the smoking hulk still drifting in the Atlantic.

Until the summer of 1914 both *Caronia* and *Carmania* were employed on the Liverpool–New York service. On 22 July the *Caronia* arrived back in the River Mersey, and did not sail again that year under the Red Ensign. On the outbreak of war on 4 August she was requisitioned by the government for service as an armed merchant cruiser. *Carmania* arrived back in Liverpool from New York three days after the declaration of war and she too was immediately requisitioned and converted for service as an AMC. She had been

due to sail again to the USA on 11 August, but this was cancelled as she prepared to go to war. Both vessels underwent conversion in the Huskisson Dock, Liverpool, and by 10 August they had been painted battleship grey, and were armed with eight 4.7 inch guns with a range of 9,300 yards. *Caronia* was the first to be completed, and she was commissioned into the Royal Navy on 8 August commanded by Captain Litchfield RN. Two days later she put to sea and on the 19th she captured her first prize of war, the German barque *Odessa* with a cargo of nitrate. By the following day she had towed the *Odessa* into Bantry Bay, before departing for Liverpool. She left the Mersey once again for Halifax, Nova Scotia, on 27 August, and after suffering a small engine room fire and having put a boarding party on to the SS *Noordam*, she arrived in the Canadian port on 14 September. On 1 October she sailed on her first 'New York Patrol' off the Ambrose Light Vessel, and she was to remain on this duty for the next six months.

Meanwhile, back in the Huskisson Dock, the *Carmania* had commissioned on 14 August 1914, commanded by Captain Noel Grant RN, with her Cunard master, Captain James C. Barr, as her navigating officer. She sailed from Liverpool for the South Atlantic the following day and arrived in Shell Bay, Bermuda, eight days later, on 23 August.

The day before, the 18,800 gross ton three-funneled German liner *Cap Trafalgar*, owned by the Hamburg–South America Line, had left Montevideo for a rendezvous at Trinidade Island in the South Atlantic off the coast of Brazil, although rumours at the time reported her heading for Swakopmund in German South-West Africa, to be used as a troop transport. Once at sea, the *Cap Trafalgar's* crew removed the ship's after funnel and disguised her superstructure, so as to give the appearance of a two-funneled Cunarder. Once he arrived at Trinidade Island, her master, Captain Julius Wirth, met several German auxiliaries and his ship was coaled and armed with two 10.5 cm guns and six 3.7 cm heavy machine-guns. In the first days of September 1914 the work was completed and the *Cap Trafalgar* sailed on her first patrol as an auxiliary. *Carmania* left Bermuda on 29 August and four days later she arrived in the West Indian island of Trinidad in the Caribbean where she stayed for two days, leaving on 4 September and heading south for the islands off the coast of Brazil, where she was to assist in the Royal Navy's search for German vessels.

At 10.30 am on Monday 14 September 1914, the *Carmania* sighted three ships off the west coast of Trinidade Island in the South Atlantic. On nearing them it was observed that there was a large liner, which was thought to be either *Cap Trafalgar* or *Berlin*, coaling from two colliers. *Carmania*'s ship's company went to action stations and as she got closer the vessels separated and made off in different directions. The large liner, which was in fact the *Cap Trafalgar*, altered course to starboard and headed towards the *Carmania*. At about 8,500 yards *Carmania* fired a shot across the liner's bows and the *Cap Trafalgar* immediately opened fire from all her starboard guns. *Carmania* replied with all her port guns and the battle was on. Most of the enemy shots passed over *Carmania* causing damage to her masts, funnel, derricks and ventilators. Owing to the decreasing range the *Cap Trafalgar*'s machine guns were becoming extremely dangerous and *Carmania* altered course until all her starboard guns were engaged.

Two of *Carmania*'s hits were seen to fracture steam pipes forward, and the German ship was observed to be well on fire forward and listing to starboard. Then a shell passed through a cabin under *Carmania*'s bridge and, although it failed to explode, it started a fire. The blaze spread rapidly since there was no water available to fight it, the ship's firemain having been fractured, and chemical extinguishers were of little use. *Carmania*'s bridge was thus abandoned and the ship was steered from aft. Fortunately she was able to continue firing, and soon the enemy ship, which was listing heavily to starboard, capsized and went down bows first with her colours still flying. *Carmania* was unable to rescue any of the survivors as the fierce fire

The shambles on HMS Carmania's *bridge after her action with the German auxiliary* Cap Trafalgar. *(Imperial War Museum)*

necessitated keeping the ship before the wind.

The battle had lasted one hour and 40 minutes and during that time 79 projectiles had hit the *Carmania* making 304 holes in the vessel. The damage she incurred was serious and included five holes in her waterline, the bridge destroyed by fire, and the loss of all steering gear forward including engine room communications, fire control and navigational instruments. Seven men were killed in the action, the most senior of them being CPO John C. Burfitt of Bourton in Dorset. Seven more were very seriously wounded and two of these died two days later. There were 21 men less seriously wounded. Fortunately by the late afternoon of 14 September, *Carmania*'s firemain system, had been repaired and the fires were extinguished. She reached the safety of Abrolhos Rocks on 16 September and the following day she left for Sierra Leone, escorted by the AMC HMS *Macedonia* (ex-P&O). During the voyage the officers and men of *Macedonia* were ordered to check *Carmania*'s position every half hour during the night, and her ship's company raised £61 for the relatives of *Carmania*'s dead. *Carmania* reached Freetown on 26 September, and two days later she arrived in Gibraltar and went into drydock.

In the meantime, off New York, the *Caronia* was having a very quiet war patrolling outside territorial waters in company mostly with HM ships *Niobe* and *Suffolk*, two armoured cruisers. In October 1914 she took three German prisoners from the Danish steamship *United States*. On 14 April 1915, when she was off the Ambrose Light Vessel, she was involved in a collision with a six-masted schooner, *Edward B. Winslow*, from Portland, Maine. There were no casualties and five days later *Caronia* completed her patrol and returned to Halifax NS. On 8 May that year she left the eastern seaboard of the United States for Liverpool where she arrived seven days later. After a thorough overhaul, which included drydocking, *Caronia* left Liverpool once again on 3 July for Halifax NS, via Bermuda. She then remained on station at Halifax, carrying out contraband patrols off New York and Chesapeake Bay, until 22 July 1916 when she left Halifax for the last time under the White Ensign and arrived back in Liverpool at the end of the month. Seven days later, on 7 August 1916, she was paid off from naval service and handed back to the Cunard company.

By 23 November 1914, *Carmania*'s battle damage had been repaired, and the following day she left Gibraltar to carry out patrols off the River Tagus and Lisbon. She carried out these duties successfully over the next five months and in fact took 21 German nationals prisoner from neutral ships which were boarded. On 4 April 1915 she left Gibraltar for a patrol off the Atlantic Isles, and regularly checked interned German merchantmen, which included the *Pamir*, inside the breakwater at Santa Cruz in Tenerife. During the patrol she spent a week at Funchal in Madeira and arrested a further 14 German nationals from neutral ships. She completed this patrol on 12 May 1915, and four days later she left for Mudros, which was the Allied base for operations in Gallipoli. On 29 May, whilst at Mudros, she ran aground on a mudbank for two days, and while stranded there the troopship *Minnewaska* collided with her but caused only superficial damage. By 1 June she had been refloated and that day she embarked the officers

and men who were survivors of HM Battleships *Goliath*, *Triumph* and *Majestic*, all of which had been torpedoed in the Dardanelles, for passage to Devonport. *Carmania* left Mudros on 2 June 1915, calling at Malta for coal two days later, and after an overnight stop she left for Plymouth, where she arrived on 12 June. During her long refit at Devonport Dockyard, Captain Grant RN left the ship and Captain Harper RN took command.

It was 6 August 1915 before *Carmania* was at sea again bound for Gibraltar and more patrols off the Atlantic Isles. On 20 September she received an urgent request for assistance in quelling a mutiny on board the British steamship *Maristan*. Fortunately *Carmania* was in the vicinity and she was able to send an armed boarding party to the ship and arrest the three ringleaders, who were landed in Devonport. In October 1915 she made one voyage to Halifax NS, to transport Canadian troops to England. In November she left Devonport once again for patrols around the Canary Isles, and she remained on these duties until May 1916, apart from two brief visits to Portsmouth in January and February of that year. On 26 May she arrived back in Liverpool, and ten days later, on 5 June, she was handed back to Cunard officials.

After long refits, both *Caronia* and *Carmania*

HMS Carmania *at Malta in June 1915.* (Imperial War Museum)

The Carmania *in the River Mersey.* (University of Liverpool)

were employed mainly on trooping duties between Halifax and Liverpool, although *Caronia* made two voyages to Bombay. When the long-awaited Armistice was finally signed in November 1918, both ships were employed repatriating Canadian troops, who were accommodated in the third class quarters on board while many first and second class berths were sold commercially by Cunard. One officer from *Carmania* remembers those days well, when all the third class berths were occupied by belligerent French–Canadian troops returning home. He says they were tough and truculent and had

The Carmania *arrives in New York, summer 1927.* (E.E. Viez)

little regard for any authority, including the military police, who had their work cut out ensuring that violence and damage were kept to a minimum, and were greatly relieved when the landed at Halifax.

In September 1919 the *Caronia* inaugurated the post-war Cunard service between London and Canada, sailing from Tilbury on the 12th of that month and calling at Le Havre to embark 4,000 Chinese labourers who were being repatriated via Canada. Three months later, on the morning of Saturday 13 December 1919, the *Carmania* was off Cape Race and approaching Halifax when, in thick fog and darkness, she was in collision with the American freighter *Maryland*. Despite avoiding action being taken by both ships, the bows of the freighter scraped the starboard side of the *Carmania* 50 feet from the stern. The only damage caused was to *Carmania*'s hull plates, which were bent above and below the line of the main deck over an area of 25 sq ft. For a time there was some excitement among the steerage passengers, where the full impact of the collision was felt. However, it soon became clear that there was no danger, the passengers were calmed by the ship's officers and *Carmania* was able to continue her voyage to Halifax and New York.

In the early weeks of 1920 both ships were completely reconditioned after their war service and several new features were introduced, including a verandah cafe and a gymnasium. Both the first and second class saloons were entirely reno-

vated with new furniture provided, and a similar transformation took place in the drawing rooms. After the refit, *Caronia* left Liverpool for Queenstown and Halifax, and on her return she reverted to London as her home port. *Carmania* was put onto the Liverpool–New York service, and in September 1921 she went to Southampton to maintain the express service in the absence of *Mauretania* and *Berengaria* which were undergoing long refits on the Tyne.

Over the next few years the two ships ran without any serious incident, and in 1923, whilst undergoing a refit at her builders' yard, *Carmania*'s boilers were converted to burn oil fuel. At the same time the passenger accommodation was altered to carry 425 cabin class, 365 tourist class and 650 third class passengers. In the following year *Caronia* was similarly converted by Vickers at Barrow-in-Furness, and both ships were put onto one week cruises between New York and Havana during the winter months. During the summer months, however, both ships returned to their normal Atlantic services, and it was on Sunday 15 June 1929 that *Carmania* was involved in a collision while homeward bound from New York. The 7,430 gross ton American Merchant Lines passenger-cargo vessel *American Banker* was steaming out of Plymouth Sound for London, as *Carmania* was coming in to her anchorage in Cawsand Bay to discharge passengers and mail before steaming on to Southampton and London. In the thick fog which prevailed that day, the two ships, running on opposite but parallel courses, scraped each other and the collision tore off *Carmania*'s shell doors which had been opened ready for the transfer of mail.

One passenger on the *Carmania* who looked out of his porthole at the time described what he saw: 'I had a shock. I expected to see the tender in the distance, but instead a huge shadow, which proved to be the bow of the *American Banker*, passed very close and if I had not withdrawn my nose I think it would have

been cut off. There was a bumping and scraping noise.' Fortunately no one was injured and both ships arrived in London on the following day. Eight months later *Carmania* was involved in another collision; this time she was at the end of one of her seven-day cruises between New York and Havana, and at just after midnight on Tuesday 25 February 1930, off Cape Hatteras, North Carolina, in thick fog, she collided almost head on with the US cargo ship *Baldbutte*. Both ships were going extremely slowly at the time, so only slight damage was caused to their bows. *Carmania* arrived in New York at noon and after a survey she was able to sail on the next cruise later the same day.

By August 1931 both ships had reached the end of their useful lives, and with the onset of the Depression both were laid up at Sheerness. In January 1932 the *Caronia* was sold to Hughes Bolckow & Co of Blyth for scrap, but later that year she was re-sold by them to Japanese shipbreakers and renamed *Taiseiyo Maru* for the voyage to Osaka, where she was broken up in early 1933. The *Carmania* was sold to Hughes Bolckow & Co in March 1932, and she was broken up at Blyth shortly afterwards.

Technical data	
Gross tonnage	19,687 (*Caronia*), 19,524 (*Carmania*)
Net tonnage	10,306 (*Caronia*), 9,982 (*Carmania*)
Length overall	675 feet (207.69m)
Breadth	72 ft 3 in (22.23m)
Caronia	Twin screw, two sets of quadruple expansion engines; 22,000 IHP, 20 knots.
Carmania	Triple screw, three direct acting steam turbines; 22,000 IHP, 20 knots.

8

Lusitania, 1907

Today, looking back over 74 years, the name of Cunard's *Lusitania* is synonymous with disaster on an enormous scale. Yet in 1907, when she left the shipyards of the Clyde, the *Lusitania* was hailed as the greatest engineering achievement in the world and placed Great Britain in the forefront of marine construction. Born out of the political race for supremacy between Britain and Germany, on 7 May 1915 *Lusitania* fell victim to a German submarine, the inevitable result of the rivalry between the two great European powers.

In 1897 the Norddeutscher Lloyd ship *Kaiser Wilhelm der Grosse* had taken the Blue Riband from Cunard's *Campania* and *Lucania*, and thereafter German ships had held the trophy without challenge. In 1902 the White Star Line, Cunard's British rival, was acquired by the American-financed International Mercantile Marine, which at that time owned a large share of the North Atlantic shipping companies. This event led to fears in Britain that Cunard might be the next company on the IMM takeover list. In addition there was a large body of public opinion which was demanding that Britain should win back the Blue Riband from Germany, and these two factors concentrated minds within the British government and the Cunard board to act in order to resolve the situation.

Negotiations between the government and Cunard to build two superliners capable of winning back and holding the Blue Riband for Britain were conducted on behalf of the company by the Chairman Sir George Arbuthnot Burns, Second Baron Inverclyde. He had a vast experience of Cunard matters, for his father had been the first Chairman of the company upon the retirement of the original partners and he had been the first to recommend that the government should adapt merchant ships for use in time of war.

By 1903 an agreement had been reached whereby the government would lend £2,600,000 at 2¾ percent interest to build two ships capable of steaming at 24 to 25 knots. In addition they agreed to make an annual payment to Cunard of £150,000, on condition that the two ships were capable of being armed and that the government would have a claim on their services in time of national emergency. Another condition was that if the ships failed to achieve the speed requirements, the annual payment would be reduced or reconsidered. In the words of a government spokesman of the day: 'It would be expedient for this country to possess, in view of certain recognized requirements of naval war, some few ships, at any rate, of great speed and lasting qualities at sea.'

The next problem for Cunard was how to power the ships in order to meet the government's strict requirements. In September 1903 Lord Inverclyde chaired a committee of experienced engineers which included the Hon C.A. Parsons, inventor of the marine turbine,

Mr James Bain, Cunard's Superintendent, and
Rear Admiral Oram, Deputy Engineer-in-Chief
for the Royal Navy. Parsons had given a con-
vincing demonstration of the marine turbine
when, in 1897 at Queen Victoria's Diamond
Jubilee Naval Review, he had steamed his vessel
Turbinia up and down the lines of assembled warships at speeds of up to 34½ knots. The Navy
had sent boats out to stop *Turbinia*, but she was
far too fast for them. However, despite this over-
whelming demonstration of the superiority of
the turbine over reciprocating engines, there
were many who remained sceptical of its future
in marine propulsion. Despite the doubters, in
March 1904 the committee came down on the
side of the turbine, and it was decided to fit the
Lusitania and her sister *Mauretania* with turbine
propulsion.

The hull of the Lusitania *on the stocks shortly before
her launch in June 1906.* (University of Liverpool)

Another problem for Lord Inverclyde was the
hull design and size of the two new ships. This
was settled after a series of private experiments
and tests by Dr R.E. Froude in the Admiralty
tank at Haslar near Portsmouth. It was decided
that the new Cunarders would be some 785 feet
long overall and have a gross tonnage of 32,000.
As was fashionable in the Edwardian era, their
size and power would be symbolized by four
massive funnels, although an early shipbuilder's
model of *Lusitania* shows her with only three.

The contract for *Lusitania* went to John Brown
& Co Ltd of Clydebank, and her keel was laid
in May 1905. Over the next 12 months work
progressed well and, in June 1906, preparations
were ready for her launch. The ceremony was
performed by Mary, Lady Inverclyde, and punc-
tually at 12.30 pm on Thursday 7 June 1906, in
the presence of 600 official guests, she sent
Lusitania stern first into the Clyde. After the
ceremony, as the ship was towed to her fitting-
out berth, the guests were entertained to lunch

Belching black smoke, the Lusitania *on her full power trials — August 1907.* (University of Liverpool)

by Sir Charles McLaren, Chairman of John Brown & Co. In his speech, Sir Charles told his audience that the *Lusitania* was 'by far the largest vessel that had ever been put into the water. In length, in breadth, depth and capacity she exceeded any other vessel that had ever been designed, whilst her engine power would be such as to send her across the Atlantic at a speed never yet accomplished, except by a torpedo boat destroyer.'

He went on to outline the government's role in *Lusitania*'s future. 'This vessel was really the latest addition to the reserves of His Majesty's Navy. It might be made with slight alterations the fastest and most powerful cruiser in the world.' He then outlined the reasons for the building of *Lusitania* and her sister ship *Mauretania*. 'Considering the important national issues at stake there was something in acquiring distinction, and I feel that no one present would be satisfied that for capacity and speed of the

Atlantic liners the record should be held by Germany. Britain was mistress of the seas; we had always been in the lead in marine construction, and there was not a Briton who ought not to feel proud that this launch had placed Great Britain in the forefront of marine architecture.'

It was to be just over a year from her launch that *Lusitania* would leave the Clyde for her trials. She was a magnificent ship of 32,500 gross tons, with a length overall of 785 feet and a breadth of 88 feet. She was also the first British passenger ship to be built with four funnels which, as was intended, gave her a look of enormous power. *Lusitania* had seven decks for the use of passengers, from the boat deck down to the lower deck. She had accommodation on a palatial scale for 552 first class passengers, and the 460 second class passengers could enjoy more comfort than was found in the first class of many ships. Even the third class quarters at the forward end of the vessel marked a distinct advance in the accommodation offered. Gone were the 'open berths', and all 1,186 third class passengers were accommodated in two, four or six berth cabins.

Most of the first class public rooms were on the boat deck and the furthest forward was the writing room and library. Decorated in the eighteenth-century Adam style, access was from the Grand Hall. The walls were punctuated by beautifully carved pilasters and mouldings, with panels in delicate grey and cream silk brocade. The windows, glazed with a specially etched glass, had pretty embroidered valances and curtains, which had been copied from an old eighteenth-century document found at Milton Abbey in Dorset. The carpet, which was specially woven for the room, was rose coloured and harmonized with the surroundings. The furniture, all of inlaid mahogany, was upholstered with the same material as the curtains and each of the writing tables had a finely engraved gilt lamp in its centre. With its leaded glass dome in the centre, this room was considered by many to be the finest in the ship.

SS Lusitania, *the first class writing room and library.* (University of Liverpool)

Aft of the Grand Hall on the boat deck was the entrance to the first class lounge and music room, which was a magnificent space decorated in Georgian style. The mahogany panelling was veneered and inlaid with specially selected woods. The furniture was of mahogany and satinwood, with inlaid tables arranged in groups. The introduction of satinwood pieces and the delicate greens of the carpets, cushions and curtains helped to counteract the heavy effect of the furniture. The roof was raised in a dome-like fashion with 12 glass panes each representing a month of the year. The fireplace, with its beautiful enamelled panels, was the centrepiece of the room.

At the after end of the first class promenade deck was the smoking room which was decorated in eighteenth-century style and panelled with Italian walnut. The furniture, consisting of luxurious sofas, settees, easy chairs and writing tables, gave the room the air of a gentlemen's London club.

The first class dining saloon was able to seat 500 passengers at one sitting, having been built

on the two levels of the upper deck and the shelter deck above. The lower saloon was 86 feet (26.5m) long and the full width of the ship, which made it almost square. The upper saloon, which was built around a central well and dome, was 62 feet (19m) long and 65 feet (20m) broad and looked out onto the shelter deck promenade. The saloon was decorated in Louis XVI style, the walls being white with gilded pilasters. At the forward end on the upper deck was a large mahogany sideboard with panels of fine gilt bronze. The dome on the shelter deck was 30 feet high and the glass was designed as four floral panels. Gone were the old refectory-style tables, and in their place were numerous round and oval tables with seating for four to 12 passengers. Just forward of the saloon on the shelter deck was a dining saloon and nursery for children, which was decorated in the same style as the main saloon.

There were 87 special cabins in the first class,

The first class lounge, SS Lusitania. (University of Liverpool)

most of these being on the promenade deck. There were two regal suites which comprised of a dining room, drawing room, two bedrooms with bathroom facilities and a pantry. There were also six *en suite* rooms, consisting of a bedroom, bathroom and parlour. All the other first class cabins were situated on the main, upper, promenade and boat decks, and were all reached

The first class dining saloon, SS Lusitania. (University of Liverpool)

by way of the Grand Staircase, the entrance to which was on the main deck convenient for gangways from docksides, landing stages and tenders.

The second class accommodation was on five decks, from the main up to the boat deck, and was situated at the after end of the vessel. The cabins were on the main, upper and shelter decks and were either two or four berth rooms. The public rooms were all decorated in similar, although simpler, styles to those in the first class. The dining saloon, which could seat 260 people at one sitting, was aft of the first class saloon on the upper deck. It was 60 feet (18.5m) long and ran the whole width of the ship. It was decorated in Georgian style, with delicately carved panels and pillars in white; overhead was a circular well surrounded by a carved wooden balustrade. The tables were arranged forward to aft in the refectory fashion and at the forward end was a large ornate mahogany sideboard. At the after end of the promenade deck were the second class gentlemen's smoking room and ladies' room, and both were designed and decorated in Georgian style. Above these on the boat

The third class dining saloon, SS Lusitania. (University of Liverpool)

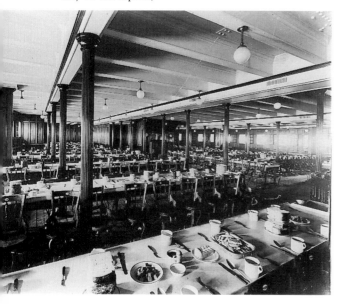

deck was the second class lounge, or drawing room. It was decorated in Louis XVI style in a light grey colour scheme, which toned admirably with the rose-coloured carpets and curtains and the satinwood furniture. The room was also furnished with writing tables and bookcases, and it served as the writing room and library as well as the lounge.

The third class accommodation was forward on four decks, most of the cabins being on the lower and main decks. The dining saloon was on the upper deck and it could seat some 350 passengers simultaneously. It ran over the whole width of the ship and the refectory-style tables were arranged athwartships, with a piano at the forward end. Above this room on the shelter deck were the ladies' room on the starboard side and a smoke room for men on the port side. The forecastle deck side-plating had been carried well aft and the side gangways of the shelter deck were enclosed and fitted with side benches for the use of third class passengers. The forward 150 feet was also enclosed, although the after half was open but still offered some shelter from the hostile elements of the North Atlantic.

It was *Lusitania*'s main propulsion machinery which was to mark her down in maritime history as a pioneer. Unlike the shipping companies which steamed out to Asia and Australia and which generally preferred the reliability of the slower steam reciprocating engines, the Cunard company, with the intense competition on the North Atlantic, could not afford to ignore technical advancements, particularly where speed was concerned. Therefore it is no surprise that Cunard fitted steam turbines into such a large passenger ship, something which had never been done before.

Lusitania was a quadruple screw ship, each propeller being four bladed and some 16 ft 9 in in diameter. They were driven by direct-drive steam turbines, the outer ones being inward-turning and the inner ones outward turning. The outer propellers were driven by HP turbines in the engine room wing compartments, while the LP turbines in the central compartment drove the inner screws. Also on the inner shafts were the astern turbines. In all, the machinery developed some 68,000 IHP and revolving at 180 rpm was capable of driving the *Lusitania* at 25 knots.

The steam was provided at 195 psi by 23 double-ended and two single-ended cylindrical boilers situated in four separate boiler rooms. The forward boiler room had two single-ended and five double-ended boilers and each of the other boiler rooms contained six double-ended boilers. In all there were 192 furnaces which consumed between 800 and 1,000 tons of coal a day. The coal bunkers ran along the sides of the boiler rooms which afforded some protection to these vital machinery spaces, as they were below the waterline and vulnerable to damage caused by collisions or enemy action.

It was the latter, perhaps, which was uppermost in the minds of the planners, for in time of war it was intended that *Lusitania* be converted to an armed merchant cruiser. For this purpose she was designed to carry 12 quick-firing 6 inch guns, two on each side on the forecastle of the promenade deck, and four on each side along the shelter deck. It was thought at the time that *Lusitania* would be a fast and powerful addition to the Royal Navy, but in fact she would never serve under the White Ensign.

By the summer of 1907 *Lusitania*'s fitting out was almost complete and she was ready to undertake her trials. She left the dock at John Brown's yard at 11.50 am on Thursday 27 June and, accompanied by six tugs, she steamed slowly down river to anchor off Greenock at 1.45 pm. It was a delicate operation and the Clyde Trust had been preparing for it over the previous 12 months by having the river dredged to a depth of 34 feet (10.5m) at high water. Huge crowds watched her progress down the river, and that afternoon at Greenock she was opened to the public, before proceeding to Liverpool and into the Gladstone Graving Dock prior to entering on her trials.

Four weeks later, after running at 25.6 knots over the Clyde measured mile, *Lusitania* anchored off Greenock on Saturday 27 July 1907 and that evening left for a cruise round Ireland with a large party of official guests. These included Sir Charles McLaren, Mr William Watson, Chairman of Cunard, the Hon C.A. Parsons and Mary, Lady Inverclyde, the vessel's sponsor. The initial cruise ended at the River Mersey on the morning of Monday 29 July, and after disembarking most of her guests off Mersey Bar she began several days of trials between Corsewall Light on the coast of Galloway and Longship Lighthouse west of Land's End in Cornwall. The trial started at midnight on the 29th and over the next 48 hours she made two runs between those points. This was followed by two runs between Corsewall Light and Chicken Rock, on the south-west tip of the Isle of Man. From first to last *Lusitania* covered well over 2,000 miles, for the most part at over 25 knots. On her two latter speed runs she averaged 26.45 knots, and it was obvious that the mail contract requirement of 24.5 knots on the Atlantic would be easily exceeded.

On Saturday 7 September 1907, over a month after the completion of her trials, *Lusitania* left Liverpool on her maiden voyage to Queenstown and New York and, in the words of the contemporary press, 'Never did a ship sail with such mighty cheers as those from the vast multitudes which lined the Liverpool landing stage last night as the *Lusitania* slowly moved from her moorings and started on her maiden voyage'. Throughout that Saturday thousands of people travelled to Liverpool from all over the country to the city's waterfront, and to the Cheshire side of the River Mersey. During the afternoon *Lusitania* was anchored in mid-stream while the elderly *Lucania* lay alongside the landing stage, and when she left for New York at 4.30 pm that day, the *Lusitania* was able to move into her berth. By 6 pm it was estimated that there were well over 200,000 people gathered to witness her departure, and through them all a steady stream of passengers embarked from the special boat trains.

At 9 pm that evening, the deep boom of *Lusitania*'s whistle indicated that she was ready to cast off. A few minutes later, assisted by tugs, she began to move slowly away from the landing stage. The cheers from the thousands of onlookers who waved hats, handkerchiefs and sticks, together with the hooting from the Mersey ferries and steam craft in the river, added to the send-off. As she moved into mid-stream she presented, with her huge funnels and brilliant lights, a picture which would never be forgotten by all those who witnessed the event.

Lusitania was commanded by Captain James B. Watt and she had on board 2,200 passengers, among whom were several Cunard directors, including Mr E.H. Cunard, a grandson of the company's founder. As well as being of great interest, because many were expecting the new ship to win back the Blue Riband for Great Britain, the voyage was also looked up as a race with the Lucania, which had left Liverpool just over four hours earlier. However, this was a most unequal contest and Lusitania overhauled the older vessel at 4.30 am on 8 September, before fog caused both ships to reduce speed considerably. Lusitania anchored at the entrance to Queenstown Harbour at 9.20 am that day and she was followed 15 minutes later by Lucania. There was considerable interest in the arrival of the two vessels and both headlands east and west of the harbour entrance were crowded with sightseers from as early as 6 am. Of course the real attraction was the Lusitania, and the sea was studded with steam boats, motor boats, yachts and rowing boats, all full of people anxious to

get a close look at the world's biggest liner.

After embarking 317 passengers and two bags of mail, Lucania left Queenstown and passed Daunts Rock Lightship at 11.35 am on the 8th. Lusitania embarked 120 passengers and 776 bags of mail and passed the same point some 35 minutes later. It was not long before she overtook Lucania once again and, although Cunard denied she was making any attempts at speed records, she steamed westward making a good speed. In fact, at 11 am on 9 September she passed the eastward bound American Line steamer Haverford, whose passengers reported the sighting of Lusitania as 'hazy, but travelling at high speed.'

Lusitania reached Sandy Hook Bar at 9.05 am on Friday 13 September 1907. She had failed to beat the Deutschland's record, but she received a tremendous welcome in New York, where crowds as great as those in Liverpool were out to see her enter the harbour. The weather in the city was glorious and Lusitania was the first big liner to use the new Ambrose Channel. An enormous crowd was at the Battery to see her steam up New York Bay, and every craft in the harbour and North River joined in a noisy chorus of welcome. In the city flags were hoisted on many buildings, and from the top of the Singer Building, which was then being built in Lower Broadway, a string of flags spelled out the word 'Welcome'. Unfortunately the day was slightly marred by crowds trying to get onto Cunard's pier. The company had issued only a few passes and the police had to be called to keep order.

Meanwhile in Germany there was also great jubilation. Lusitania's voyage had been followed keenly and the Berlin press rejoiced that she had failed to capture the Blue Riband on her first attempt. Even Albert Ballin, Chairman of the Hamburg Amerika Line, in a speech celebrating the rapid progress of German shipping said: 'Today the British government had been compelled to depart from the principle of fair and free play for all, which had made England great, and to pay a heavy subsidy to a single company in order to achieve a slight advantage over

The Lusitania *at speed.* (Maritime Photo Library)

German shipping.' The enmity which would end with the horrors of the First World War was already becoming apparent.

Lusitania left New York at 3 pm on Saturday 21 September 1907, reached Queenstown at 3.56 am on 27 September and Liverpool at 4 pm the same day, the voyage having taken five days, four hours and 19 minutes. Again she broke no records, having been forced to slow down in fog encountered throughout the crossing. One of her American passengers, who had first crossed the Atlantic on board the Cunard steamer *Asia* in 1853, said of her: 'The *Lusitania* is a veritable wonder. She seems to mark the last word in passenger ship accommodation. When I recall my impressions of the old *Asia* and compare her cabin accommodation with the luxurious appointments of this ship I consider it amazing.'

Lusitania's second voyage started at 7 pm on Saturday 5 October 1907, when she sailed from the Mersey once more. She left Queenstown at 10.25 am the following day, and again it was expected that an effort would be made to beat all the speed records for the westbound passage. This time, with weather conditions in her favour, she passed Sandy Hook at 1.17 am on 11 October, making her voyage time four days, 19 hours and 52 minutes, which meant that she had indeed won the Blue Riband for Britain. She remained at anchor off Sandy Hook until 7.12 am, when she crossed the bar and was brought up the Ambrose Channel; amidst the din of small craft blowing whistles, she anchored again off the quarantine station. Then, after an hour's delay, she moved majestically up harbour, with the deep boom of her siren answering the salutes of the smaller vessels. Later in the day Mr Gustave Schwab of Norddeutscher Lloyd, acknowledged *Lusitania*'s record-breaking crossing. During the voyage, conditions in the stokeholds must have seemed like hell on earth. Indeed, on the Tuesday night, when the turbines were running at full speed, the heat there was so intense that one of the firemen went mad, and it took six of his colleagues to restrain him. However, their work was obviously appreciated, for, to mark the occasion, the officers gave each

fireman a bottle of beer.

In November 1907, *Lusitania* was joined by her sister ship *Mauretania*, and it was not long before the slightly better performances of the latter ship began to show. In December that year she took the eastbound record, and in 1909 she broke *Lusitania*'s westbound record. But whatever the friendly rivalry between them, there is no doubt that the two ships were, at that time, unbeatable on the North Atlantic.

At the end of June 1908 *Lusitania* went into the Gladstone Graving Dock at Liverpool, where her two outer propellers were replaced. The new ones had larger blades and their pitch had been increased, which it was hoped would significantly improve her performance. Although these hopes were never fully realized, her next westbound voyage between Liverpool and New York was a record-breaking one.

In November 1908 Captain William T. Turner was appointed commander of the *Lusitania* in place of Captain Watt, who retired from the company's service. Captain Turner was a Liverpool man who first went to sea as a 13-year-old deck boy in the sailing ship *White Star*. In 1878 he joined Cunard as a third officer in the *Cherbourg* of 1875. He was holder of the Humane Society's silver medal for saving life at sea, and he had served as Chief Officer in the *Umbria* during the war in South Africa when she was a troopship. He had then gone to command *Carpathia*, *Ivernia* and *Caronia*. Although Captain Turner's command of *Lusitania* was not continuous between 1908 and 1915, it was just over seven years after he first took command of her that he was fated to take her on her last tragic voyage across the Atlantic.

On 13 January 1909, at the completion of an Atlantic crossing, *Lusitania* went into Gladstone Dock for her annual overhaul. She returned to the Atlantic service on 6 February, but just two months later she was drydocked once again at Liverpool. This time it was in order to fit new four-bladed propellers of a type which had proved so successful in *Mauretania*. This put her out of service from 8 April to 17 July 1909 and, although her performance was improved, she could never surpass the records set by her sister *Mauretania*.

Later in 1909 she started to call at Fishguard on the homeward journey, in order to land the mails and disembark her London and continental passengers. This marked the beginning of the end for Queenstown, for in January 1910 it was announced that during the winter months between November and April, Cunard liners would cease to call there, but would proceed direct to Fishguard and Liverpool. For some time there had been moves within the company to get Queenstown removed from their itinerary, and of course with the majority of passengers bound for London and the continent on the eastbound trip, and most of them eager to get to New York as quickly as possible when westbound, it was a logical move.

In August and September 1911, great efforts by *Lusitania*'s crew and by dockyard workers in New York enabled the ship to cross the Atlantic both ways three times in less than three weeks. By 4 December that year she had completed 16 round trips across the Atlantic and was about to sail on the 17th. It was a performance that not even her slightly superior sister ship *Mauretania* had achieved. However, the following year things did not go so well for *Lusitania*. Her annual overhaul in late March 1912 was delayed through adverse weather conditions, and she was unable to sail on 6 April scheduled. In the event *Carmania* was substituted and it was 27 April before *Lusitania* sailed from Liverpool for New York. Just over seven weeks later, on 25 June, *Lusitania* limped into Liverpool with damage to the blades of one of her propellers, and this put her out of service for a month. Fortunately the remainder of the year passed without further problems, but 1913 again started badly for her.

On 31 December 1912 *Lusitania* limped into Liverpool once again, this time with engine trouble. Some of her turbine blades had become twisted and extensive repairs were necessary. It was thought that the work would be completed by April, but in the event it was 23 August before she sailed once again for New York. Two

days later Cunard announced that they were to abandon completely Queenstown as a port of call for both *Lusitania* and *Mauretania*. *Lusitania* made her final stop there on Sunday 24 August 1913, when she arrived at 6.04 am, and, after embarking 179 passengers and 1,085 sacks of mail, she sailed at 9.22 am, just over three hours later. There was now less than 12 months of peacetime service left for her.

In March 1914 *Lusitania* broke her last speed record. On a voyage from New York to Liverpool she steamed 618 miles in 24 hours, making an average of 26.7 knots. The previous record had been set by *Mauretania* at 614 miles, in April 1911. *Lusitania*'s final peacetime voyage to New York started on the evening of Saturday 25 July 1914, and she arrived at her destination on Thursday 30 July. The last few days of peace were spent in New York and she sailed once again for Liverpool on 4 August 1914, the day Great Britain declared war on Germany. However, two days before this, at 9.20 pm on the 2nd, an urgent telegram had been sent from the Admiralty to Cunard which read: '*Lusitania* and *Mauretania* engaged from day of arrival in England as merchant cruisers under 3rd schedule of agreement dated 30.7.1903. You will not be required to provide or pay officers or crew. *Lusitania* will be in command of Captain Vivian H.G. Bernard RN and *Mauretania* Captain Cole C. Fowler RN. Letter follows.'

Upon *Lusitania*'s arrival in the Mersey there were rumours that the Admiralty did not want either ship as an AMC, and this was confirmed the next day by the Admiralty. But *Lusitania* could not resume her normal sailings for the Admiralty paid Cunard £37,995 to keep her at Liverpool and at their disposal until 12 September 1914. In the event, *Lusitania* did not sail to the USA again until October when the Cunard board decided that one of their two big ships, *Lusitania*, could be operated once a month if the boiler power were reduced by a quarter. The saving in coal and labour resulting from this would, it was thought, enable the company to avoid loss, though it would not make a profit either. *Lusitania* made two round voyages

CUNARD

Established 1840

EUROPE VIA LIVERPOOL

New Twin-screw Geared Turbine

TRANSYLVANIA

FRIDAY, MAY 7: 5 P.M.

Excellent Accommodations
Comfortably Appointed

Orduna, . Tues., May 18, 10 A.M.
Tuscania, . . . Fri., May 21, 5 P.M.
LUSITANIA, Sat., May 29, 10 A.M.
Transylvania, . . Fri., June 4, 5 P.M.
Orduna, . . . Sat., June 12, 10 A.M.

Gibraltar - Genoa - Naples - Piræus
S.S. Carpathia, Thur., May 13, NOON

ROUND THE WORLD TOURS

Through bookings to all principal Ports
of the World.
COMPANY'S OFFICE, 21-24 STATE ST., N.Y.

between the Mersey and New York in October 1914. She completed the second of these trips in early November, and on the 21st of that month she began a monthly service to New York. Accordingly six of her boilers were closed down, and the effect of this was to reduce the attainable speed from 24½ to 21 knots. However, this still left *Lusitania* a considerably faster ship than any other vessel plying the North Atlantic.

Lusitania was to make four more successful round voyages between Liverpool and New York before her fateful last passage, departing from the landing stage at Liverpool on 16 December 1914 and 16 January, 13 February and 13 March 1915. During the second of these voyages, *Lusitania* was involved in an 'international incident' which, although it did no physical damage, gave

Left *The Cunard sailing list as published in New York newspapers in April 1915. (Author's collection)*

Below left *The warning which appeared in New York newspapers on the day the* Lusitania *made her final departure. (Author's collection)*

Below *The reaction of* Lusitania's *passengers to the German warning. (Author's collection)*

NOTICE!

TRAVELLERS intending to embark on the Atlantic voyage are reminded that a state of war exists between Germany and her allies and Great Britain and her allies; that the zone of war includes the waters adjacent to the British Isles; that, in accordance with formal notice given by the Imperial German government, vessels flying the flag of Great Britain, or any of her allies, are liable to destruction in those waters, and that travellers sailing in the war zone on ships of Great Britain or her allies do so at their own risk.

IMPERIAL GERMAN EMBASSY.
Washington, D. C., April 22, 1915.

TORPEDO THREAT FAILS TO REDUCE LUSITANIA LIST

German Embassy's Note Telling of Peril Ignored by 1,258 Passengers.

SEAGOERS LAUGH AT DANGER WARNINGS

Lusitania's presence on the North Atlantic a very high profile. She left New York on 30 January 1915 commanded by Captain David Dow, and for the first two days the weather was calm. However, for the remainder of the voyage until just before she reached the Irish coast, *Lusitania* ploughed her way through gale force winds and heavy seas. It seems that once the coast was sighted Captain Dow was extremely concerned that his ship would be torpedoed, and so, on 5 February, in preparation for the run through the dangerous waters of the Irish sea to Liverpool, he hoisted the 'Stars and Stripes'. With the United States still neutral, and with Germany so reluctant to bring her into the war on the side of the Allies, it was considered that this ruse would guarantee her a safe passage. However, soon after the voyage ended, the use of the US flag came to the notice of the press and the incident made world news. The United States' obvious bias in favour of the Allies was shown clearly when the US administration made no diplomatic protest, but addressed a 'friendly communication' to the British government. Apparently the raising of the American flag had caused great excitement among the passengers, one of whom was Colonel Edward House, one of President Wilson's close advisors, who was on a secret peace mission to Britain and Germany.

A further two sailings from Liverpool were scheduled for 17 April and 15 May 1915, and from New York on 1 May and 29 May. However, by now the waters around the British Isles were very dangerous for Allied shipping, and in April 1915 the German Embassy in Washington sent warnings to newspapers in New York to the effect that passengers travelling on Allied ships did so at their own risk.

For her 17 April voyage from Liverpool, *Lusitania* was commanded by Captain William T. Turner, who had relieved Captain Dow when he went on leave. She made her final sailing from Pier 54 in New York at noon on Saturday 1 May 1915, with some 1,959 passengers on board, amongst whom were the usual sprinkling of the famous and wealthy. Her cargo was entered on the manifest as foodstuffs, metal rods and ingots,

and boxes of cartridges, although controversy about the true nature of her cargo would persist for many years. According to one survivor, Mrs Jane Lewis, who was travelling in the second class with her husband, 'It was very excitable at New York leaving, because it was crowded with people, and people being alarmed about things'. The German warnings to would-be passengers had obviously had their effect, for during the voyage the rumours of submarines abounded.

By Friday 7 May, *Lusitania* had entered what was called the danger zone, waters in which enemy submarines might be expected. Captain Turner took precautions, ordering all the lifeboats to be swung out and all the bulkhead doors to be closed except those required to be kept open in order to work the ship. The lookouts were doubled, two men were sent to the crow's nest and two officers were on the bridge with a quartermaster on either side to look out for submarines. Orders were sent to the engine room to keep the steam pressure very high in case of emergency and to give the vessel all possible speed if necessary.

Up until 8 am that day the *Lusitania* had been steaming at 21 knots, but now she was reduced to 18 knots. The object was to secure the ship's arrival at the bar outside Liverpool at 4 am the following morning, when the high tide would enable her to enter the Mersey at dawn. Shortly after this reduction in speed a fog came down and she was further slowed to 15 knots. Just before noon the fog lifted and speed was restored to 18 knots, which was maintained for the rest of the passage. At this time land was sighted two points abaft the beam, which Captain Turner took to be Brow Head, although he did not make a positive identification. He therefore kept *Lusitania* on her course, which was S87E and parallel with the land, until 12.40 pm when, in order to make a better landfall, he altered course to N67E. This brought the ship closer to land, and the Old Head of Kinsale was sighted at 1.40 pm, when the course was altered back to S87E. Having steadied the ship on this course, an officer began to take a four-point bearing at 1.50 pm, but this was never completed.

At 2 pm the passengers were finishing their lunch, and at 2.15 pm the ship was 10 to 15 miles off the Old Head of Kinsale with the weather clear and the sea smooth. Captain Turner, who was on the port side of the lower bridge, heard the second officer shout, 'There is a torpedo coming, sir'. Looking to starboard Captain Turner saw a streak of foam in the wake of a torpedo travelling towards his ship. Immediately afterwards there was a terrific explosion on the starboard side, between the third and fourth funnels. Almost simultaneously there was a second explosion, which was thought at the time to be a second torpedo but has since been confirmed as an internal explosion, although the cause has never been definitely established. The stricken *Lusitania* immediately took on a heavy list to starboard and in about 20 minutes she had sunk, with the loss of 1,198 lives.

Mrs Jane Lewis tells the story of those awful minutes. 'We were just inside the dining room door, so we could get out quick, because we had had rumours that something might happen. So we could get out quickly we took a table by the door. Then when the awful noise came people came pouring through the dining room from other parts of the ship. People fell down, people walked over them, you couldn't do anything because the boat was going sideways. We got out luckily, because we were near the door, otherwise we would never have got out. Then we went down the stairs, instead of going up they went down (because of the heavy list), and I fell down them. We got out onto the deck and then we stayed there, we were standing by a lifeboat, there was nobody about where we were, but there were plenty in the water. Then my husband said he'd better go down to the cabin and get our lifebelts. I said, "No, you're not going down, if you go down there you'll never get up again", and I said, "if we are going we'll all go together." We got away eventually, I was thrown into the boat, because we had to be so quick. We were rowed away from the ship, and there were people in the water everywhere.'

Mr and Mrs Lewis and their five-year-old daughter were picked up by a fishing smack and

SS Lusitania *leaving New York homeward bound on 1 May 1915. This is the last photograph ever taken of her.* (Imperial War Museum)

taken into Queenstown. Many were not so luckly, as Mrs Lewis recalls. 'There was a woman alongside me on the deck of *Lusitania*, she had a baby in her arms, but I never saw her again.' Mrs Lewis' boat was crowded with survivors and she remembers one incident clearly. 'There was an old lady, she was sitting quietly, when all of a sudden she put her hand to her mouth and said, "Oh I've left my teeth in the cabin." She had come without them, poor old soul.'

Lusitania sank bow first, with her stern almost perpendicular out of the water, just as *Titanic* had slid beneath the waves some 3 years earlier. Mrs Lewis remembers the last moments of this great ship. 'My husband said to me, "Look round now, she's going down." I said, "No I won't, I don't want to see her going." Then I thought I'd better look and she was going down fast into the water, the end of it was like that.'

Mr Charles Nash, who was 11 years old at the time, is now one of the few residents of Queenstown who remembers those far off and tragic days. 'When I got home from school at 3.30 pm, my mother told me the sad news, so I went down town which at the time was filling up with people. The post office was already besieged. On the Cunard wharf a tugboat landed people alive and dead, and the naval patrol sloop *Bluebell* landed a goodly number at the deep-water quay at about the same time. People from Cork city and all around the area came in to help and coffins were arriving as fast as they were made. A fine splendid woman with two babies lashed to her with strong rope — twins — were landed on the ballast quay near the town clock. Any-one who gazed on that scene could not keep back a tear. They were part of a big group of dead, and some alive, which were brought in by a little steam drifter, *Golden Effort*, she was navy then, under the command of Lieutenant Keble Chatterton, a famous writer of later years. His ship was well named and she got away quickly to sea again.'

Captain Turner survived and he remained on the bridge giving orders until the ship foundered. His order 'women and children first' was largely obeyed. There were complaints from some survivors about the manner in which the lifeboats were launched, their condition and the lack of leadership from the ship's officers. But considering that within seconds of being hit all the lights went out and the ship listed heavily to starboard and that she remained under way the whole time, together with the fact that she sank in 18 minutes, it is a miracle that so many did get away safely.

As always with such tragedies there were many stories of heroism, but two were officially recognized and Able Seamen Leslie N. Morton and Joseph Parry were awarded the Silver and Bronze medals for Gallantry in Saving Live at Sea. The caption to the awards read as follows: 'On 7th May 1915, the steamship *Lusitania*, of Liverpool, was torpedoed off the Old Head of Kinsale and foundered. Morton was the first to observe the approach of the torpedoes, and he reported them to the bridge. When the torpedoes struck the ship he was knocked off his feet, but he recovered himself quickly, and at once assisted in filling and lowering several boats. Having done all he could on board, he jumped overboard. While in the water he managed to get hold of a floating collapsible lifeboat, and, with the assistance of Parry, he ripped the canvas cover off it, boarded it, and succeeded in drawing into it 50 or 60 passengers. Morton and Parry then rowed the boat some miles to a fishing smack. Having put the rescued passengers on board the smack, they returned to the scene of the wreck, and succeeded in rescuing 20 or 30 more people.'

There is no doubt that the sinking of the *Lusitania* was one of the First World War's single biggest tragedies. The political repercussions were enormous, and although it did not directly bring the United States into the war on the side of the Allies, it ensured that no American administration would ever be allied to Germany.

Technical data	
Gross tonnage	31,550
Net tonnage	9,145
Length overall	790 ft (243m)
Breadth	87 ft 6 in (26.92m)
Quadruple screw, powered by four direct acting steam turbines; 76,000 SHP, 26 knots.	

9
Mauretania, 1907

Of all the Cunard liners built since 1900, the one which stands out above all the others is the first *Mauretania*. She captured the Blue Riband of the Atlantic in 1907 and remained the undisputed 'Queen of the North Atlantic' until July 1929, a record of 22 years. She was certainly a favourite of President Franklin D. Roosevelt, himself a shipping enthusiast, and she caught the public imagination on both sides of the Atlantic in a way in which no other ship had done before or has done since. *Mauretania* was, without doubt, a good-looking ship, as was her sister *Lusitania*. But *Mauretania* always appeared the more powerful of the two, due to the 30 large ventilator cowls which, ranged alongside her four enormous funnels, gave her a more streamlined profile.

The contract for the building of *Mauretania* went to Messrs Swan Hunter & Wigham Richardson at Wallsend-on-Tyne and her keel was laid in August 1904, nine months before work commenced on *Lusitania*. It was just over two years before the hull was ready for launching, and the date was set for Thursday 20 September 1906, three months after *Lusitania* had been named. The ceremony took place on the afternoon of that day, the ship being christened by Lady Anne Emily Innes Kerr, the Duchess of Roxburghe, widow of the 7th Duke. She had been one of Queen Victoria's Ladies-in-Waiting and she was the sister-in-law of Lord Tweedmouth, the First Lord of the Admiralty. Swan

Hunter had issued thousands of invitations and had to erect stands at the sides and stern of the hull for all the guests. The principal stand was reserved for the 'ladies and gentlemen', with the yard's workmen and their relatives seated in the others.

The shipyard was on the north shore of the Tyne, and the south bank was crowded with spectators, as were the quays to the east and west. Despite the fact that it was a cool, cloudy and overcast day with showers, the river was crowded with small boats, even though a considerable space had to be cleared for the launch. At 4.15 pm the Dowager Duchess of Roxburghe sent the great hull down into the River Tyne and, according to *The Times*, 'It was a magnificent sight and the vessel took 40 seconds to reach the water'. Afterwards the VIPs were entertained to a reception in the company's model room. Mr G.B. Hunter presided at the head of the table accompanied by *Mauretania*'s sponsor. Perhaps the most significant speech was given by Lord Tweedmouth, who referred to Cunard's partnership with the Admiralty and how the recent launching of HMS *Dreadnought*, together with *Mauretania*, added great strength to the nation.

The tensions building up between Britain and Germany were shown by another incident which happened on the same day that *Mauretania* was launched. The Hamburg–Amerika ship *Meteor*, which was on a cruise of celebrated sea-

The Mauretania *fitting out at Wallsend on Tyne,*
1907. (Author's collection)

coast watering places, was due to anchor off
Cowes in the Isle of Wight. However, due to very
heavy seas she was unable to do so, and she took
refuge in Portsmouth Harbour, the home of the
Grand Fleet. No sooner had she done this than
there was a 'spy scare', and with the *Dreadnought*
fitting out in the naval dockyard, it was decided
to order the *Meteor* to sea again, despite the
rough weather. This incident caused a great
furore in the German press, and was indicative
of the growing rivalry between the two countries.

Just a year after the launch, on Monday 16
September 1907, it was announced that *Mauretania* would leave the Tyne on the following day
for preliminary builder's trials. The official statement made it clear that press representatives
would not be permitted on board, and that the
results of the trials would not be published. Even
today, over 80 years later, the shroud of secrecy
which covered these trials has not been lifted.
Despite the short notice, when *Mauretania* left
her berth at 9.30 am on Tuesday 17 September,
thousands of people lined the banks of the River
Tyne to watch her progress out to the North Sea.
In North and South Shields, schoolchildren

were given a day off for the occasion. The Tyne
was decorated with bunting on every side, and
when *Mauretania* came into sight all the ships
lying in the river sounded their whistles together
in an indescribable din. The boys of the Welles-
ley training ship manned the rigging and sang
'Rule Britannia' as the great new liner passed by.
Whether this could be heard above the noise
is doubtful, but *Mauretania* responded with her
deep booming.

At 10.45 am she steamed out of the river into
the North Sea and anchored off Tynemouth.
After dark she weighed anchor and started the
first of her speed trials, which she ran between
Flamborough Head and Aberdeen. Among the
VIPs on board were Sir William White and Mr
H. Hunter from the builders, together with direc-
tors of Cunard. Each evening she anchored off
South Shields, and by the morning of Saturday
21 September 1907 all the trials were completed.
At 12.50 pm that day she steamed back into the
River Tyne and, when level with the Albert
Edward Dock, was swung round and pulled stern
first to the builders' yard at Wallsend.

It had been learned unofficially that *Mauretania* had achieved a speed of 27.75 knots, which
was well above here contract requirement. However, there had been one major problem of

excessive vibration throughout the ship at high speeds. This was overcome to a certain extent by reinforcing the stern and by weight adjustments. By Tuesday 22 October 1907, work on *Mauretania* was completed and she was ready to undergo her official trials before being handed over to Cunard. Just before 2 pm that day the great ship was pulled from her berth and towed down river. There had been problems that morning when the fireman aboard applied for an increase in wages; on being refused they had walked off the ship and did not return until early afternoon when a compromise was reached.

As *Mauretania* was towed down the river thousands of spectators lined the banks to cheer her on her way. As she passed between the Tyne piers the accompanying tugs left her and on board her departure was marked by a small ceremony. Mary Lady Inverclyde, the widow of the late Cunard Chairman, whose negotiations with the government had made the building of the two sisters possible, was invited to officially ring the signal to the engine room which set the ship in motion. She was then presented with a gold bracelet composed of replica turbine blades by Mr Thomas Bell, Chairman of the Wallsend Slipway & Engineering Company.

Once out of the river, *Mauretania* spent a few hours off the mouth of the Tyne adjusting her compasses, before steaming northwards for the Pentland Firth and then round to the Mersey. It was not a trial trip and as well as a group of VIPs there were 400 guests on board, including British and American press representatives. There were no incidents during the voyage and the weather remained fine, giving all those on board lovely views of the Scottish mainland and islands. Early in the morning of Thursday 24 October 1907 *Mauretania* arrived in the Mersey and after breakfast the guests were landed by tender before the ship went into the Canada Dock, where she was drydocked the following day.

Mauretania left Liverpool on the morning of Sunday 3 November 1907 for her official trials which were to last for four days. She ran over the same course as *Lusitania* had done just three

The Mauretania *shortly before she left the River Tyne for her trials, with the* Turbinia *alongside.* (Science Museum)

months previously, and over her four runs between Corsewall Point and Land's End she achieved a maximum speed of 27.36 knots with an average of 26.04 knots. It was quite apparent that the vessel was capable of a sustained speed of 26 knots whilst in service. The stage was thus set for her maiden voyage from Liverpool to New York.

Internally, *Mauretania*'s passenger accommodation was laid along very similar lines to that of *Lusitania*, with the main difference being the decoration of the public rooms. *Mauretania* could accommodate 560 first, 475 second and 1,300 third class passengers, which was 137 more than her sister ship. The first class passengers had access to five decks from the main deck up to the sun deck forward and amidships, which were connected by the grand staircase and two lifts both situated in the grand entrance foyer. The first class dining saloon was on two levels on the upper and shelter decks and was decorated in Francis I style, with light oak panelling. All the carving was intricate and delicate, and it was the designer's aim to have the lower room

The first class dining saloon showing the central dome,
SS Mauretania. (University of Liverpool)

The first class lounge, SS Mauretania. (University of
Liverpool)

richer in carving, leading up to the simpler upper saloon. The furniture in both rooms was upholstered in deep pink, and at one end of the lower saloon a fine sixteenth-century tapestry gave an admirable effect. In place of the old-style refectory benches, the lower saloon had tables which could accommodate from five to 14 passengers, whilst in the upper saloon parties of two to six passengers could be seated at each dining table. Between the two rooms was a large open space surmounted by a lofty dome, which gave a spacious and airy effect.

The first class lounge and music room was situated on the boat deck, and it was designed in late eighteenth-century French style. In the centre was a large oval dome with ornate bronze framing, and the ceiling around it was plainly panelled in white. The chairs and sofas were of polished beech in Louis XVI style, with variously coloured brocade upholstery. The library and writing room was on the same deck, but was smaller than the lounge. The wall panelling was silver grey sycamore, and a bookcase formed the panels on one side of the central portion. Opposite this, at the other side of the room, was a carved chimney of white marble surmounted by

a mirror similar to the design in the bookcase doors. The carpets and curtains were deep rose in colour, and this colour predominated in the furniture upholstery. In the centre of the room was a glass dome similar to that in the lounge, together with crystal chandeliers.

The smoking room was also on the boat deck and was reached either from the lounge or from the open promenade deck. This room was decorated in fifteenth-century Italian style with rich carving in the walnut panelling. At the forward end of the room there was a magnificent fireplace, the sides of which were lined with massive slabs of marble. Just aft of the smoking room was the verandah café where passengers could sit and sip coffee in the open air, but protected from the excesses of the weather. The potted palms gave the impression of a Parisian cafe. At the forward end of the promenade deck there was an observation room, where passengers could view the vessel's bows as she ran over the North Atlantic at high speeds, without being exposed to the high winds. On each side of the promenade deck there were two regal suites of rooms, which comprised a drawing room, dining room, two bedrooms, bathroom and a

An alcove in the first class smoking room. (University of Liverpool)

private corridor. The rooms were luxuriously furnished and were heated by electric radiators. On the boat and promenade decks there were 68 special and *en suite* rooms, all of which consisted of a bedroom, parlour and bathroom.

The second class accommodation, like that of the first class, was situated aft and extended from the main deck to the boat deck. Although it was not as magnificent as the first class, it was given the same care and attention, and in fact it was as good as the first class on the older ships. The public rooms were on the promenade and boat decks, and the cabins were all on the main, upper and shelter decks. The grand staircase extended from the main to the boat deck, thus giving access to all the second class accommodation.

The dining saloon was on the upper deck and opened off the grand staircase. Like the first class saloon it ran the full width of the ship, although the tables were of the refectory type and seated 250 passengers in all. The room was light and airy and this atmosphere was enhanced by a lofty dome in the centre. The drawing room was aft on the promenade deck, forward of the grand staircase. It was panelled in a variety of maple woods with gold decorations, and was decorated in Louis XVI style with the upholstery and carpets in a crimson shade. In the centre of the room the ceiling was surmounted by a dome of obscured glass with a gilded metal framework. This room was a great favourite with lady passengers. The second class smoking room was aft of the grand staircase on the same deck. It was panelled in mahogany and decorated in Georgian style, with dark blue curtains and furniture upholstery. The second class lounge was on the boat deck aft, and was an extension of the grand staircase. The whole room was panelled in teak and again the carpets and curtains were in blue.

The third class accommodation was at the forward end of the ship on the lower, main, upper and shelter decks. The two staircases extended from the main to the upper deck and one gave direct access to the dining saloon on the upper deck where 330 passengers could be accommodated at one sitting, with refectory tables and revolving chairs. On the shelter deck were situated the ladies' room and the smoking room. Both rooms were panelled in polished ash and were fitted with revolving chairs. The sleeping accommodation for the third class passengers was on the lower and main decks, and consisted of four, six or eight berth cabins.

Mauretania carried a crew of 938, which

included the master and 48 officers. The cabins for the deck officers were on the bridge deck behind the navigating bridge and chart room. The master's accommodation was directly below the navigating bridge on the boat deck, and a staircase outside his cabin led to the wheelhouse. The engineer officers had cabins on the shelter deck, above the engine room, together with a mess room on the same deck. The seamen's mess was forward on the main deck, and most of the stewards' accommodation was right aft on the lower and main decks. The firemen, greasers and trimmers had messdecks on the same decks above the after boiler room and engine room. The senior ratings such as the quartermasters, boatswains and masters at arms were all accommodated aft of the second class cabins.

Mauretania was a quadruple screw ship driven by direct-drive steam turbines. Her main propulsion machinery was identical to that of Lusitania, although there were one or two modifications which always gave her the edge over her sister ship; the diameter of the propeller blades was six inches greater and the turbines were fitted with more rows of blades than those in Lusitania. But as with Lusitania, Mauretania's outer propellers were driven by the HP turbines and the LP turbines drove the inner propellers. The machinery developed 70,000 hp, and was capable

of driving the ship at well over 26 knots. The steam for the six turbines was provided by 23 coal-fired double-ended and two single-ended boilers, with a steam pressure of 195 psi. Most of the coal bunkers ran along the sides of the ship giving protection to the boiler rooms. Like her sister ship, Mauretania was designed to be fitted with 12 6 inch guns on the promenade and shelter decks.

Mauretania made her maiden voyage from Liverpool on Saturday 16 November 1907. Unfortunately, being late in the year the prospects for good weather all the way across the Atlantic were remote. When sailing day dawned the omens were not good as the rain fell steadily all day, and the boat train from London's Euston station was nearly an hour late. However, despite the dismal weather, a good crowd turned out to cheer her off as she set sail for Queenstown at 7.30 pm that day in a blaze of lights. She was commanded by Captain John T. Pritchard and she had on board a full complement of passengers together with a record amount of gold valued at £2,750,000, the most ever carried by a single ship. The passage down the Irish Sea was very smooth and she arrived at Queenstown at 9 am on Sunday 17 November.

After embarking more passengers and the mails, Mauretania left the port at 11 am, and large crowds gave her an enthusiastic send-off. Although she had been expected to set new Atlantic speed records, it soon became evident

A magnificent port-side view of the Mauretania. (Imperial War Museum)

that the weather was not going to allow this. On Monday 18 November, she ran into a severe storm, and at 5 pm the heavy spare anchor tore away from its lashings on the forecastle at the forward end of the promenade deck, and as it crashed about in the heavy seas there was a great danger of it causing severe damage. Captain Pritchard ordered speed to be reduced, and he went forward personally to superintend the securing of the anchor. In fact, it was he who finally succeeded in getting a line around it and fixing it down once again.

During the first three days of the voyage, *Mauretania* steamed through severe gales which kept her speed down. She finally arrived off Sandy Hook at 11.13 am on Friday 22 November 1907, and was forced to anchor because of thick fog. At 1 pm, with the fog showing no signs of lifting, Captain Pritchard issued a notice that it would be impossible to land passengers until the following day. This did not please a group of financiers on board, who sent a deputation to the captain to request that he reconsider his decision. Fortunately the captain was saved from the wrath of his wealthy passengers as the fog lifted and a pilot came on board. At 6.15 pm that day *Mauretania* berthed at Cunard's pier after having been given an enthusiastic welcome, and during her stay in New York large numbers of visitors came to look over her, or just to see her at her berth.

She left New York at noon on Saturday 30 November 1907 in perfect weather. In the early hours of the following day she ran into thick fog off the Grand Banks which persisted for 30 hours, before she was able to run at full speed. At 1 pm on Friday 5 December, the last full day of the voyage, *Mauretania* passed the White Star liner *Baltic* which had left New York two days before her. The Chief Engineer, Mr Currie, was well satisfied with the performance, particularly as, despite the fog at the start of the voyage, she bettered *Lusitania*'s eastbound record by 24 minutes. She had completed the passage in five days, ten hours, 50 minutes, at an average speed of 23.69 knots.

Mauretania left Liverpool for her second westbound Atlantic crossing on 14 December 1907, and whilst she was berthed in New York on Christmas Eve, at the foot of West 13th Street, she broke from her moorings during a gale and crashed into a fleet of barges at the adjoining pier. Fortunately she suffered no damage, and on the homeward voyage, despite bed weather, she was able to set a record of 575 miles for a day's run.

On 2 May 1908, *Mauretania* left Liverpool for her seventh Atlantic voyage, and three days later she encountered trouble when, it is thought, she hit a submerged object. One blade was sheered off her port inner propeller and the 'A' bracket, which supported the propeller shaft, was damaged. It was not possible to carry out repairs immediately because, as the two remaining blades were damaged, all of them needed renewing. It was decided to take the opportunity to replace both inner shafts with four-bladed propellers, and these, together with the new 'A' bracket, were forged in Darlington. In early October that year *Mauretania* was drydocked in Liverpool and the damage was surveyed. Rumours had been circulating in the press that it was extremely serious, but fortunately this was not the case and *Mauretania* was able to make a scheduled sailing to New York on 10 October 1908, arriving back in Liverpool 17 days later on Tuesday 27 October. Two days later she was in the Canada Graving Dock for an overhaul and replacement of the inner propellers. It was decided to also replace the two outer propellers; although they were still of the three-bladed type, they were cast solid rather than detachable. It was also decided that it was an ideal opportunity to replace some of the ship's bow plating, which had been damaged some time previously whilst docking.

It was almost three months before *Mauretania* sailed for New York again. The refit had cost over £50,000, and it was hoped that as well as giving her extra speed the problem of vibration would be reduced. She left Liverpool on Saturday 23 January 1909, which once again was not the best time of year to attempt speed records on the North Atlantic. By April of that year, however, *Mauretania* had captured both the eastbound and westbound records, and was reigning supreme on the Atlantic, retaining the Blue Riband for 20 years until July 1929.

By 1909, not only were the travelling public looking for shorter crossing times on the North Atlantic, but also once at their destination they wanted a speedy land journey. It was inevitable, therefore, that ports closer to London than Liverpool would be required. As a result, the Great Western Railway Company developed Fishguard in Pembrokeshire as a port of call for the Atlantic liners. By disembarking there passengers could save five hours on the sea journey to London or the Channel ports. *Mauretania* was the first Cunard liner to use Fishguard, on 30 August 1909. She had left Queenstown at 8.10 am that day and four hours later was within sight of Fishguard Bay, and as she steamed to her anchorage there was an informal gun salute from the coastguard station and cheers from the onlookers on the cliffs, as this small Welsh town decorated the streets with bunting and turned out in force to greet her. Between anchoring just outside the breakwater at 1.30 pm and weighing anchor just 40 minutes later, *Mauretania* disembarked 240 passengers and their baggage, together with 897 mail bags. On their arrival at the quayside each passenger was presented with a small bunch of heather by eight girls in Welsh national costume, and 15 minutes later they were on the train for Paddington.

At the end of December 1909 *Mauretania*'s first master, Captain John T. Pritchard, retired and Captain William Turner assumed command. Captain Turner was to remain in command of *Mauretania* until he took over *Lusitania* shortly before her ill-fated voyage. On 10 December 1910 *Mauretania* began a round voyage between Liverpool and New York, returning to Liverpool 12 days later. Amongst her passengers were Prince Albert and Princess Radziwill, Baron de Bode, the military attaché at the Russian embassy in Washington, and Mr A.M. Carlisle, the Managing Director of Harland & Wolff Shipbuilders, who was partly responsible for designing the *Titanic*. She arrived in New York at just before

midnight on 15 December after a rough passage, and after disembarking her passengers the following morning, she left the port at 6 pm on Sunday 18 December and was able to disembark the eastbound passengers at Fishguard at 10.22 pm on the 22nd, two full days before Christmas.

In June 1911 *Mauretania* brought 2,023 visitors to Britain for the Coronation of King George V, and they were able to attend the ceremony and return to New York within a fortnight.

On Wednesday 6 December 1911, *Mauretania* was moored in the Mersey waiting to make the Christmas trip to the United States, which again involved a fast turn-round when during the evening a strong gale blew up. At 10 pm her mooring cable snapped, causing her to drift onto Pluckington Bank where she grounded firmly. Within minutes of the news, orders were given to prepare *Lusitania*, which had arrived the previous day, for the Christmas voyage. Fortunately *Mauretania* was hard and fast on a soft bottom and, at 10.30 am the following day, tugs managed to refloat her. She was taken straight into the Canada graving dock where urgent repairs were carried out. The contractors undertook to have the ship ready for sea by 14 February 1912, and they managed it — no mean feat considering that they had to replace 700 tons of hull plating. As a result of this terrific effort, *Mauretania* was able to sail for New York on 2 March 1912.

For the next 22 months *Mauretania* remained in service with few incidents. In June 1912 she was moored alongside the landing stage in Liverpool when, as a result of a sudden swell, her gangways fell into the river. Fortunately her passengers were all on board and the only casualties were pieces of luggage. Later that month her master, Captain Turner, was appointed as an honorary commander in the Royal Naval Reserve.

In December 1913, *Mauretania* made Cunard's last quick-turn-round Christmas voyage before the First World War destroyed the 'old order'. On her return to Liverpool she went into the Canada dock for her annual overhaul, part of which involved work to her main propulsion turbines.

On the evening of Monday 26 January 1914, while a number of men were brazing turbine blades, one of their gas cylinders exploded with terrific force. The Master-at-Arms, Mr George Hennessy, was closest to the scene and, after donning a smoke helmet, he went below to render assistance. The sight that met him was horrific: four men had been killed outright, one of whom had terrible injuries, six more were badly hurt and the engine room woodwork was in flames. After assisting the worst of the injured, Mr Hennessy tackled the fire and managed to extinguish it. The main damage was confined to the blades in the starboard HP turbine. By early March, *Mauretania* was once again ready for sea, and she sailed for New York on Saturday 7 March 1914, three weeks behind schedule. She had only five months' service left before war broke out.

Mauretania left Liverpool for New York on 1 August 1914 commanded by Captain Fowler, and when she was three days out, on 4 August, Great Britain declared war on Germany. An Admiralty telegram warned Cunard that the German cruiser *Dresden* was off New York so the liner was diverted to Halifax NS. Two days before this the Admiralty had sent out an order requisitioning both *Lusitania* and *Mauretania* as AMCs upon their return to Liverpool. *Mauretania*'s commander was to be Captain Cole C. Fowler RN. However, on 11 August the Admiralty informed Cunard that both ships could resume ordinary sailings as they were not going to be taken up. The letter in respect of *Mauretania* said: 'You shall cancel the arrangement for taking up the *Mauretania* and waive any claim against Their Lordships for expenses incurred by your company on her account'.

By October the reduced demand for transatlantic passages did not justify the company in now keeping both of its large and expensive ships in service, so to avoid running the two vessels at a loss, *Mauretania* was laid up at Liverpool upon her return from New York on the 26th of that month. The *Lusitania* continued the Atlantic service on a monthly basis, but when she was lost in early May 1915 it was announced, on 12 May, that *Mauretania* would sail from Liverpool to New York on the 29th. However, only a few days after this announcement Cunard cancelled it giving the reason as 'lack of demand for passenger accommodation'. This was not in fact correct, for on 11 May the Admiralty had requisitioned *Mauretania* as a troop transport for the campaign in Gallipoli.

On 25 April 1915, Anzac troops had landed on the Gallipoli Peninsula in a move which, it was hoped, would quickly end the war. Unfortunately for a variety of reasons the campaign did not go as planned, and for the next nine months, until January 1916, when the Allied troops were evacuated from the Peninsula, troopships were badly needed in the Mediterranean. Thus *Mauretania* left Southampton in May 1915 for Mudros Bay on the island of Lemnos, which was some 40 miles south of the Gallipoli Peninsula and which was to be the Allied base for operations in the area. She made two more voyages between Southampton and Mudros, in July and August, and altogether carried 10,390 troops to the area.

It was during the second voyage, whilst eastbound in the Mediterranean, that she was attacked by a submarine. Fortunately the torpedo track was seen and the ship was able to take avoiding action. It was said that the torpedo missed *Mauretania* by less than 10 feet, but what is certain is that she was saved by her high speed. This incident shows how different things might have been for the *Lusitania* had she been allowed to steam at full power.

Following her third voyage to Mudros, *Mauretania* returned to her home port of Liverpool where she was fitted out as a hospital ship with beds for 2,000 patients. Her hull was painted white with a green band and red crosses, and her funnels were painted a buff colour. She left Liverpool on 21 October 1915, once again bound for Mudros Bay and Port Augusta in Sicily to assist with the evacuation of the wounded from Gallipoli. She made two round voyages in this role and brought back 4,300 men

The Mauretania *as a hospital ship in late 1915.*
(Imperial War Museum)

from the Greek island to Southampton. Following the evacuation of Allied troops from the ill-fated Gallipoli expedition in January 1916, *Mauretania*'s role in this theatre of war was at an end, and her last voyage was completed on 25 January 1916. During her time as a hospital ship she had helped disprove allegations in the German press that British hospital ships were being used to carry combat troops and ammunition. In the event she was ordered to put into Naples where, on 29 November 1915, she was inspected by several diplomats from neutral countries, including the Swiss and US Consuls in the city. They signed a declaration to the effect that the ship was not being used improperly, and the resultant publicity was the first official announcement that *Mauretania* had been used in this role of hospital ship.

On Thursday 24 February 1916 it was announced that *Mauretania* was being returned to her owners, who immediately set about restoring her for passenger service. However, on 29 September, with an increasing number of Canadian troops requiring conveyance across the Atlantic, *Mauretania* was once again requisitioned by the Government as a troop transport. She had just completed her reconditioning at Liverpool, but within ten days she had been con-

verted once more to a troopship with accommodation for 3,200 officers and men. In October and November 1916 she made two voyages between the Mersey and Halifax NS, to carry troops of the Canadian Expeditionary Force bound for the trenches of France. On completion of these voyages she was once again laid up, this time in Gareloch on the Clyde.

Mauretania remained idle throughout 1917, and it was the entry of the United States into the war which brought her back into service. On 21 March 1918 she was given an overhaul and put into service as a troopship once again. She made seven voyages from New York between April 1918 and the Armistice in November of that year, and carried 33,610 troops of the United States Expeditionary Force bound for France.

After the Armistice *Mauretania* was once again handed back to Cunard, but she remained on hire to the Government for the purpose of repatriating thousands of American and Canadian soldiers. Her first voyage in this role was from Liverpool on Monday 25 November 1918, carrying American troops including Admiral Mayo, who had commanded the US Navy squadron in European waters. Another passenger was the singer Harry Lauder who was undertaking one of his many tours of the United States. It was to be *Mauretania*'s last sailing from Liverpool, for when she returned to England on 12 December, it would be to Southampton, her

The Mauretania *dazzle painted in her role as a troop transport in 1918.* (Imperial War Museum)

new home port. It was a logical move for the company for not only was the port closer to London, but it would also enable the ships to call at one of the French Channel ports. In fact, on 22 February 1919 Sir Alfred Booth, the Chairman of Cunard, announced that both *Mauretania* and *Aquitania* would, in future, sail from Southampton for New York calling at Cherbourg, thereby taking the place of the German liners which called there in the years before 1914. However, *Mauretania* first made numerous trips calling at Le Havre or Brest to embark American or Canadian troops for New York and Halifax NS.

In May 1919 she set a new transatlantic speed record and, after disembarking her Canadian troops in Halifax, she proceeded to New York, making the run between the two ports in just 24 hours, six hours less than the previous best time. She made her final trooping voyage from Southampton on 28 June 1919, with over 4,000 Canadian troops on board, and on her return she was reconditioned for peacetime service once more. Perhaps her most famous civilian passengers between the Armistice and the end of her Government service were John Alcock and Arthur W. Brown, who made their record Atlantic flight on 15 June 1919 — an ominous portent

for the Atlantic liners.

Mauretania was restored to her former elegance within two months, and she sailed from Southampton on 21 September 1919, commanded by Sir Arthur H. Rostron, one of the heroes of the *Titanic* disaster. Many of the passengers on this voyage were on Government service and, once again, she sailed via Halifax to New York. On the westbound passage she encountered glorious weather, with smooth seas and balmy southerly winds. However, on the homeward passage she ran through severe south-easterly gales of such violence that four lifeboats were swept away and two others smashed beyond repair in their chocks. One crew member recalls that Captain Rostron handled his ship as though she were a destroyer. He did not reduce speed and *Mauretania* stuck her nose into the oncoming seas so frequently that tons of water continually covered her forecastle.

Mauretania made her next sailing on Tuesday 19 November 1919, when she inaugurated Cunard's new Southampton–Cherbourg–New York service. In June 1920 she was to have undergone an overhaul, but the number of passengers travelling to Europe from the United States was so great that she remained in service throughout that year without a break. In the early summer of 1921 the Atlantic service was disrupted by strikes. First a miners' strike delayed sailings as the ships had to bunker on the Continent, and secondly a strike of stewards caused some problems. In the years after the 1918 Armistice *Mauretania*'s average speeds over the Atlantic had been well below her best pre-war records, which was due to two main factors. Firstly, she had spent years on Government service without proper overhauls, and secondly she had been burning inferior coal. However, an event took place in the summer of 1921 which would transform the ship and enable her to achieve even greater speeds than before.

Mauretania arrived in Southampton from New York on Friday 22 July 1921, and she was scheduled to make her next Atlantic voyage on Saturday 30 July, just eight days later. During her stay in Southampton, a great deal of routine cleaning was carried out, much of it by outside contractors. At about 2 pm on Monday 25 July, while a workman was using inflammable liquid to clean carpets in the first class cabins on the main deck amidships, it accidentally caught fire. Despite attempts to extinguish the flames, the blaze spread, and soon onlookers saw dense smoke pouring out of portholes on the port side of the ship. Both the docks' and city fire brigades attended, and were assisted by the crew members who were on board. By 4 pm the glow of flames was visible through the main deck portholes and two hours later the vessel took on a list to starboard because of the weight of water which had been pumped in. Fortunately this was dealt with by the ship's pumps and she was quickly righted, then by 8 pm the fire was extinguished and the damage could be surveyed. It was mostly confined to the first class cabin area on that deck, with the whole width of the ship for 70 feet aft of the grand staircase gutted.

The fire had started in a cabin on the starboard side, and had been carried by a broadside wind, blowing in through open portholes, to the port side. Above these cabins the deck of the first class dining saloon was severely buckled and the parquet flooring was badly charred. On a brighter note there had been no serious casualties, but it was obvious that repairs would take some time. It was only four months since Mauretania had undergone a thorough overhaul which had cost many thousands of pounds, and the question of repairs was complicated by a joiners' strike in Southampton. In the event it was decided to send the ship back to the builders' yard at Wallsend, and the opportunity would be taken to convert her from coal to oil burning.

It was late September 1921 before Mauretania sailed for the Tyne and a refit which lasted just over five months. On Saturday 11 March 1922 she left to return to Southampton where she was drydocked in preparation for her voyage to New York on 25 March. At a dinner held on board prior to sailing, Sir Thomas Royden, Cunard's chairman, said: 'Mauretania was built 15 years ago and, in spite of enormous strides that have

been made during this period, she is as good as, if not better than, she was when she came out'. He was right, for Mauretania's best days were still to come.

By 25 July 1922 Mauretania had broken her own pre-war Atlantic speed record, and she was to reign supreme on the North Atlantic for another seven years. The conversion to oil had pushed her average speeds to just above 26 knots, and they were far more consistent than when she had been a coal burner.

On 27 January 1923 she left Southampton for a routine crossing to New York and, after disembarking her passengers, she was chartered by an American travel company for a Mediterranean cruise. She left the United States on 7 February and her ports of call included Madeira, Gibraltar, Algiers, Naples, Constantinople, Alexandria and Ajaccio. It was her first voyage into the Mediterranean since the ill-fated Gallipoli campaign during 1915, only this time she actually reached Constantinople (Istanbul). The cruise ended at Southampton on 3 April, and after a break of four days most of the passengers re-joined her for the Atlantic crossing back to New York.

On 5 November, when Mauretania arrived back at Southampton after a transatlantic crossing, she was taken out of service for five months during the winter for a complete overhaul. The chief item on the agenda was the re-blading of her turbines, although the vessel was to be painted throughout and improvements made to her third class accommodation. The work was to be carried out by Thorneycrofts at Southampton, but in late March 1924, 300 workers went on strike and work on the ship came to a halt. There is no doubt that the strikers had counted on Cunard being unable to move the vessel or obtain alternative labour, but the company management were determined to sail the ship on schedule. Therefore it was decided to complete the refit at the Homet dock in Cherbourg. So, at 9 am on Friday 11 April 1924, five Dutch tugs took the great Cunarder in tow for the French port, for Mauretania was totally helpless with the work on her turbines incomplete.

Above Mauretania *at Southampton in October 1925.* (Author's collection)

Right The Mauretania *leaving New York for a cruise in 1928.* (E.E. Viez)

The journey got off to a bad start when she grounded on Calshot Spit, but fortunately the tugs were able to pull her off quickly and without any damage having been caused. She was due to reach Cherbourg later the following day, but when she was in mid-Channel the winds increased almost to gale force and the tugs were forced to reduce speed to 1½ knots. During the afternoon of Saturday 12 April, Captain Rostron sent out a radio message stating that *Mauretania* and the five tugs were 15 miles from Barfleur Point and were being driven south-east. Several tugs and tenders went out to search for them but without success. Fortunately the weather moderated and the tugs were able to get her to Cherbourg at 7 pm on the 13th, after a voyage of 58 hours. Once there the work, which entailed renewing 385,700 turbine blades, was completed quickly and by 23 May *Mauretania* was back in Southampton. She sailed for New York seven days later and ran into further troubles when one of her outer propeller shafts snapped. However, by the summer this was repaired and in August 1924 she once again broke her own Atlantic speed record, making the voyage from Cherbourg to Ambrose Lightship in five days, three hours and 20 minutes. *Mauretania*'s popularity with her transatlan-

tic passengers was not always shared in the waters around her home port. In November 1924 the Cowes Harbour Commissioners on the Isle of Wight made strong protests to the Board of Trade about the Cunarder's speed when she steamed through the Solent outward bound. It seems that when she sailed on the 1st of that month, her heavy wash had flooded Cowes main street, knocking children off their feet and carrying away small boats. However, the Government decided that, as the ship was in the charge of a pilot, the complaint should

go direct to Trinity House.

In 1926, on eastbound trips, *Mauretania* started to call at Plymouth before Cherbourg, for those impatient to reach London. In November 1928 she was taken out of service for a seven-week refit to mondernize her furnishings and decor. Work in the public rooms included re-painting, re-upholstering of furniture and the provision of new carpets. In all, 3,000 square yards of carpet and 10,000 yards of curtain silk and tapestries were used, as well as 18 valuable Persian rugs in the lounges. In the vestibule between the first class lounge and smoking room on the boat deck, an American-style bar was built, although at that time the USA was in the grip of Prohibition. She sailed again for New York on 2 January 1929, but by now her domination of the Atlantic was coming to an end.

In the twilight of her career, the Mauretania *leaving New York on a West Indies cruise, January 1934.* (E.E. Viez)

In August 1928, Norddeutscher–Lloyd launched its two sister ships *Europa* and *Bremen*, and the latter was ready for the Atlantic service by July 1929. There was much speculation as to whether the new liner would take the Blue Riband from the elderly Cunarder — the old European rivalries were being revived once again. The *Bremen* took the Atlantic speed record easily, making the crossing between Cherbourg and Ambrose Lightship in four days, 17 hours, 42 minutes, an hour better than *Mauretania*'s fastest passage of September 1928. Captain McNeil of *Mauretania* was one of the first to congratulate Captain Ziegenbaum of the *Bremen*, and although at the time it was thought that *Bremen*'s speed might never be bettered, *Mauretania* was to have one last attempt at recapturing her old record. On 3 August 1929 she left Cherbourg for New York, and actually made the entire passage in four days, 21 hours, 44 minutes. Her great effort delighted the world, and even the general director of Norddeutscher–Lloyd praised the

efforts of the Cunarder and said: 'We shall be happy and proud if in 20 years we can maintain so small a margin of time against the latest competition'. Sadly, within those 20 years the world was to go through another six years of war and the Atlantic speed record at sea was soon to be made irrelevant by the airlines.

Late on the night of Wednesday 27 November 1929, while steaming out of New York, *Mauretania* collided with a train ferry near Robbins Reef. The collision holed *Mauretania*'s bows 30 feet above the water line, and the ferry was towed to Staten Island. The impact had hurled three railway goods wagons overboard from the ferry, but no one was injured on either ship. At 4.30 am the following day the Cunarder made her way back to Quarantine where she anchored until 7.30 am, when an inspection was made of her bow damage. She then steamed back to her

pier, and within 24 hours the workers of Todd Shipyard had repaired the hole. By midnight on Thursday 28 November, *Mauretania* was able to resume her voyage. She made one more crossing that year before being docked at Southampton for her winter overhaul.

When she returned to service on 5 February 1930, with her hull painted white, she crossed to New York and then left to begin a series of cruises, the first of which took her to the Mediterranean and back to Southampton for 26 March. In November 1931, during the great depression of the early 1930s, *Mauretania* left Southampton for New York at the start of a big cruising campaign; in 47 days she was to make three cruises, two from New York to the West Indies and one to the Mediterranean. By late 1932 she was making more cruises from New York to the West Indies, and after her overhaul between 11 October and 27 December 1932, she left for the USA again. The now elderly Cunarder was back in Southampton again in

The Mauretania *at New York in January 1934.* (E.E. Viez)

September 1933 and whilst in the port she underwent what was to be her last overhaul. Her white hull was re-painted, along with the interior decoration, and most of her carpeting was replaced.

After an overhaul of her machinery *Mauretania* left for New York on Wednesday 15 November 1933 to begin her final year's service. On her arrival she made three nine-day cruises before returning to Southampton. On 27 January 1934 she began another series of cruises from New York calling at Curacao, Colon, Nassau, Trinidad and La Guira. Between then and 16 April she completed five cruises and proved a very popular ship with the American public.

Mauretania left New York for a crossing to Southampton on 20 April 1933 and on the last full day of her voyage, whilst in the Western Approaches, she met the four-masted barque *Abraham Rydberg*, on the last leg of a race from Australia. With favourable winds and her main top gallant sails set, the barque was able to stay alongside the *Mauretania*, which might almost have been seen as a humiliation for the once unbeatable greyhound of the Atlantic.

Mauretania made her final passenger sailing from Southampton to New York on 30 June 1934, the day the Cunard and White Star Lines merged. She then made five two-week cruises to the West Indies, the last one starting on 8 September. On her way south she passed the burning wreck of the *Morro Castle*, which had beached off Asbury Park, New Jersey. She arrived back on 21 September, and left again five days later, on the very day that her successor *Queen Mary* was launched. It was a rough voyage back to Southampton and she arrived back in her home port for the last time on 2 October 1934. With the merger of the two shipping lines having been made a condition of the provision of finance for the completion of *Queen Mary*, there had to be a drastic reduction in the number of ships in service and *Mauretania* was to be one of the first casualties. Although her machinery was still running efficiently, she was outdated, particularly for her cruising role. She lacked many of the refinements considered

necessary for cruise ships, and once back at Southampton she was laid up in the Western Docks.

Over the next few months there were many rumours and much speculation as to her fate. In March 1935 several potential buyers visited her, some of whom were keen to save her from being broken up. However, on 3 April 1935 it was learned that the once great *Mauretania* had been purchased for £80,000 by Metal Industries Ltd of Glasgow for scrap. Twelve days later it was announced that the following month all the fixtures and fittings were to be sold by auction at Southampton Docks. The sale started on Tuesday 14 May 1935 when a mixed array of hopeful bidders climbed the gangway and made their way to the first class lounge on the boat deck, where *Mauretania*'s finery was to come under the hammer. The auctioneer, on taking his seat on the rostrum, described the occasion as unique. He went on to say that he felt privileged to play a part in the last days of this wonderful and much loved ship. He finished by saying that it was a sad occasion, but part of the march of progress. The auction lasted eight days and two of the biggest customers were Mr Charles Boot of Bakewell, Derbyshire, and Mr Walter Martin, a hotelier from Guernsey. Mr Martin bought a number of lots including the large glass centre dome from the first class lounge. In fact, many items from *Mauretania* can still be seen in several Guernsey hotels today. Once the sale was concluded, on 23 May, the work of dismantling the fittings began and the ship's masts were shortened to allow her to pass under the Forth Bridge.

On Monday 1 July 1935, with her white hull dulled by months of neglect and streaked with rust, *Mauretania* left Southampton under her own steam for her last voyage. She carried about 60 crew members and the same number of guests, and there was a ghostly atmosphere on board with so many of her public rooms and cabins stripped bare. A large crowd gathered on the quay, amongst them Captain Sir Arthur Rostron and the mayor of Southampton. As the great liner moved slowly from her berth the band of the Southern Railway played her off and the crowd cheered. She sailed slowly down South-ampton Water to a chorus of sirens from all the other ships and boats, led by the *Olympic* which was soon to follow *Mauretania* to the breakers. The noise continued until *Mauretania* passed out of sight towards the Solent and eventually the North Sea.

She reached the Tyne during the morning of Wednesday 3 July, and the Lord Mayor of New-castle and the Mayor of South Shields were received on board by Captain A.T. Brown. The following radio message was sent to Tyneside: 'Thank you for your greeting. For 28 years I have striven to be a credit to you and now my day is done. Though I pass on, may Tyneside ever reach out to further and greater triumphs. With pride and affection I greet you. Farewell — *Mauretania*'. Further north, as she passed the port of Amble, in response to a farewell message *Mauretania* replied: 'To the last and kindliest port in England, greetings and thanks. Closing down for ever. *Mauretania*'.

During the evening of Wednesday 3 July she reached the Firth of Forth where she anchored overnight well off shore. The following day she moved into Rosyth and alongside her final berth. As she moved up the dockside she was saluted by all the ships she passed and on the quay a lone piper played the lament 'Flowers of the Forest'. It was a fitting end for a fine ship which had become a legend on the North Atlantic.

Technical data	
Gross tonnage	31,938
Net tonnage	8,948
Length overall	790 ft (243m)
Breadth	87 ft 6 in (26.92m)
Quadruple screw, powered by four direct-acting steam turbines; 78,000 SHP, 26.75 knots.	

10
The 'A' Class of 1911
Ascania, Ausonia and Albania

In the years immediately before the First World War, Cunard had been wanting to start a passenger service between London, Southampton, the French Channel ports and Canada, and in 1911 the opportunity came when the company bought three ships from the fleet of Messrs Cairns, Noble & Co's Thomson Line.

The oldest and smallest of the vessels was the 7,682 gross ton *Consuelo*. She had been launched on 2 February 1900 as a cattle carrier with wooden stalls along the sides of her weather deck. She was bought by the Thomson Line in April 1908, and was refitted to carry 50 second and over 800 third class emigrants. The *Consuelo* was a four-masted ship with a straight stem, counter stern and a single tall slender funnel. She had a maximum speed of 12 knots, and started on the Thomson Line service between Hull, London and the USA or Canada in June 1908, renamed *Cairnrona*.

On Wednesday 6 April 1910 the *Cairnrona* left London for Portland, Maine, with 850 steerage passengers who were mainly of Russian origin, and a general cargo. At about 5.30 am the following day, when the ship was off Beachy Head, there were two violent explosions in the engine room. One of the explosions damaged the third class women's quarters and caused some injuries, and one crew member, a steward, was killed. There was some panic among the steerage passengers, but the crew, helped by some US cattlemen who were taking passage, managed

to get the women and children into the boats. By now quite a serious fire was blazing in the engine room and tugs put out from Dover to assist the evacuation of passengers and crew. The emigrants were landed at the Prince of Wales Pier in Dover, where the injured were taken to hospital. Amongst those who assisted at the hospital were Vice Admiral Louis of Battenburg and Princess Louis, who had been attending a dinner in Dover. As for the *Cairnrona*, the fire was extinguished after three hours, and at 1 pm on Saturday 9 April she arrived at the Surrey Commercial Docks in London for repairs.

In March 1911 she was purchased by Cunard and renamed *Albania*. Soon afterwards she commenced the London–Canada service for the company, but she was not up to Cunard standards and within six months she was laid up at Southend and offered for sale. In 1912 she was sold to the Bank Line and was eventually broken up in 1929.

The other two ships had longer careers with Cunard, before being sunk on the company's service during the First World War. The *Tortona* of 7,907 gross tons was launched in August 1909. She was a four-masted vessel with twin screws and accommodation for 50 second and over 1,000 third class passengers. In August 1910 she arrived at Southampton and inaugurated the Thomson Line service to Canada the following day. At a dinner on board the ship that evening Mr Russel Cairns explained the reason for

The Ascania *was ordered for the Cairns Line, but launched for Cunard in March 1911. (Photographic — Stewart Bale)*

the new service. The Canadian and French Governments had signed a treaty whereby goods shipped through a British port to a Canadian port received a rebate, and it was hoped that this would prevent goods being shipped into Canada via the USA. The new service, it was hoped, could ship cargo and emigrants direct to Canada from Britain. The third ship which was to become one of Cunard's 'A' Class ships was building at Swan Hunter's yard in Wallsend when, in March 1911, Cunard purchased all three of them. It had been intended that she was to be called *Gerona*, but she was launched on 3 March that year as the *Ascania*.

Cunard's new service was started by the *Albania* on 2 May 1911, followed by the *Ausonia* (formerly *Tortona*) on 16 May, and seven days later by the *Ascania*. The cargo was loaded in London but the passengers embarked in Southampton, where there was much satisfaction that Cunard's name had been added to the port's shipping list. It was perhaps the most important development since the White Star Line had transferred its principal New York service from the Mersey to the Solent, and it was to be only a matter of time before Cunard followed suit. When the *Ascania* arrived in Southampton from Newcastle the company was able to maintain a fortnightly service to Quebec and Montreal.

Both *Ausonia* and *Ascania* were twin screw vessels powered by two sets of triple expansion engines, and both had a service speed of between 12 and 13 knots. The *Ausonia* was similar in appearance to *Albania*, but the *Ascania* was very different. She had a shelter deck with upper and main decks below, and a long forecastle with promenade and boat decks in the midships superstructure. Aft of the well deck was a poop deck. She had a straight stem and a counter stern, together with two masts and two funnels, and provided accommodation for 200 second and 1,500 third class passengers. The cabins and public rooms for the second class were amidships and each cabin was fitted with an electric radiator. The smoke room had rectangular windows, furniture and panelling in oak, and was decorated mainly in white enamel. There was also a verandah cafe on the promenade deck.

From October 1911, after the withdrawal of *Albania*, the *Ausonia* and *Ascania* continued the Canadian service, and in the winter months when the St Lawrence was closed they were diverted to Portland, Maine. In 1913 they were joined by two new ships, *Andania* and *Alaunia*, which had been purpose-built for the route.

When war broke out in August 1914, *Ausonia* and *Ascania* remained on the North Atlantic, but on eastbound passages the third class dormitories were occupied by Canadian troops. On 11 June 1917 the *Ausonia* was torpedoed off the

After a lucky escape in June 1917, the Ausonia *was torpedoed and sunk in May 1918.* (University of Liverpool)

southern coast of Ireland, but fortunately her main propulsion machinery remained intact and she was able to make Avonmouth where she was docked for repairs. Just over a year later she was not so lucky. On 30 May 1918 she was 620 miles south-west of Fastnet *en route* from Liverpool to New York when she was torpedoed by the *U 55*, which later sank her by gunfire. Although there were no passengers aboard, 44 crew members lost their lives; the remaining men abandoned ship and were in lifeboats until 8 June when they were picked up by HMS *Zinnia*, a 'Flower' Class sloop. They were landed at Berhaven later that day.

Five days later the *Ascania* was bound for Montreal from Liverpool when she went aground off Cape Ray in the Breton Strait off Newfoundland. She could not be refloated and

the seas soon ensured that she would never sail again. She was declared a total loss soon afterwards and so ended the careers of Cunard's first two Southampton-based ships.

Technical data	
Gross tonnage	9,111 (*Ascania*), 7,907 (*Ausonia*), 7,682 (*Albania*)
Net tonnage	5,699 (*Ascania*), 5,112 (*Ausonia*), 5,012 (*Albania*)
Length overall	466 ft 6 in (143.53m) (*Ascania*), 464 ft (142.76m) (*Ausonia*), 461 ft 6 in (142m) (*Albania*)
Breadth	56 ft (17.23m) (*Ascania*), 54 ft 2 in (16.66m) (*Ausonia*), 52 ft 1 in (16.02m) (*Albania*)

All three ships twin screw, powered by two sets triple expansion engines: 900 NHP, 13 knots (*Ascania*), 888 NHP, 12 knots (*Ausonia*), 783 NHP, 12 knots (*Albania*).

11
Franconia and *Laconia*, 1911

These two 18,000 ton vessels were intended as replacements for the *Ivernia* and *Saxonia* on the Liverpool to Boston service, and they were built to compete with the White Star liners on this same route. They were also designed and equipped so as to be able to take the place of the *Lusitania* and *Mauretania* when the latter were being repaired or overhauled. The decision to build the two vessels was made in August 1909, when tenders were invited from four major British shipyards. The contracts for both ships eventually went to the Tyne company of Swan Hunter & Wigham Richardson, and the keel for the first of the sisters, *Franconia*, was laid in October 1909.

Franconia was launched on Saturday 23 July 1910, exactly nine months and ten days after the keel plates were laid. The ceremony was performed by Lady Forwood, the wife of a director of the Cunard company. There were a number of spectators to witness the event, but many were prevented from attending by a strike of railwaymen in the North-East. The keel of the *Laconia* was laid on the stocks vacated by *Franconia* at the end of July 1910, and she was launched a year later, on 27 July 1911.

The two new liners had accommodation for 300 first and 2,300 third and steerage class passengers. The first class public rooms, which consisted of a smoking room, a lounge with an *en suite* writing room, which also provided an oak parquet dance floor, a gymnasium and a veran-

dah cafe, were amidships on the upper promenade deck. The interior decorations were Georgian in style and were similar in both ships. The arrangement of the first class dining saloons on the two ships differed slightly. In the *Franconia* the galley between the first and second classes extended right across the ship, but in the *Laconia* it was cut away on the starboard side and the resulting space was given over to four small dining saloons, which linked the classes. These could be used for private parties or as an overflow for the second class dining saloon. The second class smoking room and drawing room were aft of, and *en suite* with, the dining saloon. The third class accommodation was remarkably spacious and airy and all the passengers in that class were berthed in cabins fitted with wash basins. They had the use of three dining rooms, a 'social hall' with piano, a smoking room and a ladies' room.

Both were twin screw ships powered by two sets of quadruple expansion engines which gave them a service speed of 16 to 17 knots. Perhaps the most interesting engineering feature of the two vessels was the Frahm anti-rolling device. This consisted of two tanks containing over 300 tons of water placed amidships on each side of the ship and cross connected at both top and bottom. Although the device was hailed as the great saviour for those who suffered from seasickness, it was not a great success.

The *Franconia* sailed on her maiden voyage

The Franconia *and* Laconia *were built as replacements for the* Ivernia *and* Saxonia. (University of Liverpool)

from Liverpool to Boston and New York on Saturday 25 February 1911, and she was followed almost 12 months later by *Laconia*, which left Liverpool for the same route on Saturday 20 January 1912. Before she left Liverpool *Franconia* had been opened to the public at the port, for in addition to strengthening the Boston route for Cunard, it was intended that they should run cruises from Liverpool to Mediterranean ports during the winter months when demand was slack on the North Atlantic. Indeed, four days after her arrival in New York on 6 March 1911, *Franconia* began a month-long cruise, which took her to Gibraltar, Algiers, Naples, Alexandria and back to Liverpool on 9 April.

Cunard also planned to employ its new vessels in the lucrative emigrant trade between Trieste and New York. The two ships had only three years of regular passenger service with the company, which were relatively trouble free. On 24 February 1913, however, while *Laconia* was bound from New York to the Mediterranean on a long cruise, she was delayed for some days in Madeira with damage to her forward high-pressure cylinder on the port side. Then on 3 May 1914, *Franconia* rescued survivors in a lifeboat from the Leyland ship *Colombian*, which had been burned out south of Sable Island in the Atlantic Ocean.

Unfortunately time was running out for both vessels, and on the outbreak of war in August 1914 *Laconia* was in Liverpool. She remained there until 1 September, when she made one last voyage to New York before being requisitioned for use as an armed merchant cruiser. She was converted at Liverpool and commissioned on 24 November 1914, commanded by Captain C.S. Wills. Most of her ship's company were drafted to Liverpool from Chatham depot, and two days later she arrived in Portsmouth. On 16 December she left the Solent for South Atlantic and the Cape Squadron based at Simonstown. For the next four months *Laconia* patrolled between Walvis Bay and Durban, and in April 1915 she was drydocked for a refit at Simonstown. She left the Cape on 10 April 1915 and headed north up the east coast of Africa to be used as the headquarters ship for the British operations to capture Tanga and the colony of German East Africa (Tanzania). For the next four months she was anchored off Mafia Island and at Kilindini Harbour, Mombasa.

In August 1915 *Laconia* visited Aden for a few days, before returning south again to patrol between Zanzibar and Mafia Island. In December she was drydocked for another refit at Simonstown, and in January 1916 she made two trooping voyages between Durban and Kilindini, before patrolling again off East Africa. During this period she anchored in the Lindi River, in

Above *The* Franconia *in the River Thames.* (A. Duncan)

Below *A publicity leaflet advertising* Laconia's *two-month Mediterranean cruise from New York in 1913.* (Author's collection)

Bottom *The itinerary of* Laconia's *Mediterranean cruise.* (Author's collection)

Tanga Bay and at Zanzibar. It was 2 June before she finally left the East African coast for good and steamed south to Cape Town, leaving there on 22 June for Devonport. She arrived on 18 July, but after only three days, during which time a lot of her naval stores were unloaded, she left for the Sandon Dock in Liverpool, and on 28 July she was paid off from the Royal Navy and handed back to Cunard.

Franconia was in New York when the war started and for a few months she continued her regular service between Liverpool and New York. Then, in February 1915, she was requisitioned by the Government for use as a troopship, and she made her final commercial voyage from Liverpool on 29 January. After a minimal amount of conversion work she was sent straight into the Mediterranean where troopships were urgently needed for operations at Gallipoli. She was based at Alexandria and soon after her arrival she was used to carry casualties away from Gallipoli to the safety of the Egyptian port.

The author Compton Mackenzie travelled north on board *Franconia* in May 1915 and, although he was dining in the first class saloon, he was berthed in a second class cabin. When he asked the reason for this he was shown one of the empty first class cabins and, in his words. 'From floor to ceiling the white cabin was splashed with blood'. Nearly 2,000 casualties had been carried, the most severely wounded in the first class cabins, and there had been no time to clean up. Mr Mackenzie recalled that the routine in the first class was little changed from peacetime, with menus printed on cruise postcards. He remembered steaming north at full speed, to avoid submarines, and anchoring close in to Cape Helles at 6 am on 16 May 1915, where he saw shells bursting on shore as the battles raged. The troops on board were disembarked into trawlers, while wounded men and Turkish prisoners were taken on for the return voyage to Alexandria.

On 4 October 1916, while *Franconia* was still on transport duty in the Mediterranean, she was about 200 miles south-east of Malta bound for Salonika from Alexandria when she was torpe-

In early 1915 the Franconia *became a troop transport and was employed in the Mediterranean. She is seen here at Mudros with the battleship* Exmouth. *(Imperial War Museum)*

doed by *UB47*. Fortunately she had no troops on board but 12 crew members were killed by the explosion. Although the *Franconia* then sank quickly, the remaining 302 men abandoned ship and were later rescued.

In that same month the reconditioned *Laconia* resumed service between Liverpool and New York. Sadly she had only four months left before she too fell prey to a U-boat. She left New York on Sunday 18 February 1917, carrying 34 first class and 41 second class passengers, together with 217 crew members. Exactly a week later, on the evening of Sunday 25 February, she was some six miles north-west-by-west of Fastnet off Ireland, and the passengers were looking forward to arriving in Liverpool the following day. At just after 9 pm a torpedo hit the starboard side abaft the engine room. The explosion was not loud but all on board knew what had happened, and Captain W.R.D. Irvine, her master, immediately ordered all the passengers to the boats and abandoned the ship of all but himself and a handful of crew members. Fortunately the sea was calm and there was no confusion, but as the boats were lowered one of them fouled in the falls, throwing the occupants into the water and causing some casualties.

All the boats were away within 20 minutes, and soon afterwards the submarine surfaced and fired a second torpedo at the disabled *Laconia*. Even with two torpedoes fired at her it was still an hour before the liner disappeared beneath the Atlantic Ocean at 10.20 pm. The radio operators on board had managed to get distress calls out, and at 4.30 am the following morning naval vessels arrived from Queenstown to pick up the survivors. Altogether six crew members were killed, one of them a US citizen, and six passengers lost their lives, two of whom, Mrs Mary Hay and her daughter Elizabeth, were also US citizens. The fact that further American lives had been lost by the action of a German U-boat was one more step towards the entry of the USA into the war. But for Cunard, the careers of the *Franconia* and *Laconia* of 1911 were brief and they never really had an opportunity to prove themselves on the Atlantic.

Technical data	
Gross tonnage	18,150 (*Franconia*), 18,099 (*Laconia*)
Net tonnage	11,247 (*Franconia*), 11,226 (*Laconia*)
Length overall	625 ft (192.3m)
Breadth	71 ft 2 in (21.89m)

Both ships twin screw, powered by two sets of quadruple expansion engines; 18,000 IHP, 18 knots.

12
The 'A' Class of 1913-17
Andania, Alaunia and *Aurania*

As we have seen, when Cunard started its Canadian service in 1911 it was with three ships purchased from the Thomson Line which were far from ideal, and in fact the *Albania* was put up for sale within a few months. It was natural that the company would want its own purpose-built ships for the route, and in the last two months of 1911 plans were completed for the first two. The order for the vessels went to Scotts Shipbuilding & Engineering Company of Greenock and the contracts were signed on 29 January 1912.

The two liners were to be the *Andania* and the *Alaunia*, 13,000 tonners with two masts and two funnels. They were almost identical sisters with straight stems, a low superstructure amidships and counter sterns. They had an overall length of 538 feet (165,53m), and were twin screw ships powered by two sets of quadruple expansion engines which developed 8,500 IHP and gave a service speed of 14½ knots. Like the 'A' class vessels of 1911, the new ships catered for only second and third class passengers with accommodation for 500 and 1,500 respectively. The second class cabins and public rooms were amidships and included a writing room, lounge, library and smoking room, all on the promenade deck. In the third class the old-style dormitories were replaced by four-berth or six-berth cabins, with a few two-berth rooms as well. Here the passengers, most of whom were emigrants, were provided with smoking rooms, a ladies' room, a general room and a dining saloon.

The first of the two vessels to be launched was the *Andania*, and she took to the water on 13 March 1913, followed three months later, on 9 June, by *Alaunia*. Both ships entered service that same year, the *Andania* having left the Clyde in early July 1913 for her trials before arriving at Liverpool to take on stores. On the evening of Monday 14 July she left Liverpool for Southamp-

The Andania *fitting out in 1913; the battleship* Ajax *is also nearing completion.* (University of Liverpool)

The Andania *in Cunard service prior to the First World War.* (Public Archives of Canada)

A good port-side view of the Andania. (University of Liverpool)

ton, and among the guests on board were representatives of the Canadian Government. She left Southampton on Thursday 17 July and completed her maiden round voyage at Surrey Commercial Docks in London on 12 August. At that time she was the largest ship to have navigated the Thames and the approach channels were dredged for the occasion.

It was 3 December 1913 before *Alaunia* made her maiden voyage and, as the St Lawrence was closed in the winter months, she sailed from Liverpool to Portland, Maine. On her return from the United States she too went to London to join her sister sailing from that port and Southampton.

It was during December 1913 that Cunard placed an order with Swan Hunter & Wigham Richardson at Wallsend for the third ship in the class. The *Aurania*, as she was to become, was very similar to the earlier sisters and was capable of the same speeds, powered in her case by two sets of double reduction geared turbines. She was also given bulwarks forward, as the *Andania* and *Alaunia* had a reputation for being wet ships in that area. Unfortunately work on her was very much delayed when the First World War started, and it was 16 July 1916 before she was launched. She was finally completed and fit-

ted out as a troopship in March 1917, in grey livery.

Since August 1914 the first two sisters had also been employed as troopships, first of all ferrying Canadian troops across the Atlantic. For a few weeks in early 1915, *Andania* was used to accommodate German POWs in the Thames. By the summer of 1915 both ships were heavily involved in the Gallipoli campaign, and *Andania* transported the Royal Inniskilling Fusiliers and the Royal Dublin Fusiliers to Cape Helles for the Suvla landings. Later in the year *Alaunia* went east of Suez to Bombay with troops, which was a rare event for a Cunarder. In the spring of 1916 both ships were employed once again on the North Atlantic, sailing between London and Canada and the USA.

Alaunia made her final voyage from London in late September 1916, carrying cabin class passengers only. She completed the westbound journey safely and she was returning to London with 180 passengers and 165 crew members, when, on 19 October 1916, just two miles off the Royal Sovereign lightship, she struck a mine. Initially her master tried to beach the vessel and an attempt was made to take her in tow by tugs, but the inrush of water was too great. The captain ordered the ship to be abandoned and all

The Alaunia *entered service in 1913, but hit a mine and sank in October 1916.* (Public Archives of Canada)

the passengers were got safely into the boats together with 163 of her crew. *Alaunia* sank soon afterwards with the loss of two lives, a steward and a trimmer whose bodies were washed up in Pevensey Bay three days later.

On the evening of Friday 26 January 1918, *Andania* left Liverpool for New York. It was a fine clear evening and the liner was routed round the northern coast of Ireland. She had on board 40 cabin class passengers and a crew of just over 200. One of the passengers, Dr J.A. Harker of the Ministry of Munitions, tells his story of what happened the following morning when *Andania* was three to four miles north-north-east of Altacarry Light off County Antrim.

'About ten in the morning I was on the boat deck having a conversation with a steward, who was telling me that a boat drill was arranged for just after 10 am and that all passengers were to proceed to their respective boats. No sooner had he said these words than a torpedo hit the liner full amidships on the starboard side. The vessel immediately began to list to starboard and I went to my boat station, which was number six. The boat was one of the first to get away, with about 15 to 16 passengers. We rowed about for some time

and managed to pick up other survivors. After about an hour and a half we were picked up by a patrol vessel and brought to an Antrim coast town on Sunday afternoon.'

Another passenger, J.J. Holgate, recalls the attack thus:

'When the ship was torpedoed there was no confusion whatever, but we had a lot of difficulty owing to the fact that the steamer was listing badly. The next boat to ours was stoved in, and we rescued all the passengers. There were on our boat a Belgian lady of 71, a Russian lady with two children, and one of the stewardesses, none of whom uttered one word of complaint. My friend, Mr W.J. Nicholls, distinctly saw the submarine twice, once within 20 yards and again 50 yards from the boat.'

Two of the ship's company, a steward and an able seaman were killed in the explosion. For some time it was hoped that the *Andania* might be saved. A tug arrived and took her in tow, but just over nine hours after she had been hit *Andania* rolled over onto her starboard side and sank.

The newest of the three vessels, the *Aurania*, was employed on the North Atlantic. She was on hire to the Government and had made only seven round voyages before she too became a war casualty. She left Liverpool on Wednesday

3 February 1918, just six days after *Andania* had sailed. She too left in the late evening and was routed round the coast of Northern Ireland bound for New York. On the following morning she was some 15 miles north-west of Inishtrahull off the coast of County Donegal when she was hit by a torpedo fired by *UB67*. Nine crew members were killed in the explosion, and once again it was hoped that the ship could be saved. She was taken in tow by a trawler, but the towing wire was carried away, and before another could be passed over, the *Aurania* went aground off Tobermory in Scotland. At that time of the year it was not long before the seas broke her up.

Thus the war had claimed all five of Cunard's 'A' Class ships which had been the spearhead of the company's efforts to reclaim the Canadian trade.

Technical data	
Gross tonnage	13,405 (*Andania*), 13,936 (*Aurania*)
Net tonnage	8,464 (*Andania*), 8,499 (*Aurania*)
Length overall	538 ft (165.53m)
Breadth	64 ft 7 in (19.87m)

All three ships twin screw, powered by two sets of quadruple expansion engines; 8,500 IHP (*Aurania* 9,000 IHP), 14.5 knots (*Aurania* 15 knots).

13
Aquitania, 1914

Of all the Cunard liners which were built in the twentieth century, the longest serving and best-known was the *Aquitania*. Her career spanned 35 years and took her through both the First and Second World Wars and into the very much changed post-war era, and she was the only one of the giant liners to serve under the White Ensign as an armed merchant cruiser, albeit for only four weeks.

The planning of the *Aquitania* went back to 1910 and she was designed to operate on the North Atlantic express service in conjunction with the *Lusitania* and *Mauretania*. She was not meant to compete for any speed records, but to outshine White Star's *Olympic* which had been launched in October 1910. Cunard invited speci-fications for the new ship in November of that year, and approached two companies, Swan Hunter of Wallsend and John Brown at Clyde-bank. The new ship was to have a gross tonnage of 45,647, and it was estimated that she would cost £2,000,000. Three weeks after inviting tenders, on 10 December 1910, Cunard an-nounced that the order for the building of *Aquitania* had gone to John Brown & Co Ltd of Clydebank. Six months later, on 5 June 1911 the first keel plate was laid at the berth which had been specially prepared for the new ship.

As the building of *Aquitania* progressed, great publicity was given to the fact that she would be the largest vessel in the world, and as the launch date came closer the excitement grew on

Clydebank. By early April 1913 much of the scaffolding round the hull had been removed, with the launch date set for Monday 21 April, which was declared a public holiday in Glasgow. Many hours before the ceremony began, crowds gathered to view the event, and over 100,000 people watched from John Brown's yard as the Countess of Derby pressed the button which released the huge hull into the river. The liner's entry into the water was greeted by the sound-

The launch of the Aquitania *on Monday 21 April 1913. (University of Liverpool)*

ing of hundreds of whistles and hooters, together with the cheers of the multitudes of spectators. Once the ship had been safely launched she was towed to her fitting-out berth to be completed ready for her maiden voyage in the early summer of the following year.

In January 1914 the last of *Aquitania*'s four funnels was placed in position, and Cunard announced that lifeboat accommodation would be provided for all those on board, clearly as a result of the *Titanic* disaster, although Cunard said they had planned this 15 months before that tragedy. In February 1914 it was announced that *Aquitania*'s first master was to be Captain William Turner, who became better known as the master of the *Lusitania* when she was torpedoed in May 1915.

By Saturday 10 May 1914 work on the new ship was completed, and the following day the delicate task of transferring her from Clydebank to Greenock was undertaken. There was great public interest in the event and the churches in the area had to alter the times of their services so that the congregations could witness the great ship passing down the Clyde. With four tugs ahead and two astern, *Aquitania* set out at 11 am and reached Greenock at 1.30 pm. Once

Aquitania *fitting out in the spring of 1914.* (University of Liverpool)

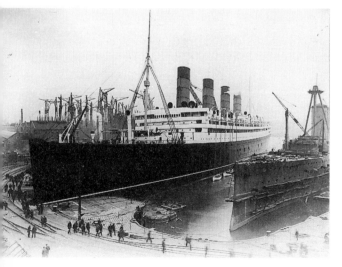

there the tugs were cast off and the liner proceeded under her own power to Wemyss Bay where she underwent trials. When these were completed she set course for Liverpool and arrived in the Gladstone Dock on Wednesday 13 May 1914, to prepare for her maiden voyage which was scheduled for the end of that month.

For the 3,230 passengers who could be accommodated on board, the facilities were very generous and surpassed anything seen before on the North Atlantic. The 618 first class passengers were berthed in cabins or staterooms amidships on 'A', 'B', 'C' and 'D' decks, and on 'B' deck there were also special suites of rooms with bath and toilet facilities. Most of the public rooms were on 'A' deck and included lounges, writing rooms, a smoking room and garden lounges. Just aft of the No 1 funnel casing was the drawing room which was decorated in the Adam style copied from certain features in Lansdowne House in London. Aft of this room was the main staircase and the Georgian lounge, which was flanked on both sides by the garden lounges. Continuing aft came the long gallery which stretched from the lounge to the smoking room. On the port side there were large sash windows which overlooked the promenade and sea. The inside walls were adorned with prints of English seaports in the eighteenth century and engraved portraits of Prince William Henry, the third son of George III, Lord Nelson, Handel and others. The whole room was 150 feet (46.15m) long and also contained showcases which held exhibits of china, lace and art work. Next came the smoking room which was modelled on Greenwich Hospital with oak panelling and beams. The restaurant, which was on 'D' deck, was decorated in the Louis XVI style. Aft of it was the grill room, decorated in early Jacobean style with several features derived from a carved oak room in the seventeenth-century palace at Bromley-by-Bow. On 'E' deck, below the first class foyer, was a swimming pool and gymnasium.

The 614 second class passengers were accommodated aft on 'A', 'B', 'C', 'D' and 'E' decks. Their lounge was on 'A' deck and was decorated

Top *The Louis XVI restaurant*, SS Aquitania. (Author's collection)

Above *The grill room on 'D' deck*, SS Aquitania. (Author's collection)

Above right *The Carolean Smoking Room*, SS Aquitania. (Author's collection)

in the Adam style. Beneath the lounge on 'B' deck there was a drawing room, smoking room, and right aft a verandah cafe. The second class dining saloon was on 'D' deck, aft of the galley areas which were situated between the first and second class saloons. The 1,998 third class passengers were accommodated on 'C', 'D', 'E', 'F' and 'G' decks, and both the public rooms and cabins were of a high standard. The third class entrance was forward on 'C' deck, from which stairways led to the general room on 'D' deck. The three third class dining saloons were on 'F' deck, with cabins on 'E', 'F' and 'G' decks. Most of them had two or four berths, but a few larger rooms could accommodate six passengers. There were 972 officers and crew members, most of these being engine room and pursers' staff.

Aquitania had a gross tonnage of 45,647 with an overall length of 901 feet (277.23m) and a beam of 97 feet (29.84m). She was a quadruple screw ship and was powered by direct acting steam turbines. Her port outer shaft was driven by the high-pressure turbine, the starboard outer by the intermediate-pressure and the two inner shafts by a low-pressure turbine. The 21 double-ended coal-fired boilers were arranged in four boiler rooms and they supplied steam at 195 psi. In all, the main propulsion machinery developed 60,000 SHP and gave the vessel a service speed of 23½ knots.

Aquitania left Liverpool for maiden voyage on Friday 30 May 1914, but the event was over-shadowed by the tragic sinking of the *Empress*

Above left *The first class smoking room, SS Aquitania.* (University of Liverpool)

Far left *One of the paintings in the first class smoking room.* (University of Liverpool)

Left *A second class two-berth cabin, SS Aquitania.* (University of Liverpool)

Above *A third class six-berth cabin, SS Aquitania.* (University of Liverpool)

of Ireland in the St Lawrence River the previous day, with the loss of over 1,000 lives. On board *Aquitania* were a sprinkling of VIPs and titled people, one of whom, Lord Eversley, a former MP and member of Mr Gladstone's government, had first crossed the Atlantic in 1851 on the little Cunarder *Nigara*. *Aquitania* berthed in New York on the morning of Friday 5 June, a glorious summer's day, and she made her way up harbour to the whistles and salutes of the hundreds of boats which had turned out to see the latest

addition to the Cunard fleet. The voyage had taken five days, 17 hours and 43 minutes, but as there had been an ice warning she had steamed further south than usual, and added nearly 100 miles to the journey. On the homeward run she called at Fishguard to land passengers, and then made two more round voyages to New York before the First World War, the second between 11 and 27 July 1914. She was in Liverpool when the war started, and was requisitioned by the Government for service as an armed merchant cruiser; she was converted for this role in the Gladstone Dock, being fitted with ten six-inch guns, four of which were mounted on the forecastle, two on 'B' deck amidships, two on 'B' deck aft and two on 'C' deck aft.

Aquitania was commissioned into the Royal Navy at 9 am on Friday 7 August 1914, commanded by Captain E.K. Loring RN, and the main body of her crew joined the ship from

Portsmouth that same day. At 12.10 pm the next day she left Liverpool for two days of exercises at sea between the Clyde and Isle of Man, before leaving to patrol the Western Approaches. Among the ships she sighted on this first patrol were the Cunarder *Laconia*, with her funnels disguised, and the *Olympic*. On 16 August she returned to the Mersey to coal, and leave was granted to the civilian stokers.

Four days later, on 20 August, she left Liverpool for her second patrol of the Western Approaches. On Saturday 22 August she was in dense but patchy fog when, at 7.06 am in a position 50° 20′N/17° 30′W, she sighted a cargo ship inward bound, so altered course to close and identify her. Both ships were then hidden by fog, and seven minutes after first sighting her, despite putting her engines full astern, *Aquitania* collided with the other vessel on her starboard side abaft the engine room. The cargo ship turned out to be the 9,300 ton Leyland ship SS *Canadian*. Neither ship was in any danger of sinking and the *Aquitania* went astern to clear the *Canadian* and examine the damage. Her stem was buckled and the plates were torn away from 'C' deck downwards and aft to frame 304. After her carpenters had strengthened the bulkheads, *Aquitania* set course for Liverpool at 12 knots, and the following day she was escorted by HMS *Caronia*. On the morning of 24 August she anchored in Liverpool Bay, where she remained for the next eight days while a court of inquiry was held into the collision. As a result of this it was decided that the *Aquitania* was too big for a role as an AMC, and on 2 September she entered Gladstone Dock where the crew were employed landing stores and ammunition and dismantling her guns. By 10 pm on Thursday 3 September all her guns had been landed on the quayside, and the following afternoon she went into drydock for repairs. At 11.30 am on 5 September the White Ensign was hauled down and all the RNR officers and ratings left the ship for the naval barracks at Portsmouth. *Aquitania*'s days as an armed merchant cruiser were over.

By the end of 1914 her damaged bows had been repaired, and she was laid up in Gladstone Dock until a useful role could be found for her. This came in the spring of 1915, with the Allied landings on the Gallipoli peninsula to which huge numbers of troops had to be transported. Along with *Mauretania*, *Aquitania* was urgently required to carry three divisions of troops to Mudros, so she was requisitioned by the Government on 18 June, and the Ministry of Transport asked Cunard to fit 800 more berths. Secret Government documents which have now been released show that the cabinet was deeply divided on the question of using the two Cunarders in such a role. It was only weeks after the *Lusitania* disaster and fears were expressed about the loss of life if the ships were torpedoed. However, under pressure from the Admiralty it was agreed that the two vessels would be used as troop transports.

Exactly a week after she had been requisitioned, *Aquitania* left Liverpool with 4,872 men and 521 officers of the 13th Division on board. She made three trooping runs to the Mediterranean, before being fitted out as a hospital ship and given a white livery with a green riband and buff-coloured funnels. She was commanded by Captain C.A. Smith, with Captain E. Britten as her Staff Captain, and she served in this role until the following January. She regularly arrived at 44 berth in Southampton Docks with nearly 5,000 patients, and 20 ambulance trains were required to convey them to various hospitals. Her final departure from Mudros with invalids was on 27 December 1915, and she arrived in Southampton Docks on 8 January 1916. After undergoing engine maintenance she went up to Liverpool on 22 January for a refit, and when this had been completed in mid-February it was decided to lay her up in Loch Goil on half hire.

However, on 10 April 1916 she was discharged from Government service altogether and was ordered to Southampton where Harland & Wolff had undertaken to recondition her for Cunard's service. The Government gave the company £90,000 to cover the cost of the work and for three months' hire while it was undertaken. One of the conditions of this grant was

The Aquitania *at Mudros as a troop transport. The* Mauretania *is in the background.* (Imperial War Museum)

The Aquitania *as a hospital ship at Southampton.* (Imperial War Museum)

that Cunard had the reconversion work completed by mid-June and the ship moved out of the port. In the event Harland & Wolff revealed that they could not complete the work until 7 August, and a dispute arose between Cunard and the Admiralty Director of Transports, who insisted that the liner be moved as she was hampering troop movements.

With the Admiralty threatening to remove the half-reconditioned vessel to a Solent anchorage, the dispute was resolved on 21 July 1916, when *Aquitania* was once again requisitioned by the Government for further service as a hospital ship. It had been decided that more such vessels were needed in the Mediterranean, and although the *Aquitania*'s reconditioning as a passenger liner was complete except for internal painting, orders were given to stop the work and start fitting the ship out as a hospital ship once again. On 21 November 1916 the *Britannic* was mined in the Aegean Sea and *Aquitania* was ordered to the Mediterranean to replace her. She left Southampton empty for Port Augusta to embark invalids, calling at Gibraltar to embark more nurses and at Naples for coal.

A month later, at the end of December 1916, the *Aquitania* was again laid up, this time in the Solent. The costly lesson learned earlier in the year, when the Government had paid Cunard

to recondition the ship, was heeded and this time she was left fitted out as hospital ship and Cunard were paid half the normal rate of hire, which was £6,000 monthly. She remained in the Solent for the whole of 1917, and in November of that year she almost went aground when, in gales, she lost an anchor and 120 fathoms of cable.

It was the United States' declaration of war in December 1917 which brought the *Aquitania* back into service, and for the remainder of the war she was commissioned under the White Ensign as an American Expeditionary Force transport. On 15 December 1918 she was back in the Gladstone Dock at Liverpool, then on 10 January 1919 she was paid off from Government service and the White Ensign was hauled down once again. Ten days later she was bound for Halifax NS under Cunard management, but with most of her accommodation reserved for the Government.

In May 1919 she was still employed in the repatriation of Canadian and US troops, and it was announced by Cunard's Chairman that when she returned to commercial service *Aquitania*, together with the *Mauretania*, were to be based at Southampton. The reason given was that the company wished to capture the share of passenger traffic which had been taken by the German ships prior to August 1914. However,

The Aquitania *dazzle painted as a troopship.* (Imperial War Museum)

it was a logical move as Southampton was a better port and it was more convenient for the Channel ports and London. On Sunday 13 July 1919 the *Aquitania* left Southampton on her final trooping voyage before returning to Liverpool to start her reconditioning.

When she had been hastily converted into an AMC in the early days of the war, 3,000 men had been employed to strip the ship of her luxury fittings, which had then been put into store. These were now to be fitted back into the liner, and this work lasted until Wednesday 26 November 1919, when she left Liverpool for the yards of Sir W.G. Armstrong Whitworth & Co Ltd for conversion from coal to oil burning. She arrived on the Tyne on the last day of that month and work began at once on one of the biggest contracts the yard had ever undertaken. The refit on the Tyne lasted 30 weeks and during that time 300 tons of old material was removed and 11,300 yards of steel pipes were installed. The conversion for oil fuel greatly reduced the engine room personnel, as nearly 300 firemen and trimmers became redundant.

It was on Sunday 27 June 1920 that the work was completed, and *Aquitania* was towed stern first down the Tyne for a trial voyage round

the north of Scotland to Liverpool. During the reconditioning, each of the eight furnaces in the 21 double-ended boilers had been fitted with a brass oil fuel burner, which sprayed the oil into the furnace. Among the structural alterations were the installation of a bank and an enquiry office on 'D' deck, in the foyer outside the Louis XVI restaurant. On 'B' deck all the first class cabins were rebuilt and, although they were reduced in number, they were increased in size and some had private dining rooms added. The Palladian lounge, Louis XVI restaurant, Carolean smoking room and the long gallery were seen again, resplendent in their pristine glory.

After drydocking in Gladstone Dock, *Aquitania* began her first fully commercial post-war voyage when she left Liverpool for New York on Saturday 17 July 1920. Her return voyage terminated at Southampton on 7 August, where she joined the *Mauretania* and *Imperator* (later to be re-named *Berengaria*) in what Cunard described as their express Channel service to New York, provided weekly by the three ships. *Aquitania*'s performance as an oil burner was extremely good, enabling her to keep a remarkable continuity of speed over long distances, and to re-fuel in under 20 hours with only six men being employed on the task.

In May 1921 *Aquitania* left Southampton on schedule despite a strike of stewards on board, the company enlisting the help of the Liverpool clerical staff to act as stewards for the voyage. One of the managers, Mr E.C. Cotterell, went on board as the chief library steward, and despite this makeshift arrangement the voyage was a success. During her annual winter refits of 1926, 1927 and 1928 her first class accommodation was extensively modernized, particularly the staterooms on 'B' deck which were enlarged once again. In November 1930 the liner was turned into an art gallery for one voyage, when 350 sketches, water colours and oil paintings by national artists were put on display. They were to be auctioned in New York in aid of the British Legion, and the US authorities agreed to waive any duty payable on them. The exhibition was opened at Southampton by Prince

George, the Duke of Kent, who visited the ship together with the US Ambassador in London.

In February 1932 the *Aquitania* was used for cruising for the first time with her second class accommodation re-designated 'tourist class'. She left New York for the first cruise on 3 February and steamed into the Mediterranean calling at Gibraltar, Port Said, Villefranche, Naples and Piraeus. She made two such cruises during February and March 1932, both of them starting and finishing in New York. Most of the passengers were Americans, but bookings were also taken from Britons who were wintering in the Mediterranean and who wished to travel from port to port. Later in the year *Aquitania* made shorter cruises between New York and Bermuda. In November 1932 she was given an eight-week overhaul at Southampton where she underwent some internal reconstruction. Her first class accommodation was reduced to 650, and 55 new outside cabins with bathrooms were constructed. The tourist class area was greatly enlarged, with a reduction in passengers to 600, while her third class accommodation was altered to cater for 950. A new theatre was built with a 300 sq ft stage for the production of plays, live entertainment and cinema shows, and was accessible to all passengers. In addition, all the public rooms were completely renovated.

On 24 January 1934, while outward bound from Southampton, *Aquitania* grounded briefly on the Brambles Bank in the Solent, but she was refloated quickly and was able to continue her voyage. In the following year, on 9 March, she left New York for a Mediterranean cruise which was due to end in Southampton at 4 pm on Wednesday 10 April. She left her last port of call, Villefranche, on 5 April and five days later at 3.30 pm, just as she was turning up into Southampton Water, she was caught by strong winds and ran aground on Thorne Knoll, part of the Bramble Bank. Her engines were immediately put full astern but she was stuck fast, and for some hours seven tugs tried to free her, but without success. As the tide went out, her stem could be seen high and dry on the bank while her stern was low in the water, and at 9 pm that

evening her 300 passengers were landed by lighter. It was 5 pm the following day before she was refloated, aided by ten tugs pushing and pulling and with black smoke pouring from her funnels. Fortunately she had been resting easily on mud, and after a full survey it was revealed that she was none the worse for the ordeal, and was able to sail for New York on schedule on 17 April.

In 1937 and 1938 she continued with a mixture of Atlantic crossings and cruises, and on 23 August 1939 she left Southampton for New York on what was to be her last voyage as a crack express liner. She had on board the newly appointed British Ambassador to the USA, and after calling at Cherbourg that same day, she arrived in New York on 29 August. *Aquitania* left the port on the following day carrying very few passengers, and each evening the ship was blacked out. She arrived back in Southampton on 5 September 1939, two days after the start of the Second World War. She sailed for New York again two days later, arriving there on 13 September with hundreds of American citizens on board who had all left Europe before the storm broke. She then returned to Southampton where she remained until 21 November when she was once again requisitioned for service as a troop transport.

Without a doubt the outbreak of war in 1939 provided a reprieve for the *Aquitania*, for with the *Queen Elizabeth* due to enter service in the summer of 1940, she would almost certainly have been withdrawn. *Aquitania* left Southampton on 29 November 1939 for Halifax NS to bring back Canadian troops. It was on a second such voyage, at 4.30 am on 17 December 1939, that she was involved in a collision with the *Samaria*, while in a convoy with the *Empress of Britain* escorted by three destroyers and the aircraft carrier HMS *Furious*. It was a very dark, overcast night and the *Samaria* collided with both the *Furious* and *Aquitania*. Fortunately damage was minimal and the convoy was able to continue its voyage to Halifax.

In early 1940, *Aquitania* underwent an extensive refit in the USA, during which she was

The Aquitania *as a troopship during the Second World War.* (Imperial War Museum)

defensively armed with two six-inch guns and smaller armament. In March 1940 she was despatched to Sydney, and in June of that year, with the *Queen Mary* and *Mauretania*, she formed part of the biggest convoy ever to leave Australia with troops for the Middle East. Over the next 18 months she was based at Sydney carrying Australian and New Zealand troops to Singapore, Ceylon, India and Suez. With the entry of Japan into the war at the end of 1941, the waters of the Far East became extremely dangerous, and in the early weeks of that phase of the conflict she made two fast passages between Pearl Harbor and San Francisco carrying women and children. By the spring of 1943 she was employed with the two *Queens* on the shuttle service across the Atlantic, transporting many thousands of US troops to Europe. For most of these crossings she formed part of an unescorted convoy of four fast passenger ships, relying on speed alone to avoid U-boats.

In May 1945, with the end of the war in Europe, the shuttle service was reversed as *Aquitania*, the two *Queens* and over 300 smaller vessels repatriated the US and Canadian troops. In October 1945 the *Aquitania* was withdrawn

from the Atlantic run in order to assist with bringing home British and Imperial troops. She left Southampton for Sydney in late October with some 3,000 Anzac troops on board. Initially it had been intended that she would call at Cape Town, where the civic authorities had arranged a great welcome. However, in view of the awkward tides and the fact that the Admiralty would not provide indemnity against any damage caused to the ship, Cunard decided to anchor her in the roadsteads while the ship fuelled and embarked stores. Officially denied their shore leave, the 3,000 troops took matters into their own hands and swarmed into tugs and lighters despite the efforts of the Military Police to stop them. However, the majority of the men wanted to get home and when the ship sailed the following day only 21 had failed to get back on board. She arrived in Sydney towards the end of November 1945, and on the return voyage from that port in early December she carried 90 British children who had been evacuated to Australia five years previously, together with 4,000 RN officers and ratings and 450 civilian passengers. On her return to Southampton in January 1946, it was announced that in the following month *Aquitania*, together with other ships, would take the wives and children of Canadian servicemen across the Atlantic to their new homes in Canada. She sailed on the first of these voyages on 25 February, and returned with 3,000 German POWs coming to work in Britain.

Between April and June of that year, *Aquitania* was refitted and partially returned to her pre-war condition. The first class area was restored to its former glory with accommodation for 400 passengers, and the tourist section was partially restored, but the third class was left with its large dormitories. Her hull was painted black once more, after nearly six years of dull battleship grey, and her funnel took on the rich Cunard red. After one voyage to Halifax NS in late July 1946, *Aquitania* went back into dock at Southampton for further restoration work, and when she sailed for New York in October of that year it was with the Foreign Secretary and other delegates who were going for the first few days of the UN

General Assembly. On her return she lay idle for over four weeks before making another voyage to Halifax NS with Canadian war brides and Government passengers.

By now *Aquitania*'s future was seriously in question as her charter to the Ministry of Transport was due to end in April 1948, and one possibility which arose was a charter to the Australian government to carry emigrants to Sydney, as there were 400,000 prospective settlers awaiting passage. However, this was not to be, and on 1 April 1948 she was released by the Ministry of Transport and returned to Cunard. After a short overhaul, the Canadian Government chartered the liner for a series of 11 voyages between Southampton and Halifax NS, carrying mainly emigrants. The Canadian government paid Cunard a fixed sum to maintain the ship in the Canadian service and to provide an option for further voyages. Up to 1,150 berths were to be reserved for the Canadian emigration authorities, and the company was free to sell any spare berths on their own account. She sailed westbound on the first of these voyages on Tuesday 25 May 1948 commanded by Captain G.E. Cove. All the first five voyages were fully booked, and on the eastbound journeys she brought very welcome dollar-spending tourists back to Southampton. In February 1949 there was another reprieve for *Aquitania* when the Canadian government renewed the emigrant contract for a further 14 voyages, which assured her future until the end of that year.

Aquitania had her final overhaul and drydocking in February 1949, and resumed her Canadian service on 8 March. In early April the ship and a rather unusual stowaday made headlines, and even a leading article in *The Times*. It seems that in the Western Approaches, a weary migrant swallow boarded the ship and found shelter in the first class lounge. The unexpected guest left the ship in Southampton and it was thought to be one of the first swallows to arrive in England that year! By 29 November 1949 *Aquitania* was making the last of her voyages with Canadian emigrants, and she arrived back in Southampton on Thursday 1 December. By

The Aquitania *in the final years of her service after the Second World War.* (Imperial War Museum)

now the number of emigrants to Canada had fallen, and as there were plenty of vessels serving the Australian trade, the end was in sight for *Aquitania*. After a full survey in Southampton, the following announcement was made at Cunard head office in Liverpool on Wednesday 14 December 1949: 'After full consideration of all the circumstances, it has been decided to withdraw the *Aquitania* from active service.' This came as no real surprise, for the liner was 35 years old and the cost of refitting her for further service on the North Atlantic would have been prohibitive.

Aquitania lay at 108 berth in Southampton's Western Docks for the whole of December, then on 9 January 1950 it was learned that Messrs Hampton & Sons Ltd, of Arlington Street, London, had been instructed to auction the vessel's furnishings and equipment which included the panelling, ceilings and floorings of all the first class rooms. In the event, the auctioneer's catalogue ran to 85 pages, with 2,875 lots. Later in the month Cunard sold the *Aquitania* to the British Iron & Steel Corp (Salvage) Ltd for £125,000. At noon on Saturday 18 February 1950 the formal transfer of ownership took place and

The Aquitania *shortly after her arrival at the breaker's yard at Faslane in February 1950.* (WSPL)

the Cunard house flag was lowered.

On the following day *Aquitania* left Southampton for the last time, bound for the Clyde breakers yard, commanded by Captain R.B.G. Woollatt, who had been her master since November 1948, and with a crew of 200 Cunard men. She had been scheduled to leave at 9 am, but fog delayed the departure for four hours. Quite a crowd had assembled to wave farewell, but as the fog did not clear most drifted away, and when she finally sailed at 1 pm the event passed almost unnoticed. As she left, the signal 'Goodbye with regret' was hoisted from the signal station and both the *Edinburgh Castle* and *Empire Windrush* sounded their whistles in salute. Once out of the Solent, compasses were adjusted and then courses were set for Land's End and the west coast. The voyage was made at 14 knots, and as *Aquitania* rounded Land's End she dipped her stem into the Atlantic swell for the last time. Apart from the emptiness of the ship, with all the rooms stripped of their fittings, it was obvious that this was no ordinary voyage. Arrows chalked on the decks directed the few press representatives on board to the lounge where there were deck chairs, which had escaped the auctioneer's hammer, for them to relax in.

Fire hoses had been laid out ready for use and a few paintings still hung on walls. As the old ship arrived in the Firth of Clyde, in perfect weather on the morning of Tuesday 21 February 1950, a passing submarine signalled 'RIP', a frigate 'We are proud to have met you', and a Royal Fleet Auxiliary 'Goodbye old faithful'.

Aquitania anchored at the Tail of the Bank at 10 am and she remained there until early afternoon when she was taken in tow by tugs. For the next four hours she made her way slowly through the narrows to Gareloch, where hundreds of people lined the banks to see the last of the great four-funnelled Atlantic liners, a product of a bygone age, move to her final resting place — not many miles from where she had been built. She was the largest ship to have entered Gareloch at the time, and as she was edged to the wharf at Faslane the deep boom of her whistle echoed around the Scottish hills. As 'Finished With Engines' was rung for the last time there were more than a few eyes with tears in them. She had been built when the *Titanic* was still fresh in people's minds, and she had almost survived to see jet airliners winging their way across the Atlantic in a matter of hours.

On the day after *Aquitania* arrived at Faslane, the auction at Southampton of all her furniture and fittings ended, having raised £20,000. By October that year all her superstructure had

gone, and at 3 am on the 12th fire was noticed in the stern of the hulk. Within an hour of the first outbreak two fires were raging, the second in the forward well deck. According to eyewitnesses the fires were spectacular and lit up the whole area. Later that morning firemen from Metal Industries (Salvage) Ltd, who were breaking up the ship, and local fire brigades managed to put out both conflagrations. Early in 1951 the *Aquitania* had ceased to exist, but she had provided industry with 31,000 tons of ferrous and 1,300 tons of non-ferrous scrap.

The Aquitania with her funnels and superstructure gone, but before the hulk caught fire. (WSPL)

Technical data	
Gross tonnage	45,647
Net tonnage	21,998
Length overall	901 ft (274.62m)
Breadth	97 ft (29.56m)
Quadruple screw, powered by four sets of direct acting steam turbines; 60,000 SHP, 23.5 knots.	

14
Berengaria, 1920

Between 1920 and the entry into service of the *Queen Mary* in 1936, *Berengaria* was the pride of the Cunard fleet, although she had not been built for Cunard but for the Hamburg–Amerika Line, as that company's prestigious ship on the North Atlantic intended to compete directly with White Star Line's *Olympic* and Cunard's *Lusitania* and *Mauretania.* She was the brainchild of Albert Ballin, the Director General of Hamburg–Amerika, who decided to build three great passenger liners which, although they would not take any speed records, would be the biggest and most luxurious passenger ships afloat, at a time when the rivalry between Britain and Germany was nearing its height.

The keel of the first ship was laid in June 1910 at the Vulkan Werft shipyard at Hamburg on the River Elbe. Originally it had been intended to name the vessel *Europa*, a name which had been used by the Hamburg–Amerika Line as far back as 1880. However, with the intense rivalry in Europe, a much grander name was sought for what would be one of the world's largest ships, so the title *Imperator* ('Commander' or 'Emperor') was chosen. The other two ships were to be called *Vaterland* ('Fatherland'), and *Bismarck* (after the 'Iron Chancellor' of Germany from 1884–1890). *Imperator*'s launching ceremony took place on Thursday 23 May 1912, and it was performed

The Imperator *in the River Elbe, before her maiden voyage.* (Hapag-Lloyd AG)

by Kaiser Wilhelm II himself. The Kaiser was received by Albert Ballin and, accompanied by a number of distinguished military officers, including Grand Admiral von Tirpitz, the German Emperor sent the great hull down into the River Elbe. The strong military presence at the ceremony reflected the Kaiser's keen interest in military affairs and the strong militarism in Ger-

Right *A view of* Imperator's *bows dominated by the eagle.* (Hapag-Lloyd AG)

Below *A close-up of the eagle which adorned the* Imperator's *bows in the early months of her career.* (Hapag-Lloyd AG)

many at that time. It was certainly not the style of Ballin, who disliked the rivalry between the great European powers.

It should be remembered that the launching of the *Imperator* took place just over five weeks after the *Titanic* disaster, and subsequently changes were made to both the hull design and equipment on board. In the hull a five foot double bottom was fitted, and 83 lifeboats, including two motor boats, were added, sufficient to accommodate everyone on board and with many positioned in the lower part of the superstructure. In outward appearance the *Imperator* was impressive, with her straight bow dominated by a huge eagle, and her counter stern decorated with ornate gold scrollwork. She had three tall, slightly raked funnels (the after one of which was a dummy and housed ventilator shafts) and two masts.

Imperator was now the world's largest ship, with a gross tonnage of 52,117. She had an overall length of 909 feet (277.06m) (including the eagle at her stem), a breadth of 98 ft 4 in (29.97m) and a depth of 57 ft 1 in (17.4m). She was a quadruple screw ship powered by four direct acting triple expansion turbines. The HP and IP turbines drove the inner propellers and the LP turbines drove the outer screws. The steam was provided by 46 coal-fired watertube boilers in four boiler rooms, and altogether the main propulsion machinery developed 62,000 SHP, which gave the vessel a service speed of 23 knots.

Internally the ship was decorated with elegance and charm, and although the magnificence was designed to eclipse all competition, little thought was given to the stability of the ship. The 714 first class passengers were accommodated on six decks amidships. Most of the first class public rooms were on 'B' deck and consisted of a ladies' lounge, library, lounge and the exclusive Ritz Carlton restaurant. The most striking room on this deck was the famous Palm Court, which boasted a ceiling 21 feet (6.4 m) high. At the after end of the lounge there was a marble bust of the Kaiser, which was duplicated in *Imperator*'s sister ship *Vaterland*. The first class dining saloon could seat over 700 passengers in one sitting, and was on both 'C' and 'D' decks, linked by the grand central staircase, so that the diners on 'C' deck could look down through a central balcony to those below. On 'D' and 'E' decks there was a magnificent Pompeiian swimming pool, surrounded by small changing cubicles. The 401 second class passengers were also provided with luxurious accommodation situated just aft of the first class. The 962 third class passengers were berthed right astern, while the 1,772 steerage passengers were accommodated in the bows. In total *Imperator* carried 1,500 more passengers than Cunard's *Lusitania* and *Mauretania*, and, with her crew of 1,200, there were 4,335 souls on board when she sailed with a full complement.

In December 1912 it was announced that the *Imperator* would leave Hamburg for her maiden voyage to New York on 7 May 1913, calling at Southampton the following day. By late April the vessel was ready to undergo her trials and be handed over to her owners, but she was soon to be hit by a series of misfortunes which would delay her entry into service. The first of these happened on 22 April as she left Hamburg for Cuxhaven and the open sea to undergo her trials, when she ran aground at Altona in the Elbe. However, no damage was done and she was quickly refloated. At the time the company did not admit to what had happened and they issued a statement saying that, 'In consequence of east wind and low water the vessel will remain in harbour at present'. Fortunately, the following day she was able to get to Cuxhaven, but then on 25 April there was an explosion of benzine on board which killed two men and injured

The first class dining saloon, SS Imperator. *(Hapag-Lloyd AG)*

The first class lounge of the Imperator, *showing the bust of the Kaiser. (Hapag-Lloyd AG)*

five others. *Imperator* was nevertheless able to start her trials the next day, but three days later a very serious problem arose when it became clear that the turbines were seriously overheating, and the trials had to be abandoned. This also meant that a cruise south, on which the Kaiser was to be the chief guest, had to be cancelled, and the ship was returned to her builders. Many disappointed passengers who had been booked for her maiden voyage were re-allocated berths on the older and much smaller *Cleveland*.

It was 10 June 1913 before *Imperator* was able to leave Cuxhaven for her maiden voyage to New York. She then left Southampton at 2.45 pm on Thursday 12 June, and after calling at Cherbourg passed the Nantucket Lightship at 12.50 pm on Wednesday 18 June. After spending the night anchored off Quarantine, *Imperator* made a triumphant passage up the harbour before docking at her berth in Hoboken. Thousands of people lined the shores and crowded the windows and roofs of tall buildings to see the new ship. During her maiden voyage the *Imperator*, in spite of delays caused by fog and rough weather, had averaged 21.13 knots. She left New York at 1 pm on Wednesday 25 June,

with 1,242 first and second class passengers, the largest number of these classes ever carried in one ship. On the homeward passage British passengers were disembarked in Plymouth, and *Imperator*'s first Atlantic voyage ended back in Cuxhaven. One serious problem had been the ship's lack of stability with a tendency to roll heavily, even in calm weather.

Imperator made several Atlantic crossings and arrived in New York at the end of the fifth one very late on the evening of Tuesday 27 August 1913. She berthed at Hoboken and her first and second class passengers were disembarked before midnight, but the 1,500 steerage class passengers had to remain on board until the following day when the immigration authorities could deal with the necessary formalities. At 4 am on the Wednesday morning, when all but the duty watch were asleep, smoke was seen coming from a storeroom beneath the second class accommodation. The alarm was raised and the crew attempted to fight the fire which was spreading rapidly. The New York fire brigade were alerted and firefloats came alongside to assist.

The fire raged for five hours and it was only extinguished after tons of water had been pumped into the compartment, giving the ship a 15 degree list to starboard against her berth. At one time it was thought that the liner would

The Imperator *arrives in New York early in her career.* (Hapag-Lloyd AG)

have to be towed into midstream to give the fire-floats better access, but fortunately this was not necessary. When the blaze became very intense and threatened the superstructure, the steerage passengers were landed and taken to Ellis Island to await the immigration officers. The only casualty was the ship's second officer, Hans Gobrcht, who had directed the firefighting in the early stages. He had donned a smoke helmet and gone in to ascertain the extent of the fire. Unfortunately, due to a misunderstanding, he was attempting to gain access to an adjoining compartment when the watertight door was closed from above, crushing his leg. His body was later recovered by the city firemen.

Most of the fire damage was in the stores compartment, but other areas were also affected by the heat, smoke and water. The second class dining saloon had suffered, as well as some of the alleyways in that section. In the event *Imperator* left for Hamburg as scheduled on 30 August 1913, but without any second class passengers. The cause of the fire was almost certainly defective wiring in the storeroom, and after undergoing repairs at Cuxhaven she was able to sail once again for New York with a full complement of passengers on 11 September.

Rumours started to circulate that at the end of October 1913 *Imperator* was to be taken out of service for a thorough reconstruction of her boilers and for conversion to oil burning. This was strongly denied by Albert Ballin, but he confirmed that the vessel would be berthed for her annual overhaul from 10 November 1913 to 14 January 1914. Negotiations also took place to get the work done at Liverpool where the *Imperator* could be accommodated in the Gladstone Dock. Unfortunately the political atmosphere was such that there was little real chance of getting the contract completed in Britain, and this presented a problem for the Hamburg–Amerika Line because it was in dispute with Vulkan Shipbuilders over the performance of the liner's boilers. The company also announced that it was considering using the *Imperator* for a service between New York, Monte Carlo and Naples during the summer season, but the First World

War broke out before this plan could be implemented.

Imperator reached Cuxhaven on completion of her final transatlantic crossing in 1913. She had been very successful and had shared fully in the North Atlantic trade; on her last voyage to New York she had carried 3,601 passengers and had earned £65,000 in passage money, a record for a vessel on a single voyage. Soon after her arrival in her home port, she was taken back to her builder's yard to be almost completely rebuilt internally.

During the refit the differences between the owners and builders were settled; the result was heavy losses for the shipbuilding company, who were not able to pay any dividend to their shareholders in 1913. When *Imperator* emerged on 9 March 1914, she looked a very different ship. The large incongruous decorative eagle on the stem had been removed and her funnels had been shortened by 3m (10 feet). Inside the liner, almost all the passenger accommodation had been reconstructed. All the heavy marble pillars and panelling had been removed and replaced by lighter wood and metal fittings. The crew's quarters were also rebuilt to provide more accommodation for the ship's stokers. To provide more stability, hundreds of tons of cement were poured into the vessel's double bottom. Altogether the work had cost Vulkan Shipbuilders £200,000, as it had been carried out under a five-year guarantee.

Imperator started her second and final season for the Hamburg–Amerika Line on Wednesday 11 March 1914, when she left Cuxhaven for New York. She called at Southampton the following day, before sailing west into violent south-westerly gales. When she was about 240 miles south-west of Brow Head, four lifeboats were torn from their davits and found intact four days later by a small cargo vessel. The liner was never in any danger and, in fact, her master reported that she was now a far more stable ship. She returned to Cuxhaven on 29 March 1914, with only four more month's service ahead of her before war broke out in August. After that she did not sail again under the German flag, being laid up in the River Elbe at Cuxhaven for the duration of the war.

By February 1916 she had lain for over a year in the Elbe in all weathers. Her central funnel had been painted grey to prevent recognition by Allied airmen, and anti-aircraft guns were positioned on the neighbouring shores to give further protection. The ship herself looked neglected and dilapidated, compared to her pre-war condition while on the North Atlantic.

After the Armistice in November 1918, the Allied forces of occupation found *Imperator* rusted, decaying and stuck in the Elbe mud. The Allied Control Commission temporarily allocated her to the United States, and men of the US Navy, assisted by a number of Hamburg–Amerika seamen, boarded her. Strangely enough, once she had been refloated it was found that her machinery was in reasonable condition. The great ship left the river under her own steam on April 27 1919, and was taken to Brest where, on 5 May, she was commissioned as the US Navy Transport USS *Imperator*. Several days later she met her sister ship, the former *Vaterland*, now re-named the *Leviathan*, which had spent the war in the United States and was in excellent condition. The two vessels were to spend the next four months repatriating US troops.

The *Imperator*, commanded by Captain J.H. Robinson USN, left Brest on the morning of 13 May 1919 for New York, with the *Leviathan* sailing almost nine hours later. However, *Leviathan* easily overtook her sister, a measure of how the latter's machinery had been neglected. *Imperator*'s role as a troop transport was completed by 21 August 1919, and the US Navy made it known that they wished to keep her along with the *Leviathan*. However, Cunard was also pressing a claim for the ship, which many thought would be a just reparation for the loss of the *Lusitania*. Thus on 29 August the Allied Naval Commission in Paris announced that the USS *Imperator* was to be transferred to Britain, and it was made clear by the Shipping Controller in London that the vessel would be managed by the Cunard Line.

However, the United States Shipping Board and War Department did not welcome the news, and maintained that the vessel had been given under the terms of the peace settlement to the USA. The dispute lasted for almost four weeks before the announcement was made in Washington on 21 November 1919 that *Imperator* was to be handed over to Cunard by the US Shipping Board three days later on Monday 24 November. The controversy was still not over, however, for the United States Government had spent almost £300,000 to refit and refurbish the ship and they were reluctant to part with her. A Cunard crew, commanded by Captain C.A. Smith CBE RD RNR, took her over on the day she was formally handed to the company, but it was to be another 17 days before she sailed.

The USS Imperator *in 1919.* (Imperial War Musuem)

She had been originally scheduled to sail on Wednesday 10 December 1919, but another dispute arose, this time between Cunard and New York port officials. There had been a strike of coal miners in the USA, which had started on 31 October, and under emergency regulations in the country at that time *Imperator* had too much coal in her bunkers. Urgent diplomatic activity took place behind the scenes and, after a promise that Cunard would replace all the coal in excess of 250 tons, clearance was given for her to leave.

Imperator left New York at 9 am on Thursday 11 November 1919 sailing for the first time under the Cunard flag with 3,967 passengers on board, including 1,171 who had booked to Cherbourg. The whole voyage took ten days which was due to the poor quality coal on board and the fact that the ship had not been drydocked since February 1914 for the bottom to be cleared of marine growth. In the event, the calls at Plymouth and Cherbourg were cancelled as it was thought that her fuel supplies might not last, so there were hundreds of disgruntled continental passengers on board. Furthermore, there were many complaints that beers, wines and spirits

had run out early in the voyage. However, despite the problems, *Imperator* arrived off 46/47 berths of Southampton's Eastern Docks at 10 am on Sunday 21 December 1919, flying the Stars & Stripes at the foremast and the Cunard flag at the mainmast, with the Red Ensign at the stern. She was scheduled to sail again for New York on 10 January 1920, but first she had to undergo an overhaul.

The work was carried out in Liverpool, and it was from this port that she made her first transatlantic trip for Cunard which was, at this stage, only managing the ship on behalf of the Shipping Controller. She sailed at 1 pm on Sunday 22 February 1920, arriving in New York nine days later on 2 March, and leaving there for Southampton six days later. The voyage home took ten days, and at one stage she developed a list which was traced to defective ash injectors which were leaking. It was obvious that the *Imperator*'s machinery needed a complete overhaul before her speeds would be back to those which she had achieved in the pre-war years. One other interesting feature of the voyage was the appearance of the first bank on board a British passenger ship, with the London City & Midland Bank having a fully equipped branch in the first class and a sub-branch in the second

Cunard's Berengaria. (Author's collection)

and third classes.

Soon after her arrival in Southampton, her next scheduled sailing on 27 March 1920 was cancelled and work was started in the port to recondition the liner. The refit was carried out by Messrs Thorneycroft and Armstrong Whitworth. By Saturday 5 June *Imperator* was once again set to re-join the transatlantic service, and she sailed that day for New York with a full complement of passengers. She remained in service now for over a year then, on 27 March 1921, after Cunard had purchased the vessel, she was re-named *Berengaria*. Her first sailing under her new name was on 16 April, when she left for New York, but shortly after this she lay idle at Southampton for several weeks, unable to fill her bunkers with coal owing to a miners' strike. In early June it was decided to send her to Cherbourg for bunkering, and she was then able to resume her service.

It may have been this industrial trouble which brought Cunard to the decision that *Berengaria* should be converted from coal to oil burning, and so at the end of October 1921 *Berengaria* joined *Mauretania* at the yards of Sir W.G. Arm-

strong Whitworth & Co on the Tyne for the conversion work to be carried out. She was the largest ship to enter the river and it was a delicate operation as she was towed upstream to the Walker Naval Yard. Each of *Berengaria*'s 46 water-tube boilers were given five oil burners — 230 in all — and her ash ejectors were removed. Thirty-two fuel tanks with a capacity for 6,200 tons of oil were fitted at the sides of the boiler rooms, and all the boilers were re-tubed. Improvements were made to the stowage of lifeboats and all the cabins were refurbished. Perhaps the most notable alteration, as far as the passenger accommodation was concerned, was the conversion of the former Ritz Carlton restaurant into a parquet-floored ballroom for 250 dancers.

The work was completed on 25 April 1922, and the following day she was towed down the River Tyne stern first. The river had been cleared of ships and buoys for the operation which took over two hours. Once clear of the Tyne she anchored for compass adjustments and embarked several guests, among whom were Cunard and Armstrong Whitworth directors and the US Consul from Southampton. She sailed from her home port the next day and, after a pleasant voyage down the North Sea, she arrived in the Solent on Saturday 29 April, and began her first voyage on 20 May.

The Pompeiian swimming pool on the Berengaria. (Author's collection)

In August 1922, whilst homeward bound from the USA, the liner struck a submerged object which damaged one of her propellers. She eventually arrived a day late and was immediately docked; her next sailing was postponed for five days. Later in 1922 she lost 36 feet (11m) of guard rail in heavy weather in the Atlantic, but nobody was injured and this was only a minor incident.

For the next six years *Berengaria* operated successfully on Cunard's express service on the North Atlantic in conjunction with *Mauretania* and *Aquitania*. In November 1925 she met the full force of an Atlantic storm, with hurricane-strength winds and furious seas which lasted for over 48 hours. Furniture was literally thrown about the rooms, and fixtures were torn from their supports. Many portholes of thick glass were blown in and 25 passengers were injured. When the vessel arrived in Southampton she was almost 12 hours behind schedule and a row of ambulances awaited her to take care of the injured. Nearly four years later, in September 1929, she carried the Prime Minister, Mr Ramsey MacDonald, and his daughter Isabel from Southampton to New York for a conference with President Herbert Hoover. Three months later *Berengaria* was again exposed to the full force of an Atlantic storm, and this time many of her ventilators on the upper deck were carried away by 50 foot waves.

On Tuesday 7 April 1931, *Berengaria* was nearing the end of another eastbound crossing of the Atlantic when, at 4.30 pm, she ran aground on the Boulder Bank about four miles east of the Nab Tower off the Isle of Wight. The mishap occurred in thick fog and it appears that the ship was carried off course by strong currents. Tugs were unable to release her and the ship's position caused some anxiety. The passengers were landed by tenders, and it was decided to await high tide the following morning before attempting to refloat her. Fortunately, by 10 am that day *Berengaria* was afloat again and was berthed in Southampton just before noon. Divers went down to examine the hull, which was found to be virtually undamaged, and the vessel was able to make her next voyage as

scheduled three days later on 11 April.

Just over 12 months after this incident, *Berengaria* went aground once again in the Solent. This incident occurred on Wednesday 11 May 1932, and again *Berengaria* was inbound for Southampton Docks from New York. She had taken the bend from the Solent to Southampton Water when she was carried too far towards the Calshot side and stuck in the mud off Calshot Spit. Tugs sent from Southampton were able to pull her off after about half an hour and many of her passengers were unaware of the incident. Again she was undamaged and was able to sail on her next scheduled voyage.

In the first three months of 1933 *Berengaria* underwent a major overhaul at Southampton, which was completed on 12 April 1933, when a special party of guests and press representatives were shown round the ship. Many of the first class staterooms were enlarged and fitted with bathrooms. The Palm Court was completely redecorated and refurnished, and the walls of other public rooms were covered with rick silk damasks and printed linens. In the tourist class 70 new cabins were installed and a Tudor gallery was constructed with timber from the New Forest. In addition, a cinema was installed which featured new 'talkie' equipment. The third class accommodation was also redecorated and altogether the refit employed some 2,000 workmen for nearly three months. When the ship sailed two days later on Saturday 14 April, she again carried the Prime Minister, Mr Ramsey MacDonald, on his way to see President Franklin D. Roosevelt, who had been inaugurated in office the previous month.

At 9.23 am on 11 November 1933, whilst *Berengaria* was homeward bound through roaring gales and mountainous seas, she received an SOS call from the Swansea registered cargo ship SS *Saxilby* of 3,630 grt. Her message that she was flooding rapidly and trying to get her lifeboats away sent *Berengaria* racing to her position 400 miles west of Valentia off Ireland. Preparations were made to receive the 28 crew members from the Welsh ship and the liner reached her last known position, 51° 50′N/19° 15′W, some two hours later. Despite a long and exhaustive search there was no sign of the *Saxilby* or her crew, and after 12 hours Captain Britten called off the rescue mission and continued his voyage to Southampton. No trace was ever found of the stricken vessel.

With the withdrawal of the *Mauretania* in 1934, *Berengaria* and *Aquitania* were left to maintain Cunard's express service from Southampton to New York, and a speedy turn-round in each port was called for. In September 1935 *Berengaria* set a record when she arrived at her berth in Southampton at 10 pm on Tuesday 11 September, and sailed again for New York at 11 am the following day, just 13 hours later. On 7 October 1936, after having completed an Atlantic voyage, *Berengaria* underwent an overhaul in Southampton's Ocean Dock. On 20 October, at about 3.30 pm, fire broke out in the first class cabins on the starboard side of 'B' deck. Both the docks' and the city fire brigades attended, and the blaze was soon under control and extinguished. The fire had been confined to cabins B123 and 125, although several others suffered smoke and water damage. It was ascertained that the cause was defective wiring, which was eventually to lead to *Berengaria*'s demise.

Although *Berengaria* was able to sail on schedule in November, she had just 15 months' service left. She made her final passenger sailing from Southampton on 21 February 1938 and arrived in New York eight days later on 1 March. Two days later, at 3 am on Thursday 3 March, fire was again discovered in the first class lounge on the upper promenade deck. The ship's crew, together with city firemen, fought the blaze for three hours before the outbreak was extinguished. *Berengaria* had been due to sail at 11 am that day, but there were only about 100 passengers on board at the time and they were in no danger. The lounge was completely gutted, and 20 first class cabins on 'A', 'B' and 'C' decks beneath, which included the luxurious Imperial and Prince of Wales suites, were damaged by water and deck buckling. Inevitably her sailing was postponed and the first class passengers were offered berths in the *Alaunia*, which was also sailing that day. However, many of them were faithful to *Berengaria* and they chose to transfer to second class berths in the ship. It was announced that *Berengaria* would sail on the following day, 4 March, with second and third class passengers only. However, when port and Lloyds officials examined the vessel, it was clear that they could not give her clearance to embark passengers at all. In the event she sailed on the evening of Friday 4 March with no passengers on board and arrived in Southampton on the

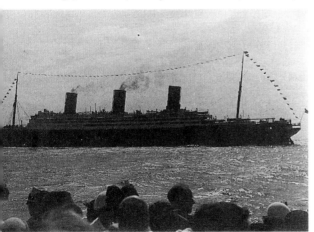

The Berengaria *anchored off Five Fathom Hole, St George, Bermuda, in September 1936.* (E.E. Viez)

Cruising in September 1936 — looking forward from the second class area. (E.E. Viez)

Looking forward from the stern docking bridge. (E.E. Viez)

found that defective wiring had been to blame. *Berengaria* was scheduled to sail on 13 April, but by now it was obvious that the ship would need to be re-wired throughout before she could ever go to sea again. However, in the days following this latest fire the decision was taken to withdraw *Berengaria* from service altogether, as the cost of renovation would be too great. This was two years earlier than had been intended, for she was to have remained on the North Atlantic until the *Queen Elizabeth* entered service in 1940. So, on 23 March 1938, *Berengaria* was removed from the Cunard sailing lists for good.

For the next seven months the once great liner lay idle in Southampton's Western Docks until, on 19 October, it was announced that the decision had been taken to dispose of her. In the following month she was bought by Sir John Jarvis MP for demolition at Jarrow on the Tyne. Sir John was the Member of Parliament for Guildford in Surrey, and among the companies he had interests in was Sir W.G. Armstrong Whitworth Ltd, in the industrial North-East of England. When the great depression hit the country in the early 1930s with its subsequent terrible problem of unemployment, particularly in the Tyneside area, he took energetic steps to help alleviate the problem. His plan was called the 'Surrey Scheme' and it was designed specifically to help the unemployment problem in the Jarrow area. One of the ways the scheme accomplished this was the buying of old ships for scrap and giving the job of demolition to the people of Jarrow. The *Berengaria* was the third such ship purchased by Sir John, and he paid £108,000 for the vessel.

Berengaria made her final voyage from Southampton to Jarrow on Tuesday 6 December 1938, leaving her berth at 10 am. She had on board 12 passengers and 160 crew members, most of whom were employed in the boiler and engine rooms. As she steamed slowly away from the dockside, her neighbour, the *Empress of Australia*, another ex-German liner, bade farewell with her siren and *Berengaria* responded with three deep booms. Other ships in the port took up the farewell and *Berengaria* answered each one

afternoon of Thursday 10 March. Once again, faulty wiring had caused a serious fire on board.

Initially some work was started to clear up the fire-damaged lounge, but seven days after her arrival in Southampton, fire once again broke out on the ship. This time it was in the second class cabin area on 'C' deck, and only prompt action by a crew member confined the damage to one cabin. Upon inspection it was again

The view aft from the first class promenade deck. (E.E. Viez)

— no ship or boat was too insignificant to be denied the courtesy of a reply from the great vessel. Captain George Gibbons, who had commanded *Berengaria* since 1935, took her up to the Tyne on her final voyage. He described her as a 'grand ship' and the atmosphere on board was happy, for she was going to play a small part in alleviating the problem of unemployment. It was a strange trip north, with a ghostly atmos-

phere on board, which was highlighted on the first night out when most of the cabins, alleyways, staircases and public rooms remained in darkness.

As she steamed down Southampton Water, *Berengaria*'s funnels belched forth black smoke as her boilers, which had been shut down for eight months, refused to give of their best for a short time. However, once clear of the Solent speed was maintained until she arrived off the mouth of the River Tyne on the afternoon of Wednesday 7 December, just over 24 hours after leaving Southampton. Hundreds of people had gathered at the end of Tynemouth Pier, round the Spanish Battery and at other strategic points to see the *Berengaria* towed up river. Unfortunately the area was blanketed in fog and the Tyneside pilot decided it was not safe to enter harbour, so she was anchored a mile from Tynemouth Pier for the night.

Next morning the weather was not much better, and by then there were worries that her fuel supply might run out. Fortunately by 1.45 pm on Thursday 8 December the fog had lifted and *Berengaria* started the final leg of her voyage. By 4 pm she was alongside her berth in the disused Palmer's Yard at Jarrow. Sir John Jarvis watched the ship arrive, although he did not go on board, and shortly afterwards the quayside was deserted.

The furniture and fittings from *Berengaria* were auctioned in January 1939, and over 200 Jarrow men were employed in breaking up the old ship, which furnished 35,000 tons of scrap for what had by then become a frantic re-armament programme. On 3 September 1939 Britain declared war on Germany, and Jarrow's men were required for more urgent tasks. Work on breaking up the lower part of the *Berengaria*'s hull just above the waterline, which was all that was left of the ship, came to a halt and nothing further was done at Jarrow. On 10 July 1946, after the war had ended, the remains of the hull were towed to Rosyth in two parts for the final process of dismantling. But by this time, very few people were interested in the remains of an old liner which had been built in the Imperial Germany of 1913.

Technical data

Gross tonnage	52,117
Net tonnage	21,506
Length overall	909 ft (277.06m)
Breadth	98 ft 4 in (29.97m)

Quadruple screw, powered by four sets of AEG–Vulkan steam turbines; 62,000 SHP, 23 knots.

15
Albania, 1921

Cunard's second *Albania*, like the first ship of the name, had a relatively short career with the company. Perhaps her only claim to fame was the fact that she was the first passenger ship to be built for Cunard after the First World War. She was launched from the yards of Scott's at Greenock on Saturday 17 April 1920, and by Christmas of that year she was ready for service.

Albania had a gross tonnage of 12,768 and an overall length of 539 feet (164.28m). She had a straight stem, a counter stern, one funnel and four masts. Although she had been ordered in 1916 as a coal burner, this was altered during building so that she would burn oil. The ship's twin screws were driven by double-reduction steam turbines which developed 6,800 SHP and gave her a speed of 13 knots. She was fitted to carry 480 cabin class passengers, and while the accommodation was not as luxurious as that found in the larger ships, it was very comfortable. The public rooms included a spacious dining saloon, which was panelled in Louis XVI style and painted grey with ivory decorations, a smoking room, a social hall and a lounge. The smoking room was panelled in oak with a marble fireplace and furniture modelled on early eighteenth-century styles. The decoration and furniture for both the social hall and lounge were modelled on the style at the time of William and Mary.

Albania made her maiden voyage from Liverpool to New York, commanded by Captain F.G.

Brown, on Tuesday 18 January 1921. She sailed via Queenstown and took 11 days, then she returned to London from where she settled in to a regular service to Halifax and New York.

Albania remained with Cunard until the autumn of 1925, when she was laid up. She had not proved particularly successful, and with the three 'A' Class ships of 1925 now on the Canada route, it meant that she was in effect redundant. In 1930, with the onset of the Depression, Cunard had to get rid of excessive tonnage and *Albania* was sold to an Italian shipping company, Soc Anon Navigazione Libera Triestina. She was renamed *California* and was rebuilt for their

The Albania *was the first Cunard liner to be built following the First World War.* (Public Archives of Canada)

A port-side view of the Albania. (University of Liverpool)

Trieste to Seattle service. Her short broken decks were combined into one continuous boat deck from the bridge aft to her aftermast, and the accommodation was altered to provide berths for 130 first and 30 second class passengers. *California* left Genoa on 11 December 1930 and arrived in Seattle in the following month.

In December 1935, with the outbreak of war in Abyssinia, *California* was requisitioned by the Italian Government for use as a hospital ship. In December 1936, after the reorganization of the main shipping companies in Italy, she was transferred to the ownership of Lloyd Triestino but continued in her same role. By 1938 she was laid up with all her medical equipment intact, and with Italy's entry into the Second World

War in May 1940, she was once again requisitioned as a hospital ship. On the night of 10 August 1941 she was at Syracuse when she was hit by a torpedo during an air raid, and she sank in shallow water. There was only one casualty and the hulk was subsequently raised, but it was considered fit only for scrap.

Technical data	
Gross tonnage	12,768
Net tonnage	7,519
Length overall	539 ft (164.3m)
Breadth	64 ft (19.5m)
Twin screw, powered by two sets of double reduction geared turbines; 6,800 SHP, 13 knots.	

16
Scythia, 1921

Scythia was the first of three 19,000 tonners built for Cunard as part of the programme to replace First World War losses. She was built by Vickers Ltd at Barrow-in-Furness for the passenger and cargo service to New York, and she was launched on Tuesday 23 March 1920 by Mrs S. Maxwell, the wife of a Cunard director. *Scythia*'s completion was delayed for two months by industrial disputes and it was not until 5 pm on Saturday 20 August 1921 that she left Liverpool on her maiden voyage.

Scythia, like the other ships of the class, was

an oil burner and her twin screws were driven by Brown–Curtis double reduction geared turbines which gave her a speed of 16 knots. She could carry 12,500 deadweight tons of cargo, and had accommodation for 337 first, 331 second and 1,538 third class passengers. Perhaps the most notable features of the first class section were the two garden lounges which enabled passengers to watch the sea and storms from the security of these glass-enclosed compartments. Overall, the *Scythia*, although she had only one funnel, was a handsome vessel, and she has been described by one well-known author as 'dignified', which is perhaps very appropriate.

In February 1922, only six months after she entered service, *Scythia* was *en route* to Halifax

Scythia was the first of three 19,000 tonners to replace war losses. (J.K. Byass)

NS and New York when she suffered damage to her port turbine which delayed the voyage. The following year, on Sunday 30 September 1923, she was outward bound for Boston and due to call at Queenstown that afternoon to embark 100 passengers when she encountered dense fog all the way down the Irish Sea. As she was preparing to enter harbour, the 21,073 gross ton White Star liner *Cedric* was leaving the port for Liverpool at the end of her passage from America, and as the two ships manoeuvred outside Queenstown they collided, and some damage was caused to *Scythia's* starboard side forward of the bridge above the waterline. Although neither vessel was seriously damaged, *Scythia* could not continue her voyage and she returned to Liverpool for a survey and repairs. Her passengers were transferred to the *Berengaria* at Southampton and *Caronia* at Liverpool, and repairs to the *Scythia* took over three weeks.

In February 1924 *Scythia* made her first cruise from New York to the Mediterranean, arriving back in the Mersey from Gibraltar on 30 March. Later in the year the vessel's second class section was re-designated 'tourist cabin'. Four years later, on 31 March 1928, when the King and Queen of Afghanistan visited Liverpool, they were accommodated overnight on board the *Scythia* which was moored at Princes Landing Stage. In June 1932 the vessel was used for experiments which, at the time, were hailed as a breakthrough in the search for new fuels. The material was known as 'colloidal' and it was a mixture of furnace fuel oil and pulverized coal. It was thought that the new fuel would offer hope to the British coal industry which had suffered severely through the drop in demand for bunker coal. Unfortunately, at the end of two round voyages, the fuel was not used again and despite great publicity having been given to the start of the tests, very little more was heard of it.

On Saturday 7 July 1934, as *Scythia* was leaving Liverpool for Galway and New York, she collided with the inward bound Isle of Man Steam Packet Company's ferry *Viking*. Damage was very slight and *Scythia* was able to continue her passage after only a short delay. Her final voyage

before the Second World War started on 5 August 1939, and eight days later she arrived in Boston. On her return she left New York on 18 August, calling at Galway and Belfast and reaching Liverpool on the 27th. Five days later she left for New York again, and this time she had a full complement of passengers, mainly US citizens eager to get home before Europe was plunged into war once more. She made three further voyages to New York before being taken over by the Government in November 1939 for use as a troop transport. She was converted for this role in Glasgow and, as a troopship, she was used in many theatres of war.

During the summer months of 1940 *Scythia* carried children from Liverpool to New York as part of the evacuation programme set up by the Children's Overseas Reception Board. In November 1942 she took part in the landings on the North African coast code-named 'Operation Torch', and it was during this period that she had a very lucky escape. She had sailed from Greenock to Algiers with 4,153 troops and 700 tons of equipment. At 10 am on 22 November she anchored about a mile off the south entrance to Algiers Harbour, with several other ships all waiting instructions on the disembarkation of troops. During that afternoon she discharged several bomb disposal squads, but the main body of troops remained on board. At 5.30 pm there was an air raid warning, but no aircraft were seen and the 'all clear' was soon given. However, the next air attack began at 8.30 pm that day and this time planes were heard approaching. All the naval escorts were putting up a heavy barrage and *Scythia's* gunners joined in with the ship's six Oerlikons and Lewis guns. Despite this, half an hour after the first warning had been received, a bomb exploded about 50 yards off *Scythia's* port quarter, and the concussion caused damage to steam pipes in the engine room.

After this attack there was a quiet spell until 2 am the following day, 23 November, when a heavy high-level air attack started. This lasted for over two hours, and at 4.30 am *Scythia* was hit by a torpedo from one of the attacking aircraft. It struck the ship on the starboard side in No 1 hold, and she immediately started to settle by the head. Emergency alarms were rung and within four minutes all the troops were at their stations. After a thorough investigation it was decided that there was no immediate danger, although the crew and troops remained at their stations. There were seven casualties, all among the troops, two of whom died later in hospital.

The 'all clear' went again at 6 am, just as it was beginning to get light, and the action stations were dismissed. Scythia's master signalled to the shore authorities stating that he wished to dock the ship as soon as possible, and he was told to be off the harbour's north entrance by 10 am that morning. In the event he was kept waiting in this position until just after noon when Scythia steamed through the breakwater and tied up alongside a berth at 3 pm. Had the ship been attacked and hit again whilst outside the breakwater it is not difficult to imagine the horrific casualties which would have resulted. Upon inspection it was found that the torpedo had torn a hole in the ship's side extending from the bilge to the lower 'tween deck. Happily the 4,000 troops were disembarked without any further casualties.

After being towed to Gibraltar, where temporary repairs were carried out, she was then able to steam across the Atlantic to the USA where the work was completed. During the remainder of 1943 and the first half of 1944, Scythia was employed on the North Atlantic ferrying American troops to Europe. Once the war was over she joined the many ships carrying the GIs back home. In February 1946 she made her first voyage to St John's in Newfoundland with 480 wives and children of Canadian servicemen — the first contingent of 'post-war settlers' to join their husbands and fathers in Canada. Shortly after leaving Liverpool, Scythia had to put into Belfast Lough with engine trouble which delayed her by several days. On her return voyage she brought 2,500 German POWs for employment in England, before sailing for Bombay to repatriate British troops who were not required in the East after the defeat of Japan.

She made several voyages to India and the

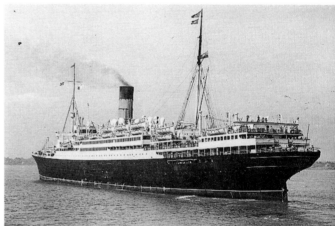

Top *The* Scythia *in March 1948, still in her troopship colours.* (Michael Cassar)

Above *The* Scythia *leaving Southampton after the war.* (Maritime Photo Library)

Mediterranean before being chartered, in August 1948, to the International Refugee Organization and the Canadian Government to carry European displaced persons to Canada, where they were being accepted as immigrants. She continued in this role for over a year, making ten round voyages and carrying over 11,000 of these unfortunate people from Bremerhaven to Canada.

On the evening of Sunday 16 October 1949 she arrived in Liverpool after completing her final voyage with the European refugees, and after being stripped of all her surplus stores she went up to the Clyde for reconditioning by John Brown & Company. When this was finished in August 1950 she had accommodation for 248 first and 630 tourist class passengers. Many new amenities were installed, including a cinema which seated 150 and could be used by both classes. The tourist class dining saloon was given new wood panelling and there were now large children's playrooms for both classes. Her outward appearance was altered slightly by the provision of glass screens on her 'A' deck promenade space. *Scythia* made her first post-war voyage from Liverpool to New York on Thursday 17 August 1950 carrying 880 passengers, and she returned to London to inaugurate the Cunard service to Quebec via Le Havre in the following month.

By 1952 *Scythia* had been joined on the route by the *Samaria*, which had also been reconditioned, and it was in June that year that *Scythia* was involved in a serious collision. At about 11.20 am on 5 June 1952, commanded by Captain Donald M. McLean and with 875 passengers on board, *Scythia* was in the Gulf of St Lawrence outward bound for Le Havre and London when, in dense fog, she collided with the Canadian registered 7,178 gross ton SS *Wabana*. The two ships had plotted each other's courses on radar for about 20 minutes, but this did not prevent the accident and *Scythia*'s bow struck the *Wabana* about 30 feet (9m) from the stern of her starboard quarter. One seaman on the Canadian ship was killed outright and two were thrown overboard but were subsequently rescued. *Scythia*'s stem was buckled, but about 36 feet (11m) of *Wabana*'s stern was torn away, and *Scythia* took her in tow until tugs arrived. After putting back into Quebec, temporary repairs were made to *Scythia*'s bow, after which she was able to continue her voyage. In the subsequent inquiry both ships were apportioned blame equally for faulty navigation.

The Scythia *at Southampton during the 1950s.* (F.R. Sherlock)

For the remaining six years of her career, *Scythia* ran without any serious problems. In November 1955 she again carried Canadian troops from Europe to Quebec, and in early 1957 she was transferred to Liverpool once again for the Cobh–New York service. However, her 36-year career was almost over and she sailed into Southampton for the last time on 22 December 1957. In the following month she was sold to the British Iron & Steel Corporation and was broken up by Thomas W. Ward, arriving at Inverkeithing for demolition on 23 January 1958.

Technical data	
Gross tonnage	19,730
Net tonnage	11,938
Length overall	625 ft (190.5m)
Breadth	74 ft (22.55m)
Twin screw, powered by two sets of double reduction geared turbines; 13,500 SHP, 16 knots.	

17
Samaria, 1922

Samaria of 1922 was the second of Cunard's post-war intermediate liners, and a sister to the *Scythia*. Originally she should have been launched and completed within a month of her sister ship, but continual industrial disputes during her construction delayed her by six months and added £250,000 to the building costs. Sadly this resulted in Cunard refusing to put another order with Cammel Laird & Co of Birkenhead. The *Samaria* was launched by Mrs J.H. Beazley, the wife of a Cunard director, on a very wet and dismal Monday, 27 November 1920. While the new vessel was being towed to her fitting-out berth she passed close to the former German liner *Kaiserin Augusta Victoria*, which was then being chartered by Cunard, and this sight, together with the necessity for the new ship, served to remind people of the losses suffered by Cunard during the First World War.*

The *Samaria* finally ran successful trials in Liverpool Bay on the weekend of Saturday and Sunday 8–9 April 1922, and made her maiden voyage from Liverpool to Boston on Wednesday 19 April. Her layout and appearance were identical to that of *Scythia* and she could accommodate 330 first, 330 second and 1,500 third class passengers. All the first class public rooms were on 'A' deck and comprised a drawing room and reading room forward with the smoking room further aft and a lounge in between. On each side of the lounge were sections partitioned with sliding glass windows which were called the garden lounges or verandah cafés. Many of the staterooms had private facilities and the decoration throughout was described as 'handsome without being ornate'. The second class passengers had their own drawing room, smoking room and a verandah café. The dining saloons for both first and second class passengers were on 'E' deck with lifts serving both compartments. Like her older sister, the *Samaria* was oil fired and driven by double reduction geared turbines, giving her a service speed of 16 knots.

The Samaria *first entered service in 1922.* (J.K. Byass)

---

* *Kaiserin August Victoria* later became Canadian Pacific's *Empress of Scotland.*

Two months after making her maiden voyage, *Samaria* had one passage cancelled because of engine trouble and her passengers were transferred to the *Laconia*, which was making her second voyage to Boston and New York. In January 1923 *Samaria* became a 'one class' ship for a world cruise out of New York with many of her berths sold to the travel agent Thomas Cook. This was obviously a great success for it was repeated the following year. Over the next 15 years the *Samaria* maintained her service to Boston and New York and made a large number of cruises from both the USA and England, thus becoming a well-known and popular vessel on both sides of the Atlantic.

On 26 August 1939 *Samaria* made her last sailing before the outbreak of war, when she left Liverpool for New York via Cobh and Galway Bay. She arrived in the United States shortly after the outbreak of war, and thus had few passengers for the return voyage. For the first four months of the war *Samaria* continued in Cunard's service and made a number of transatlantic voyages unescorted. She left Liverpool for one such crossing on Saturday 16 December 1939, with several hundred American passengers on board, bound for the USA. She steamed overnight around the north coast of Ireland, and at 4.30 the following morning she was off the north-west coast of Ireland, in a position 55° 30′N/6° 54′W, when she encountered a convoy bound for Halifax NS consisting of the *Aquitania* and *Empress of Britain*, led by the aircraft carrier HMS *Furious* and screened by four destroyers.

The night was overcast and very dark and all the ships were totally blacked out; furthermore, the convoy, which had sailed from Glasgow, had not been told of the *Samaria* making her lone voyage. Suddenly the officer of the watch on board the *Furious* sighted a darkened ship right ahead and approaching rapidly; as he turned the aircraft carrier to starboard in order to avoid a collision, the *Samaria* crossed from port to starboard. The navigation lights on board the *Furious* were switched on and two blasts were sounded on her siren, but almost simultaneously

the *Samaria* passed along her starboard side carrying away three side radio masts which had been lowered. Shortly afterwards *Samaria* collided with the *Aquitania*'s port quarter, the sparks being seen by the escorting ships. HMS *Eskimo* signalled the *Samaria* to ask if she was in danger of sinking and as she replied in the negative the convoy continued on its way. The *Samaria* had suffered damage to her bows, superstructure and starboard lifeboats, which had been swung out in readiness. Fortunately there were no injuries on any of the vessels involved, but the *Samaria* had to return to Liverpool for repairs, and these kept her out of service for the remainder of that year.

In January 1940 the *Samaria* was chartered by the Ministry of Transport for service as a troop transport, and over the next five years she saw service in all theatres of the war. In the summer of 1940 she transported children to New York under the Government-sponsored evacuation scheme. At the end of 1944 she was trooping to the Mediterranean Sea, and in March 1945 she steamed through the Dardanelles and into the Black Sea to Odessa in order to embark 1,110 POWs who had been liberated by the Red Army. The majority of them were men of the British Army, but there were also members of the Canadian Army and Air Force and the Norwegian Army. *Samaria* arrived in the Mersey on 30 March to a subdued reception, and after spending the night on board the men travelled by train to reception camps and 42 days' welcome leave.

Later that year the *Samaria* was in Bombay to embark over 3,000 army and civilian passengers who were returning to England after long service overseas. Although the war was over, *Samaria* was still needed as a troopship and in April 1946 she brought 600 WAAF, WRNS and ATS members from Alexandria to Liverpool. In fact, this was the largest contingent of servicewomen embarked in any one ship during the war years and the immediate aftermath. Later that year she carried 500 wives of Canadian servicemen to Halifax NS, and in January 1947 she was in the Mediterranean once again transporting more British troops back home from Port

Said. By this time, although *Samaria* was still
in grey livery her funnel had been repainted in
Cunard colours.

On 2 July 1948 she arrived in Liverpool flying the Jolly Roger from her signal halyards. In
fact, she had a detachment of the 17/21 Lancers
on board, and the regiment had flown that flag
since the Crimean War. The Lancers were returning from Palestine and had embarked in
Haifa. *Samaria* subsequently made only one
more trooping voyage before being released from
these duties by the Ministry of Transport on
Friday 6 August 1948.

Samaria's next task was to take part in the
scheme sponsored by the British and Canadian
Governments for the transfer of European refugees to Canada. For this her hammocks and
standee bunks in the dormitories were replaced
by double-tier metal bunks, and after completing a short refit she made her first voyage in this
role in September 1948. The enormity of the
problem of displaced persons after the Second
World War can be shown by the fact that the
Samaria and a number of other vessels were fully
employed for two years. On 20 February 1950,
as *Samaria* returned to London from Halifax NS,
she was in collision with the Electricity Authorities collier *George Balfour* at the entrance to King
George V Dock. Fortunately damage to both
ships was not serious and *Samaria* was soon able
to continue carrying emigrants to Canada.

In October 1950 *Samaria* was finally refitted
for her normal peacetime service again, and for
this she went up to John Brown & Co at Clydebank. Like the *Scythia*, she was converted to
carry 250 first and 650 tourist class passengers,
and on 14 June 1951 she sailed from Liverpool
to Quebec. On her return to England she joined
the *Scythia* on the Southampton–Le Havre–
Montreal roue, calling occasionally at Boston
and New York. On 24 March 1953, while she
was temporarily on the Liverpool–New York
route again, she was in collision with the Anchor
liner *Caledonia*. Both ships were inbound,
Samaria from New York and the *Caledonia* from
Karachi. The *Samaria* was just going alongside
the landing stage with the *Caledonia* being man-

Top *The* Samaria *trooping in the Mediterranean in
June 1948.* (Michael Cassar)

Above *The* Samaria *in the River Thames after the
Second World War.* (A. Duncan)

oeuvred past her by tugs, when a line snapped
and the latter swung across, hitting the *Samaria*.
After undergoing repairs in the Gladstone Dock
she returned to Southampton and the Canadian
service.

Just over two years after this incident, on 16
November 1955, Cunard announced that the
Samaria was to be withdrawn from service. In
early December that year she was laid up at
Southampton and in the same month she was
sold to the British Iron & Steel Corporation

Left *A fine aerial view of the* Samaria *in the Channel.*
(Skyfotos Ltd)

(Salvage) Ltd for £317,500. In January 1956 she
went to Inverkeithing for breaking up, after a
career of over 43 years on the North Atlantic.
Her hulk provided the nation with 12,500 tons
of ferrous and 400 tons of non-ferrous scrap.

Technical data	
Gross tonnage	19,597
Net tonnage	11,834
Length overall	624 ft (190.2m)
Breadth	74 feet (22.55m)
Twin screw, powered by two sets of double reduction geared turbines; 13,500 SHP, 16 knots.	

18
Laconia, 1922

Cunard's second *Laconia* of 1922 is best remembered today for her sinking in September 1942 by a U-boat, and the subsequent rescue operation by that and other enemy submarines which was disrupted by Allied aircraft on bombing missions. As a result of these events, Grand Admiral Karl Dönitz issued his 'Laconia order', instructing his U-boats not to attempt any other such rescues, and in October 1946 he was acquitted of war crimes in connection with the order.

Laconia's story begins on 1 May 1919, when the Tyneside· shipbuilders, Swan Hunter & Wigham Richardson of Wallsend, received the order to build the 19,000 gross ton vessel. She was virtually a sister ship to the *Scythia* and *Samaria*, and identical to them both internally and externally. Originally the *Laconia* was to have been launched in November 1920, but this had to be postponed for five months as the slipway was blocked by the burnt-out hulk of the French liner *Meduana*. This was eventually moved in early April of the following year, and the *Laconia* was launched on 9 April 1921.

She made her maiden voyage from Southampton to New York on 25 May 1922 and after this she transferred to Liverpool as her terminal port, also occasionally using Hamburg, where she loaded cargo and embarked emigrants in her third class accommodation. In January 1923 she made a world cruise from New York, which took her to 22 ports and lasted over four months. This voyage was repeated in the following year, and

in May 1924 she joined the transatlantic service from Liverpool once again.

In September 1934, over 12 years after she had first entered service, the *Laconia* was involved in a collision off the US coast. At 3.43 am on Monday 24 September, when she was seven miles NNW off Cape Cod bound for New York from Boston, she rammed in dense fog the port side of the US freighter *Pan Royal*. *Laconia's* stem plating was badly crushed and was split open from her hawsepipe to below the waterline, while *Pan Royal* suffered serious damage to her port side. Both vessels were able to proceed under their own steam and *Laconia* continued her voyage to New York, where she was drydocked for repairs. Just over a month later, on 28 October, she left the USA for Liverpool before resuming cruises in early 1935.

In the weeks immediately prior to the Second World War, the *Laconia* was sailing on the route between Liverpool–Galway–Boston and New York, and she arrived in the latter port for the last time on 22 August 1939. After the declaration of war the following month, the *Laconia* was requisitioned by the Admiralty for service as an armed merchant cruiser. The conversion was carried out at Portsmouth and was completed in early January 1940. By the 8th of that month she had embarked ammunition for her eight six-inch and two three-inch high angle guns and two days later she left the port to carry out trials in the Channel off the Isle of Wight.

The Laconia *of 1922 was one of Cunard's Second World War losses.* (E.H. Cole)

Following this she had to return to the South Railway Jetty in Portsmouth for repairs to damage caused by the blast of her guns during the trials. After embarking gold bullion, she left Portsmouth at 10.27 am on Tuesday 23 January 1940, and after a few days at Portland she left for the 3rd Battle Squadron at Halifax NS.

Over the next months she escorted convoys to Bermuda and to points in mid-Atlantic where they were taken over by other escorts for the remainder of their voyages. On Sunday 9 June 1940, at 11.57 am, the *Laconia* cast off to escort a convoy which had left Halifax NS about three hours earlier. She had been alongside No 9 extension berth at Halifax and seven minutes after casting off, whilst going upstream to turn in Bedford Basin, she went aground on uncharted rocks. After soundings had been taken it was clear that the ship was seriously damaged forward and was leaking. It was 1.27 pm before she was refloated and anchored, and all hands were set to removing ammunition from forward to aft and discharging her fuel into lighters.

By midnight she was alongside once again and the following day, when divers examined the damage, it was clear she would have to be docked for repairs. So, on 11 June, two days after the accident, the *Laconia* put to sea under her own steam bound for St John, New Brunswick. One crew member, Mr A.H.E. Townshend, recalls the uncanny sight of sealed oil drums, which had been stowed to provide buoyancy, popping out of the damaged hull like corks as the *Laconia* limped round to St John. It was 23 July 1940 before the vessel was repaired and at sea once again to continue her convoy escort duties.

As with most AMCs the conversion work had been done quickly and further improvements were carried out later. In October 1940 the *Laconia's* crew were employed dismantling disused passenger accommodation, and some weeks afterwards the old third class dining saloon was filled with oil drums for additional buoyancy should she be damaged. In April 1941 the *Laconia* escorted a convoy to Hvalfjord and from there she was employed on the Northern Patrol before returning to Halifax NS in the following month. In June 1941 she returned to St John, New Brunswick, for a refit which lasted from 23 June to early August. Following this refit she

A *port-side view of the* Laconia. (University of Liverpool)

spent only a short time with the Halifax Escort Force before leaving Canada at the end of August as part of a convoy escort bound for Liverpool. It had been decided that she was to become a troop transport for the remainder of her war service.

The *Laconia* arrived in the Bidston Dock at Birkenhead on 12 September 1941, and after disembarking RAF personnel who were on passage, work began to unload ammunition and stores. The C-in-C, Admiral Sir Percy Noble, visited the ship on 16 September and nine days later, on Thursday 25 September at 9 am, the White Ensign was lowered and the ship paid off. Her ship's company were sent on foreign service leave and the *Laconia* was taken over by Cammell Laird & Co for conversion to a troopship. By early 1942 she was at sea once again and, although she was still requisitioned by the Government, she was back under the management of Cunard.

For the next six months the *Laconia* made several trooping voyages to the Middle East, making her final outward passage to Suez in June 1942, as part of a convoy of 17 ships escorted by the battleships *Nelson* and *Renown*. She had on board 3,000 troops along with their equip-

ment and they were disembarked at Port Tewfik in the Bay of Suez. At that time the Germans were about to launch the offensive on Alam Halfa to encircle the Eighth Army and capture Egypt, and all the shipping off Suez was under constant air attack. In view of this, her turnround in the port had to be made quickly. She embarked 697 passengers who were mainly returning service personnel and a number of families. The officers and most of the families were berthed in what had been the old first class accommodation and conditions were somewhat cramped. Also embarked were 1,800 Italian POWs who had been captured in North Africa, for it must be remembered that the bulk of Rommel's forces in that theatre of war were Italian. The prisoners were locked into makeshift accommodation in the ship's holds, which must have been unbearable in the terrific heat of the Red Sea.

In command of the *Laconia* was Captain Rudolph Sharp CBE RD RNR, who had been master of the *Lancastria* when she was lost off

St Nazaire in June 1940. On that occasion Captain Sharp had stayed on the bridge until the ship turned over and sank, and he had spent over three hours in the water before being rescued. On 12 August 1942, just as soon as embarkation was completed, the *Laconia* weighed anchor and set a course down into the Red Sea for Cape Town. For Captain Sharp there were the same problems he had faced on the *Lancastria*; his ship was seriously overloaded and his passengers included invalids as well as women and children. In addition to this he was well aware that there were not nearly enough spaces in the lifeboats or enough lifejackets for everyone. As well as these problems, despite the fact the ship was virtually run by the military, the boat deck was encumbered with all sorts of inessential sports gear. These included tennis nets stretched athwartships, shuffleboards, deck chairs, camp beds and even the boats' falls were often used as swings and seats — it was almost as if the *Laconia* was on one of her peacetime cruises.

She arrived in Cape Town towards the end of August after calling at Aden, Mombasa and Durban, and on 1 September 1942 she left the port to proceed independently to Freetown. During daylight hours she followed a zigzag course, and after dark she undertook what was described as 'evasive steering'. Soon after leaving Cape Town she received a signal from the authorities diverting her from her original course, but still instructing her to proceed to Freetown. There were no incidents at all for the first ten days out of Cape Town, and on the first class boat deck families sunbathed and children played. The main reminder of the war were the Italian POWs who were now in the custody of 100 Polish guards, and who were exercised in groups during the day in what had been the third class section.

At 8 pm on Saturday 12 September 1942 the *Laconia* was in a position 5° 05′S/11° 30′W, in mid-Atlantic and some 130 miles NNE of Ascension Island, proceeding at 15 knots on a course of 290°. At 8.10 pm she was hit by a torpedo, fired by *U156*, on the starboard side abaft the

bridge. The missile exploded violently in No 4 hold, and most, if not all, of the 450 Italian prisoners in the hold must have been killed outright. The vessel immediately took on a 15 degree list to starboard and before Captain Sharp could take stock of the damage to his ship, and only a minute after the first explosion, a second torpedo hit the ship and exploded in No 2 hold on the starboard side, killing hundreds more Italian prisoners. By now the engines had been stopped and all the watertight doors closed, but no radio distress call could be sent as the aerials had been carried away by the explosions.

Ten minutes after the first torpedo struck Captain Sharp ordered the ship to be abandoned and ensured that all precautions were taken to get the women and children into the lifeboats first, together with the hospital cases. A number of the Italian POWs tried to rush the lifeboats but the Polish guards, with bayonets fixed, managed to hold the great majority of them back. The vessel had 32 lifeboats, but a number of these had been destroyed by the explosions and in all it was believed that 22 were launched with their occupants. There was a certain amount of confusion, which was compounded by the panic-stricken prisoners, but the situation would have been far worse had it not been for the magnificent efforts of the Polish guards. Then, at 9.11 pm, just over an hour after she had been hit, the *Laconia*'s stern rose high out of the water and she sank by the head. There were hundreds of people still on board, mainly the Italian POWs, and as the ship disappeared beneath the waves there was a terrific explosion, probably the boilers blowing up. For those in the water there was little hope of survival as sharks were prevalent in the area, and for the survivors in the lifeboats and on the liferafts the prospect was not much better as they were adrift in the Atlantic with only a faint hope of rescue.

Meanwhile, the *U156* surfaced and went closer, mainly for Lieutenant Commander Werner Hartenstein to get some idea of the ship he had sunk. Whilst doing this his crew heard the cries of Italian survivors, and the knowledge of the Italian POWs set in motion one of the most unusual rescue operations of the Second World War. The U-boat commander sent out a signal to his HQ at Lorient and as a result *U506* and *U507* were sent to assist. Arrangements were also made through the Armistice Commission for Vichy French warships to help with the rescue mission, and the Italian submarine *Capellini* also set course for the area.

On the morning of 13 September, *U156* surfaced alongside the boat which contained 48 survivors, including Mr J.H. Walker, *Laconia*'s Senior First Officer. 'A submarine surfaced and ordered us alongside. We were given hot coffee and the commander told us to keep together as a French warship would come along and pick us up.' Acting Leading Seaman H.J. Vines, a gunner from the *Laconia*, also saw the U-boat 'very close on the surface, evidently picking up survivors'. By 15 September both *U506* and *U507* had arrived and all three submarines were packed with survivors from the *Laconia*.

At 11.25 am on 16 September, *U156* had 110 survivors on board and four lifeboats in tow when a USAF Liberator bomber was sighted. A large red cross flag was unfurled and displayed, and the aircraft flew over. About an hour later, what was presumed to be the same aircraft attacked the submarine and dropped six bombs. One of the lifeboats was destroyed and the submarine itself was damaged. Lieutenant Commander Hartenstein ordered all the survivors on board to go over the side and the lifeboats were set adrift, before the U-boat left for the damage to be repaired.

Despite this, the other U-boats continued the rescue operation, and altogether 1,111 people survived the disaster, 450 of these being Italian POWs. The French cruiser *Gloire* took 1,039 of those rescued to Casablanca, and the sloop *Annamite* carried 42. The last four survivors to be rescued were picked up by the armed trawler HMS *St Wistan* on 21 October 1942, and they were the only ones alive in a boat which had contained 51 people. Of the four, L/S Harry Joseph Vines and A/B Anthony Vincent Large, both RNVR personnel, were awarded the BEM, their citation reading as follows: 'They spent 38½ days in a lifeboat from the *Laconia*, during which time 47 of the 51 occupants perished. They displayed qualities of leadership and character which inspired their companions to carry on and maintain their self control and hope of rescue.' The other two survivors, A/Bs E.A. Riley and H.E. Dobson, were mentioned in despatches for great fortitude. Captain Sharp, who had been lucky to survive the *Lancastria* disaster, was not amongst those who were picked up from the sea when he went down with his ship. According to Mr Walker, 'he had remained calm and quite the master of the situation throughout'.

Technical data	
Gross tonnage	19,695
Net tonnage	11,804
Length overall	623 ft (189.9m)
Breadth	73 ft 2 in (22.3m)
Twin screw, powered by two sets of double reduction geared turbines; 13,500 SHP, 16 knots.	

19
Tyrrhenia/Lancastria, 1922

Throughout the history of the Cunard company there is no shipping disaster more horrendous than that of the *Lancastria* in June 1940 and, indeed, the tragedy was one of the worst in world maritime history. The origins of the ship go back to November and December 1911, when the Cunard company acquired the share capital of the Anchor Line, a company which supplied shipping services to many areas of the world but primarily to India. As with most shipping companies, the Anchor Line suffered heavy losses during the First World War, and so, in the years which followed, a large building programme was put in hand to replace the lost vessels.

In 1919 the Anchor Line ordered two 16,000 gross ton ships which were to be sisters, designed for the company's service between the Clyde and New York. The order for the ships went to William Beardmore & Co of Dalmuir on the Clyde, and the *Tyrrhenia*'s keel was laid on 2 June 1919. Her launching ceremony was to have taken place on Tuesday 18 May 1920, but when the day arrived gale force winds prevented it. Instead, Lady Beardmore, the wife of Sir William Beardmore, the chairman of the builders, performed the naming ceremony while the *Tyrrhenia* remained on the stocks. She was floated on Monday 31 May, being released by Colonel J. Smith-Park, acting for Lady Beardmore. Once into the water the vessel was towed to the fitting-out berth alongside her sister ship *Cameronia*, and the cruiser HMS *Raleigh*.

The *Tyrrhenia* had a gross tonnage of 16,243, and an overall length of 572 ft 6 in. She had accommodation for 265 first, 370 second and 1,150 third class passengers. Her first and second class passengers had public rooms which included lounges, smoking rooms and a verandah café. For third class passengers there were a general room and ladies' room, together with two dining saloons which could seat 1,000 people at one sitting. The saloons for the first and second classes could seat 220 and 300 passengers respectively.

The vessel was driven by twin screws which were powered by two sets of Brown–Curtis double reduction geared turbines. Each set developed 6,250 SHP which gave her a speed of 16½ knots. The steam for the turbines was provided by six double-ended boilers which were oil fired but which could, if necessary, be readily converted to burn coal. Having originally been intended for the Anchor Line, she was taken over on the stocks by Cunard when they acquired the company and, as such, she was very different from any previous Cunarder, becoming a 'one off' ship in the company's pre-war fleet. With a slightly raked bow, two masts and a single funnel, she was the first Cunarder with a cruiser stern, and she was a handsome ship.

Just over two years elapsed between her launch and her maiden voyage, due to industrial trouble at the builders' yard which seriously delayed her fitting-out. However, by early June 1922 she had completed her trials off the Clyde and was ready for her maiden voyage from Liverpool to Quebec and Montreal, which took place on 13 June that year. Subsequent voyages during 1922 took her to Boston, New York, Halifax and Montreal and in early December she left New York on a cruise to the Mediterranean calling at Gibraltar, Naples and Genoa among other ports. The *Tyrrhenia* arrived back in Liverpool on 27 December, and after a three-week overhaul she sailed for New York on 20 January 1923. It had been a successful start to her career.

For a while during 1923 the *Tyrrhenia* was placed on the Hamburg–Southampton–New York service and once again during the year she was used on other routes as well as for cruising. At the end of January 1924 she made her final transatlantic crossing as the *Tyrrhenia*, arriving in New York on 5 February. She left four days later and returned to the Mersey on 18 February. She had been due to sail again on Saturday 23 February as the *Tyrrhenia*, but this was cancelled as Cunard had decided to convert the ship to carry cabin and third class passengers. This change would make her more suited to the

cruising role, which was to take up more of her time in the years prior to 1939, so during the overhaul she was redesigned to accommodate 580 cabin and 1,000 third class passengers. Two swimming pools were built aft on the promenade deck, one each on the port and starboard sides, and the area was called the sun bathing deck. The name *Tyrrhenia* had not proved popular, so the opportunity was now taken to change it, and she sailed for New York on 23 March 1924 as the *Lancastria*, having been re-named in the last few days of February.

Over the next few years the *Lancastria* sailed a variety of routes on the Atlantic, and in the winter she made cruises from both New York and Liverpool. On Saturday 8 October 1932 she

Right The Lancastria *under tow in the River Thames.* (Museum in Docklands)

Below and below right *Fine side views of the* Lancastria *dressed overall.* (A. Duncan and Maritime Photo Library)

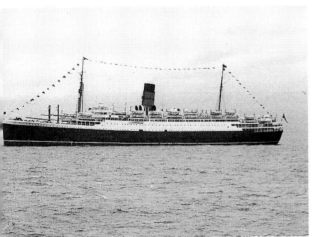

left Liverpool for a 14-day Mediterranean cruise, and two days later was involved in a rescue at sea. At 3 am on 10 October, whilst in the Bay of Biscay and at the height of a gale, she received a distress call from the 4,800 gross ton Belgian steamer *Scheldestadt*, which was in a position 45° 30′N/8°W and her engine room was flooded. Although the *Lancastria* was 50 miles away, Captain G.R. Dolphin raced to the scene, and on his arrival he pumped oil overboard to windward and leeward of the *Scheldestadt*. A volunteer crew was lowered in a boat under the command of Mr A.J. Denby, the *Lancastria*'s first officer, and after battling through heavy seas they manoeuvred alongside the disabled vessel and managed to take off the master and the 21 crew members. Later that morning they were landed at Lisbon, *Lancastria*'s first port of call, and the *Scheldestadt* was eventually taken in tow by salvage tugs for her journey to the shipbreaker's yard, which is where she had been bound.

The *Lancastria*'s cruise ended on 22 October and after further cruises she re-joined the Liverpool to New York route on 24 December. Four years later, on 20 October 1936, whilst returning to Liverpool after a 16-day cruise, she was herself involved in an incident. She had already been delayed 17 hours by gale force winds, and as she followed the *Scythia* up the Mersey at just after 4 am, a gust of wind caught her and gently grounded her off Egremont in Cheshire. Most of the passengers felt nothing and did not know the vessel was aground until they were told by stewards. Fortunately she was refloated at 11.30 am the same day and was pulled the final half mile to the landing stage. After examination in the Huskisson Dock it was confirmed that no damage had been done and after an overhaul she sailed for Boston and New York on 21 November.

The summer and autumn of 1938 were spent cruising to the Mediterranean and the Atlantic Isles from both Liverpool and London, with prices for a 13-day cruise starting at 13 guineas. After undergoing a refit in Liverpool in the early weeks of 1939 the *Lancastria* made her last peacetime Atlantic crossing on 3 March, when she

left Liverpool for Queenstown, Boston and New York, arriving there on the 15th. Three days later she started a series of four-day and five-day cruises to Bermuda, which continued until late April when the destination was changed to Nassau, in the Bahamas, and the cruises were extended to six days.

These were happy times for both passengers and crew; the cruises were not expensive and many cabins were taken by honeymoon couples and young people. A number of the passengers would stay over in Bermuda and Nassau and catch the ship when she returned on another cruise. The crew made many friends among the passengers, some of whom would cruise several times on the *Lancastria* during the summer. The last of these cruises ran from 2 September to 8 September 1939, and on her return to New York she remained alongside her berth for the next 13 days, during which time her hull was painted grey and her portholes were blacked out.

When she sailed at 12.45 pm on 21 September she steamed north to Halifax NS to load cargo, before leaving for England alone and unescorted on 25 September. When she arrived in the Royal Victoria Dock in London at 4.30 pm on 5 October, she was taken on hire by the Government as a troop transport. Over the next three months, now armed with a number of defensive guns, she sailed between Liverpool and Halifax NS. On her westbound voyages she carried mainly Canadian civilians returning home, and on the journey back to Liverpool she would be loaded with cargo, which often included aircraft in wooden crates on deck.

In the spring of 1940 the *Lancastria* was moved up to the Clyde and then to Scapa Flow where she was to have embarked troops for the landings in Norway, although this plan was then altered as it was considered that large liners would prove to by easy targets in the restricted waters of the Norwegian fjords. However, in early June 1940 she was to be found off Narvik assisting with the evacuation of troops. On the voyage back to the Clyde the convoy of troopships was attacked by German aircraft, but the *Lancastria* came through unscathed. Following this operation she made one voyage to Reykjavik with troops and returned to Liverpool with civilian internees on 12 June 1940. The intention was that she should be refitted and a large number of her crew were paid off.

As the shipyard prepared to start work on the *Lancastria*, the situation in France became desperate. The French Army was decimated and Paris was about to be occupied. Although the Dunkirk evacuation was complete, there were still thousands of British and Allied troops to be brought out from the Channel and Atlantic ports, and with France on the verge of collapse all available troopships were needed to assist in the last minute evacuation. In Liverpool an emergency call went out for *Lancastria*'s crew to rejoin her, and she sailed for Plymouth at 5 pm on 14 June 1940. The story is now best taken up by Captain Rudolph Sharp, whose report to the Shipping Casualties Section of the Department of Trade dated 26 June 1940 ran thus:

'We left Plymouth at midnight on the 15th June for Quiberon Bay where we arrived at 6 pm on the 16th. We left Quiberon Bay that night at midnight and anchored in the Carpenter Roads, St Nazaire, at 4 am on the 17th June. We lay at anchor in 12 fathoms of water and from 8 am on the 17th until noon we embarked 5,200 troops and a number of refugees including women and children.* After 12 o'clock we had to wait for completion of our embarkation and for the other ships and the destroyers which were to escort us to our destination. The Oronsay was lying four cables from us at anchor. At 1.48 pm the enemy flew over and dropped bombs which hit the Oronsay. After that, we expected an air attack at any time. The boats were turned out ready for lowering, and the crew divided into two watches with instructions to do nothing else but stand by the boats, except when the ARP signal was sounded, when they were to go down to their fire stations, clearing everyone off the upper deck.

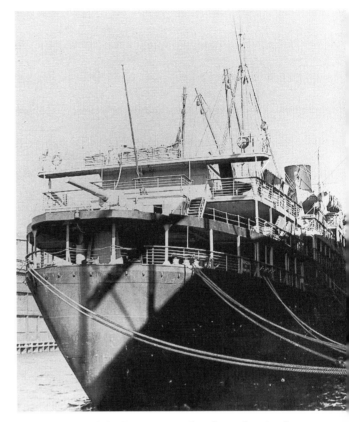

A stern view of the Lancastria *after the outbreak of war in 1939; her stern gun can be clearly seen. (Public Archives of Canada)*

'Our own planes were flying over all the time. The crew had been going to and from their ARP stations at intervals from 2 pm. At about 3.45 pm the ship's ARP alarm was blown on mouth whistles and the electrically operated gongs were rung below. At this signal everyone was to take cover but we had so many on board that actually it was impossible for everyone to get under cover. I was in my cabin when the officer on watch gave the alarm. I immediately went on to the bridge and had just reached the wheelhouse when the ship was struck by a salvo of four bombs which cut off all communication and started fires fore and aft. I did not even see the aeroplane. The four bombs, which were all high explosive, struck the ship simultaneously in the most vital parts, one went down the funnel, the other three strik-

---

*The refugees were in fact British nationals and their families who had been employed by the Fairey Aviation Co in Belgium.

ing No 4, No 3 and No 2 hatches, shattering the hatch boards, which were covered with steel plates, timbers and ladders. We had a number of three-inch high angle guns on board and at least a dozen machine guns. The two officers on watch, one on the bridge and another on the after bridge, let go all their ammunition, and the rest of the guns were all blazing away. From that time until the ship sank the the scene was one of confusion and disorder, as I could make no communication with any part of the ship. Some of the soldiers who were unable to swim became somewhat panicky and came to the bridge for lifebelts. I did my best to reassure them although I knew we only had 2,000 lifebelts on board. The ship began to sink rapidly by the head, listing from side to side, probably caused by the passengers rushing from port to starboard as the ship rolled. About ten minutes after we had been hit, at about 4 pm, the ship heeled over onto her port side and sank.

'I had on my Kapok lifejacket and for the next three or four hours I was in the water, surrounded by those who had managed to escape with lifebelts, or by hanging on to rafts and floating debris. The loss or life amongst the troops must have been high, I should think between 3,000 or 4,000, principally due to shortage of lifebelts, and also to the 1,407 tons of oil fuel from the deep tank which rose to the surface and was the cause of many casualties, adding greatly to the difficulties of rescue workers. There were numbers of ships and several destroyers all round us, but the air attack was still going on, so they were unable to help while this lasted. I could hear all the surrounding ships firing at the enemy; the attack lasted for two hours after we were in the water. Several calcium flares which had become detached from lifeboats and rafts were drifting on the sea of oil, and I was afraid they would set it on fire. I had asked, when at Glasgow, to be relieved of this surplus oil, but there had never been time to discharge it. This oil proved to be fatal in the end.

'A number of small boats, operating from the beach, were carrying out rescue work, but their work was greatly impeded as the rescuers could not get a grip on the men owing to the greasy oil. I saw many men in the water with me who had

slipped through their lifebelts, probably through not having time to tie them on properly. The troops had been on the ship so short a time to give them instructions. The first thing they had needed was food and they were at their fourth sitting when the ship was attacked. Whilst I was in the water, boats would come within 20 feet of me and then go away; they were picking up everyone they could find.

'The spirit of the men in the water was wonderful, they even managed to sing whilst waiting to be picked up. After about three or four hours, I suddenly recognised my Quartermaster, Murphy, in one of our boats, No 10A. I hailed him and he immediately came along and picked me up. Apparently ten of our boats had got away from the ship. He himself had been picked up out of the water soon after the ship sunk, he had somehow managed to get hold of a boat and was assisting with the rescue work. There were a number of naked soldiers in the boat who were covered with oil. We went over to a French trawler and they sent us to the destroyer Havelock. A number of women and children were already there. I was waiting my turn for the bathroom when the order was given that the crew of the Lancastria were to go on board the Oronsay, which, although hit, had not been sunk. Her bridge was wrecked by a bomb which struck, but no one on board had been hurt. She brought us safely back to England, by means of a boat's compass on the bridge.

'I spoke to many of the engine room ratings of the Lancastria to enable me to form some opinion as to why a 17,000 ton vessel, with her bulkhead doors closed, should sink in so short a time. My conclusion is that each of the bombs which struck the ship passed through the upper deck and hatches, bursting in the ship and blowing holes in her sides. Then, apparently, a further bomb exploded in the water close to her side, just abaft the bridge, which probably added to the damage. The weather at the time was light NW wind, slight sea and swell, cloudy with bright periods. We were heading WNW with the sun in that quarter. Not everyone who had a lifebelt was saved. A lot of men were hurt. I should estimate

Cunard's worst tragedy — at about 4 pm on 17 June 1940 the Lancastria *heeled over onto her port side and sank. Hundreds of survivors can be seen on the hull and in the water.* (Imperial War Museum)

that 2,000 were saved by lifebelts and another 500 in boats and rafts, so that 2,500 people were saved out of a total of about 5,500. I lost 70 of my crew of 330.'

In fact nobody will ever know how many people lost their lives in the tragedy, but some estimates give the figure as high as 4,400. Whatever the true figure, the loss of life was horrific and the Prime Minister, Winston Churchill, felt that there had been so much bad news that he forbade the publication of the loss of the *Lancastria*. However, on 26 July 1940 it was finally published in the British press.

Perhaps the last words in the terrible story should go to Madame Ruth Audra, a French resident of Prefailles near St Nazaire: 'The *Lancastria* sank before our eyes; for nearly a month, both before and after the Germans entered our village, my gardener helped rescue the bodies that came ashore along the coast. The sea was calm and lovely all that summer, the fuel oil with which they were covered was apparently protective; none of the bodies was injured or disfigured, and my gardener came in again and again dead tired, and heart sick as we all were, to say to me, "Madame, indeed I'm telling you the truth, he looked like a child asleep." There are 72 of these Englishmen in our cemetery. The last time I was allowed to go there, in 1942, when there were some 2,000 Germans in the village of 450, there lay on the long grave a wreath of China roses with on it the one word, "Reconnaissance".'

Technical data	
Gross tonnage	16,243
Net tonnage	9,645
Length overall	572 ft 6 in (174.5m)
Breadth	70 ft 3 in (21.4m)
Twin screw, powered by two sets of double reduction geared turbines; 13,500 SHP, 16.5 knots.	

20
The 'A' Class of 1922
Andania, Antonia and *Ausonia*

The next three intermediate liners launched by Cunard in the early 1920s were all 13,000 tonners and were intended for the London–Canada route. All three ships were, however, to end their days serving under the White Ensign, and there are many ex-naval men who will remember the fleet repair ship HMS *Ausonia* which served at Malta in the late 1950s and early 1960s. Indeed, in my early years in the Royal Navy I can recall seeing the *Ausonia* moored in Grand Harbour and can remember her being spoken of with affection by those who had served in her.

The *Antonia* and *Ausonia* were both launched

The Antonia *was launched in March 1921. (A. Duncan)*

in March 1921, the former at Vickers Armstrong's Barrow-in-Furness yards and the latter in Newcastle upon Tyne, at the yards of B & E Armstrong Whitworth & Co. The *Andania* was built by Hawthorn Leslie & Co at Hebburn-on-Tyne. Despite the fact that she was the last to be launched, the *Andania* was the first to be completed and she made her maiden voyage from London to Montreal on 1 June 1922. Two weeks later, the *Antonia* followed her and on 31 August the *Ausonia* sailed from Liverpool to Canada, then returned to join her sisters sailing from King George V Dock in London.

All three liners had accommodation for 500 first and 1,200 third class passengers and essentially they were emigrant ships with a good cargo space. They were twin screw vessels powered by double reduction geared turbines and they had a speed of 15 knots. All three ships remained mainly on the London to Montreal route during the 1920s and 1930s, and in the winter months, when the St Lawrence River was frozen up, they terminated their voyages at Halifax NS. They all frequently called at Hamburg to embark third class passengers and load cargo. In January 1923 the *Antonia* was employed between Hamburg and New York, and she had called at Cherbourg *en route* from New York on New Year's Day. On the following day, whilst she was bound for Hamburg, fire broke out in a linen room near the third class quarters. Fortunately

It was 31 August 1922 before the Ausonia *made her maiden voyage from Liverpool to Canada.* (A. Duncan)

it was discovered quickly and extinguished by the crew, and over the next seven days repairs were carried out in Hamburg.

In April 1924 the three ships added Queenstown to their route, which was a service for the new Irish Free State. Five years later, on 27 September 1929, the *Antonia* was involved in a collision with the Norwegian ship *Brio* near the Princes Landing Stage in Liverpool. The *Antonia* suffered some damage to her port quarter, but she was able to continue her voyage, which on this occasion was to Belfast, Quebec and Montreal. With the onset of the Depression in the early 1930s, trade to Canada fell off, and in the autumn of 1932 the *Andania* was laid up for over two years in London. She did not come back into service again until after Cunard had merged with the White Star Line and the latter company's ships *Georgic* and *Britannic* had transferred from Liverpool to Southampton. In the spring of 1935 the *Andania* replaced them, sailing from Liverpool to New York.

Meanwhile, on 3 October 1934, the *Antonia*, bound for Belfast and Liverpool from Montreal, had gone to the aid of the small British collier *Ainderby* which was in distress 500 miles from

The Andania *was the first of the 1922 trio to be completed and she made her maiden voyage on 1 June 1922.* (Photographic — Stewart Bale)

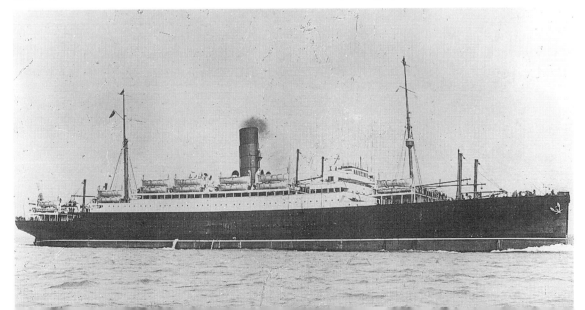

St John's, Newfoundland. In the event the *Antonia* stood by the vessel overnight but was not required to give assistance, and the *Ainderby* was able to continue her voyage to Montreal. Three years after this, on 14 December 1937, the *Andania* was involved in a collision, this time in the Thames. She was on her way up river in thick fog to the Surrey Commercial Docks at the end of a voyage from Halifax NS, when she collided with the tanker *British Statesman* which was moored at Purfleet Jetty. There were no passengers on board as they had already been disembarked at Tilbury, and fortunately no one was injured on either ship. The tanker was seriously damaged in her starboard quarter while the *Andania* suffered damage to her bows and had to anchor in mid-stream, unable to proceed further until the fog cleared on the following day. Over the next few days she underwent repairs and was able to sail once again for Halifax NS on 20 December, only two days later than had been scheduled.

In August 1939, when the dark clouds of war were once again gathering over Europe, the *Andania* was on the Liverpool, Belfast and New York route, whilst the *Antonia* was sailing

Left The *Andania at London's docklands.* (Museum in Docklands)

Below left The *Ausonia in the River Thames.* (Museum in Docklands)

Below *A Cunard advertisement of the 1930s.* (Author's collection)

between Liverpool and Montreal and the *Ausonia* was plying the Atlantic between London and the Canadian ports. The *Antonia* left Liverpool on 26 August and she had almost completed her voyage when war broke out. On her return to England she was chartered for service as a troopship, and for the first 12 months of the war she brought Canadian troops to England and carried Government passengers and child evacuees westbound to Canada and the United States. Both the *Andania* and *Ausonia* were requisitioned by the Admiralty for service as armed merchant cruisers when they returned to England in September 1939, and they remained under the White Ensign for the remainder of their careers.

The *Andania* went to Cammel Laird's yard at Birkenhead for conversion and she commissioned under Captain D.K. Bain RN on Thursday 9 November 1939, the same day that most of her ship's company arrived in a draft from Devonport. She was armed, like most AMCs in the early weeks of the war, with eight elderly six-inch guns and two three-inch high-angle anti-aircraft guns. On Sunday 12 November she left her berth and moved into the Alfred Dock for the final stages of her conversion. Four days later she left the Mersey and after nine days of trials in Liverpool Bay she left for Greenock and the Northern Patrol.

Seven months later, on 15 June 1940, HMS *Andania* was on patrol in a position 62° 36′N/15° 9′W, steering a course 240° at 15 knots. It was 11.30 pm and Captain Bain had just arrived on the bridge, when a heavy explosion shook the ship as a torpedo hit her on the starboard side aft, between five and six holds. The alarm was sounded, the crew closed up to their stations and the starboard guns opened fire on a periscope about 1,500 yards away. HMS *Andania* then settled by the stern, with a list to starboard, and lost headway, but this was rectified by the engineers transferring fuel oil. Her rudder was out of action and the main generators in the engine room were flooded and of no use. At 11.45 pm a second torpedo was sighted approaching from starboard, but this passed harmlessly 100 yards astern. Half an hour later,

at 12.15 am, a third torpedo passed 50 feet astern and at 12.50 am a fourth and last torpedo also passed astern. The track of this projectile was clearly visible and the gunners opened fire; obviously this had some effect, for no more missiles were fired.

When the damage was assessed it was found that five, six and seven holds were flooded, and despite the fact that all pumps were set to discharge, the water level elsewhere was rising, particularly in the engine room. At 1.15 am Captain Bain ordered all personnel who were not required to abandon ship and to stand off close by. At 2.30 am, with the water gaining rapidly, the engine room too was abandoned. By 2.40 am the vessel was down 15 degrees by the stern and Captain Bain gave the order to abandon ship; most of the crew were picked up by the Icelandic trawler *Skallagrinur*. At 6.55 am HMS *Andania* was standing vertical in the water, and within a minute she had sunk by the stern. Later that day the crew were landed at Scapa Flow and five days afterwards the Admiralty announced the news to the press.

The *Antonia* was finally requisitioned by the Admiralty in October 1940, and originally she was to have been an AMC. However, the urgent need for repair vessels took priority and she went to Portsmouth Dockyard for conversion to a fleet repair ship. The conversion work took ten months and early on it was decided that the vessel would be purchased outright from Cunard. By early August 1942 work on the ship was almost completed and advance parties of her company joined her. At 9 am on Wednesday 19 August 1942 she was commissioned into the Royal Navy as HMS *Wayland*, and at 5 pm that day the main draft of the ship's company went aboard.

During September 1942 she sailed in and out of Portsmouth as she completed her trials, then on the last day of the month she left for the Clyde. After further trials HMS *Wayland* joined a convoy for a passage to Trincomalee in Ceylon, via Cape Town. In May 1943 she arrived in Kilindini Harbour, Mombasa, and whilst there her destination was changed and she

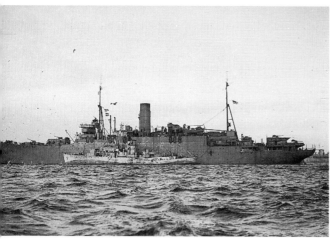

Above left *The armed merchant cruiser HMS Ausonia in October 1941.* (Campbell Finley)

Left *The* Antonia *became the Royal Navy depot ship HMS Wayland.* (Imperial War Museum)

Above *HMS Ausonia in the Atlantic during 1941.* (C.G. Thompson)

steamed north through the Suez Canal to Ferry-ville in Tunisia (now Menzel Bourguiba in the Gulf of Tunis), where she remained for the rest of that year supporting the final moves in the defeat of the Axis forces in Tunisia and the Allied operations to capture Italy. In early 1944 she made her postponed voyage to Trincomalee in Ceylon, where she remained for the rest of the war, supporting the Far East Fleet in the conflict with Japan.

On 26 October 1945, the *Wayland* left Trincomalee for Bombay, where she underwent a refit, having been dogged by mechanical trouble. When this was completed she remained in the Indian port until 7 February 1946 when she left for the UK. The voyage across the Indian Ocean was plagued with problems for her engine room

staff and she took ten days to reach Aden. She finally arrived in Gareloch via Suez and Gibraltar on 3 April, and she remained there until 21 May when she sailed for Chatham by way of the Irish Sea and the English Channel. On 31 May she was paid off at Chatham and laid up pending disposal, and was finally broken up at Troon in Scotland in 1948.

After the *Ausonia* had been requisitioned, she went up to the Tyne where she was fitted out as an AMC. The work was completed on 7 November 1939, when her ship's company joined from Chatham, and the following day, at 9 am, she was commissioned into the Royal Navy under Captain D. Wizey RN. After carrying out some trials off the mouth of the Tyne, HMS *Ausonia* left the area for Portsmouth at 3.45 pm on 13 November, passing through the dangerous waters off The Downs at just before midnight. After spending eight days in the Solent she fuelled at Portland on 24 November and the following day, in storm force winds, she left for Halifax NS to commence her role as an escort for Atlantic convoys.

Over the next two years HMS *Ausonia* escorted numerous convoys from the Canadian east coast to a position south of Iceland. She would then refuel at Hvalfjord and return to Halifax NS with a westbound convoy. Very often on these runs she would carry RAF personnel to and from the training stations in Canada. By late 1940, Captain G. Freyberg CBE RN (the brother of the New Zealand Major General Bernard Freyberg VC) had taken command, and in November 1940, when HMS *Jervis Bay* was sunk whilst protecting an Atlantic convoy, HMS *Ausonia* was escorting another convoy in the same area. However, good fortune was with her at the time for neither she nor the convoy were located by the pocket battleship *Admiral Scheer*.

In early March 1941 she made a patrol in the Denmark Strait before refitting at Harland & Wolff's Belfast yard. During her stay in Belfast, both the city and shipyard were bombed by German aircraft. Between 8 November 1941 and 15 January 1942 she underwent a refit at Cardiff and when this was completed she returned once again to Halifax NS. In mid-February she sailed south to Bermuda where she carried out patrols in the Sargasso Sea. By now there was an urgent need for repair and depot ships, and the first two AMCs to be earmarked for this role were the *Ausonia* and the *Aurania* (HMS *Artifex*).

In March 1942 approval was given for HMS *Ausonia* to be converted and she left Bermuda on the 24th for Portsmouth, arriving there on 6 April at 6.24 pm. On 20 April dockyard contractors started work on discharging the buoyant ballast, and she paid off as an AMC on 3 May. Owing to the heavy demands on the dockyard services it was to be two years before the work was finished and when she commissioned again she would be almost unrecognizable as the former Cunard liner.

Meanwhile, in June 1942, the Admiralty purchased the vessel from Cunard as they had done with the *Antonia*. When the conversion work was finished in May 1944, HMS *Ausonia* was an extremely effective repair ship. She had a number of workshops including plate shop, welding, plumbers, smithy, coppersmiths, patternmakers,

electrical and drawing office. She re-commissioned at Portsmouth on 2 May 1944, and one shipwright, Mr C.J. Baker, recalls joining her: 'On our arrival at Portsmouth we were marched in a body through the dockyard. On turning a corner we saw the *Ausonia* for the first time. She had a very high freeboard and towered above the workshops and adjacent buildings.'

Over the next few weeks work went on storing the ship, and all that time there were air raids on both the city and dockyard. On one occasion a mine exploded quited close to the ship. At the end of May, HMS *Ausonia* sailed north to the Clyde for trials, and at one time it was thought she might support the naval forces in the Normandy landings, but this was not to be and on 11 June 1944 she sailed east of Suez for the war against Japan. She was routed via the Suez Canal and arrived at Kilindini on 12 July. She remained in the port for two months before steaming north to Aden where she stayed for eight months until May 1945, during which time her crew were given the task of repairing LCTs for the campaign in Burma. After a four week refit in Bombay, HMS *Ausonia* arrived in Trincomalee in June 1945 and remained there for the next 12 months.

At Trincomalee she was berthed quite close to the wreck of the SS *Sagaing*, sunk by Japanese aircraft in the dark days of April 1942. During her time there her crew carried out repairs to ships of the fleet with some repairs to vessels damaged by kamikaze attacks. At one time it was thought that the *Ausonia* would follow the fleet to Singapore for the re-occupation, because it was anticipated that all the dockyard equipment would be destroyed, but in the event she was not required. However, Mr Baker can recall that soon after the war his ship rendered assistance to a French troopship on its way to Indo-China loaded with troops of the Foreign Legion. They had a seven-year posting in front of them, and would have served it but for the débâcle of Dien Bien Phu.

On 14 June 1946 HMS *Ausonia* left the East Indies Fleet for home; she arrived at Greenock on 2 August, subsequently becoming part of the

Above *The heavy repair ship HMS Ausonia at Trincomalee during her commission with the East Indies Fleet in 1945-46.* (E.A. Chappell)

Above right *HMS Ausonia as the flagship of the Flag Officer Mediterranean Flotillas at Grand Harbour, Malta.* (Michael Cassar)

Below *HMS Ausonia laid up at Sheerness in April 1950.* (Maritime Photo Library)

reserve fleet in the Gareloch. Between July 1947 and June 1949 she was at Chatham, where she was the flagship of the Officer Commanding the reserve fleet in that port. In July 1949 she was transferred to Sheerness and in July the following year to Rosyth. After six months in Scotland she returned to Chatham on 1 February 1951 to undergo a refit, which was completed in May 1954. The work was extensive and it included the fitting of new boilers which had been taken from an old destroyer. HMS *Ausonia* was then taken to the yards of W. Badger & Co at Millwall for preservation, and she remained there until the end of June 1957. Her future looked very uncertain, but a long reprieve came with the decision to use her as a replacement for HMS *Ranpura* (ex-P&O), the fleet repair ship at Malta. According to Mr L. Sklenar, one of the *Ranpura*'s crew members, she was in poor shape and her boilers were a continual cause for concern.

HMS *Ausonia* was towed to Devonport and, after a further refit, she re-commissioned on 16 September 1958. After undergoing trials she left Devonport on 3 October, arriving alongside the *Ranpura* in Grand Harbour, Malta, two weeks later. Mr Sklenar recalls that there then followed two weeks of hard work as all the stores and equipment were transferred from the *Ranpura* to

Malta, took *Ranpura* back to Devonport. Mr Sklenar remembers with satisfaction the newly furnished and equipped messdecks of the *Ausonia* and the large recreation room, which was most welcome after the poor conditions on board the *Ranpura*.

From June 1962 HMS *Ausonia* became the flagship of the Flag Officer Mediterranean Flotillas, and she also acted as an accommodation and repair ship for the 5th Submarine Division which was based at Malta. At the end of July 1964, with the gradual rundown of British forces in Malta, the submarine division was disbanded. Soon after this, on 7 August that year, HMS *Ausonia* left Malta bound for Portsmouth where she arrived ten days later, to be immediately paid off for disposal. In September 1965 she was sold the *Ausonia*, and he remembers how the former vessel rose higher out of the water, and the latter sank lower as the heavy equipment was moved from one ship to the other. Once this had been

completed, on 1 November 1958, *Ranpura*'s crew themselves transferred to the *Ausonia* and the latter's steaming crew, who had brought her to to Spanish shipbreakers and on the 13th of that month she left Portsmouth under tow for Castellon and the cutting torches of the scrap yard. So passed the last of Cunard's 1922 trio.

Technical data	
Gross tonnage	13,950 (*Andania*), 13,867 (*Antonia*), 13,912 (*Ausonia*)
Net tonnage	8,391 (*Andania*), 8,445 (*Antonia*), 8,527 (*Ausonia*)
Length overall	520 ft 2 in (158.54m)
Breadth	65 ft (19.8m)
All three ships twin screw, powered by two sets of double reduction geared turbines; 8,500 SHP, 15 knots.	

21
Franconia, 1923

The *Franconia* was very similar in design to the *Scythia* and *Samaria* of 1921. She was built for the service between Liverpool and New York, but she was also designed with cruising in mind, and before the Second World War she became renowned for her long world cruises. The *Franconia* was built on the Clyde by John Brown & Co and she was designed by Cunard's naval architect, Mr L. Peskett. She was launched on 21 October 1922 by Lady Royden, the wife of the company Chairman, Sir Thomas Royden. Just under eight months later, on 8 June 1923, she was ready to run her acceptance trials in the form of a cruise from the Mersey, where she had

The Franconia *in the River Mersey.* (J.K. Byass)

been drydocked, north to Oban and back to Liverpool. There was a large party of guests on board, including the vessel's sponsor and her husband. In the ten days which followed this cruise she prepared for her maiden voyage to New York.

Franconia was a ship of 20,175 gross tons and she carried 331 first, 356 second and 1,266 third class passengers. The first class public rooms were on 'A' deck and they consisted of a writing room, garden and main lounges and a smoking room. The later was a reproduction of an old English inn, half-timbered and oak panelled with a real wood fire in a brick inglenook fireplace. On 'B' deck there was a long promenade space and most of the first class cabins, whilst further aft were the second class public rooms, and right aft was a promenade space for third class passengers. The second class cabins were on 'D' deck, and the dining saloons for the first and second classes were on 'E' deck. In place of what would have been one of her forward holds was a swimming pool with gymnasium and squash court. As no cargo hatch was necessary, her superstructure continued unbroken from the bridge aft to the well deck, which improved the appearance of the vessel. The *Franconia* was oil fired and propelled by two sets of Brown Curtis double reduction geared turbines with a speed of 16 knots.

On Saturday 23 June 1923 the *Franconia* left Liverpool for her maiden voyage to New York via Queenstown, and she remained on this route

An excellent drawing of the Franconia *which was reproduced as a postcard by Cunard.* (Author's collection)

until late October that year. She left Southampton on 24 October 1923, with passengers but no cargo, for Boston and New York, arriving in the latter port on 4 November; 11 days later she left for a world cruise which set the pattern for the years to come. During the cruise she called at Havana, Panama, San Francisco, Honolulu, Japan, Manila, Singapore, Calcutta, Colombo, Suez, Alexandria, Naples and Gibraltar and then crossed the Atlantic again to New York.

In June 1926, whilst on a cruise from New York, the *Franconia* ran aground at San Juan in Puerto Rico in a heavy swell. She was refloated but returned to New York for a survey, and the cruise was cut short. Three years later, on 10 April 1929, whilst on a world cruise, she was leaving Shanghai when she was involved in a collision. As she put out from the wharf she dug her nose into the mud and her stern swung round on the strong tide. Before tugs could control her she crashed into the Italian gunboat *Libia* and a Japanese cargo ship. The latter was torn from a buoy and the chain from this became entangled with *Franconia*'s propellers. The buoy was momentarily forced under the water and it surfaced under a lighter which sank, taking its four Chinese crew members with it. Later that day *Franconia* left for Kobe in Japan, having sustained damage to her hull above the waterline and to her starboard stern tube. She

was, however, able to complete the cruise, crossing the Pacific Ocean and returning to New York via Panama.

In June 1931 she was chartered to the Furness Withy subsidiary, Furness Bermuda Line, to replace its ship *Bermuda* which had been damaged by fire at Hamilton. This charter lasted until the end of the year and on Boxing Day she left Southampton on a six-month world cruise with fares starting at £375 per person. At the end of 1932 she was given a thorough overhaul during which her first class accommodation was redesignated cabin class and she was altered to carry 350 cabin, 350 tourist and 930 third class passengers. She was also given white livery, which looked very effective with her red and black funnel.

Over the next six years *Franconia* made numerous cruises, and her final world cruise ran from 24 December 1938 until June 1939 when she returned to England. In the last weeks before the Second World War she was employed on the Liverpool to New York route via Belfast and Galway. After the war started in September 1939, she was chartered by the Government as a troopship and some conversion work was carried out at Liverpool, including painting the hull black. Her first trooping duty was to transport men to reinforce the garrison at Malta, and she left

The Franconia *in white livery.* (E.H. Cole)

Liverpool in late September 1939 in convoy with the *Empress of Australia* and the Royal Mail Lines ship *Alcantara*. The latter vessel had been requisitioned by the Government as an AMC and she was carrying troops to Malta where, after disembarkation, she was to be taken over by the dockyard for fitting out for her new role.

On 5 October 1939 the convoy was in the Mediterranean in a position 37° 40½′N/9° 18½′E, and steering a zigzag course which at 5.45 pm required altering from 126° to 81°. The three ships were in line abreast in the order *Franconia*, *Alcantara* and *Empress of Australia*. The latter two vessels put their wheels to port and started to swing towards the new course, but as a result of a misunderstanding by the quartermaster on the *Franconia* (who thought the order was to steer 181°), his ship was turned to starboard. She had swung to 131° before the error was noticed and the wheel was put hard to port. However, she had hardly started to move in that direction when her starboard bow collided with *Alcantara*'s port side level with No 2 hold. She also delivered a glancing blow further aft before the two ships parted and were able to continue the voyage.

The *Franconia* arrived at Malta late on the following day and the full effect of the collision was

The Franconia *as a troopship in Malta's Grand Harbour shortly before she was returned to Cunard.* (Michael Cassar)

revealed; the fore peak was opened to the sea, with damage also extending below the waterline. She was put into drydock and temporary repairs were carried out. At the subsequent inquiry it was decided that the ships had been placed too close together by the officer at Gibraltar.

Franconia's next voyage was to transport Polish troops to Marseilles, and in June 1940 she was involved in the evacuations from Narvik and Britanny. During the latter operations she took 8,000 troops on board at Quiberon, and during air raids she was damaged by near misses, which necessitated repairs to her machinery. In the following month she conveyed troops from the Clyde to Suez via Cape Town, and she followed this with other trips to the Middle East and India. In September 1942 she took part in the invasion of Madagascar, and in early 1943 she made more trooping voyages to North Africa. Later that year she assisted with the Allied invasion of Sicily and Italy, and during 1944 she transported US troops from New York to the Mediterranean.

In January 1945 came the highlight of *Franconia*'s wartime career. In late 1944 she had gone into the dockyard in Liverpool for some modifications to fit her for her next duties. She was to act as the headquarters for the British delegation to the Yalta conference, where Churchill, Roosevelt and Stalin were to draw up Europe's new political maps in anticipation of the end of the war. For the occasion, her first class smoking room was converted to a radio room, with map and conference rooms also being provided. She sailed from Liverpool on 17 January 1945, and before she reached the Dardanelles all the service personnel on board were ordered to change into plain clothes for the passage through neutral Turkish waters. The actual conference was held in the Livadia Palace, the former summer residence of Tsar Nicholas II, and it was March 1945 before the *Franconia* returned to Liverpool.

For over two years after the end of the war the *Franconia* continued trooping on Government charter. In February 1947 she was out of action at Liverpool for a month following a fire

The Franconia *was sold for scrap in December 1956 after a career of 33 years.* (Maritime Photo Library)

on board, and in June 1948 she arrived in Liverpool from India, having made her last voyage before being released by the Government. During her war service she had steamed 319,784 miles and had carried 189,239 troops. She was sent up to John Brown's yard at Clydebank for reconditioning which took nine months, and she was the last of Cunard's ships to be refitted for peacetime service.

She emerged on 2 June 1949 with her hull, superstructure and interior refurbished and repainted, and her accommodation altered to take two classes of passengers, 250 first and 600 tourist class. By now Cunard had 350,000 gross tons of shipping in service and a third of this was put onto the Canadian service, including the *Franconia*, which reflected the great demand for passages on this route. In the following year,

on the morning of Wednesday 12 July 1950, when she was leaving Quebec for Liverpool with 780 passengers on board, she grounded by her stern at the western end of Orleans Island, which juts into Quebec Harbour. All the passengers were landed and it was hoped that the ship would be refloated at high tide the next morning. However, this could not be done and at the next low tide it was possible to walk across the rocks and touch the ship without getting wet. Operations began to remove her cargo, and the vessel was finally refloated on Sunday 16 July, four days after she had run aground, and she was towed to the Dovic Shipyard at Lauzon for repairs.

It was early September 1950 before she emerged, and she arrived in Liverpool on Wednesday 13 September, having been out of service for eight weeks of the busy summer season. In June 1954 she suffered engine trouble on an eastbound voyage and arrived in the Mersey three days late. In June the following year she was transferred to Southampton and she added Le Havre as a port of call on her Canadian route.

In November 1955 she was chartered by the Canadian Government to carry troops between Rotterdam and Quebec. On Thursday 28 April 1956 the *Franconia* left Southampton for Halifax NS with 670 passengers and, after three days at sea, when she was 450 miles west of Le Havre, she suffered problems with her main engines again. Her port turbine had to be shut down completely and Captain Donald Mclean decided to return to Southampton where she arrived early on 4 May. This time she was out of service for two weeks before she was able to sail again, but it was clear that her career was drawing to a close.

On Friday 12 October 1956 it was announced that the *Franconia* and the *Ascania* were to be withdrawn from the company's service in the following month, and the former left Liverpool for her last Atlantic crossing, to New York, on Saturday 3 November that year. The return voyage was plagued with trouble, once again caused by her main engines. She finally reached Liverpool on Wednesday 28 November, four days late, and then she had to ride out a gale off the Mersey Bar for a night before she could go alongside the landing stage. It had been intended that she make a trooping voyage to the Middle East, in the build-up of troops for 'Operation Musketeer' (the Suez Crisis), but with her engines now totally unreliable this was cancelled.

On 13 December 1956 she was sold to the British Iron & Steel Corporation and was allocated to Thomas W. Ward's yard at Inverkeithing for demolition. She left Liverpool the following day and arrived there six days later, on 19 December, after a distinguished career of just over 33 years.

Technical data	
Gross tonnage	20,175
Net tonnage	12,162
Length overall	625 ft (190.5m)
Breadth	73 ft 3 in (22.33m)

Twin screw, powered by two sets of double reduction geared turbines; 13,500 SHP, 16 knots.

22
The 'A' Class of 1925
Aurania, Alaunia and *Ascania*

The second group of three intermediate steamers launched for Cunard in the post-war building programme of the 1920s entered service in 1925, and two of them ended their careers under the White Ensign after the Second World War. All three ships were 14,000 tonners and they were similar in appearance to the earlier vessels of 1922, with a straight stem, two masts, single funnel and counter stern. The *Aurania* was built for the New York Service, with the *Alaunia* and *Ascania* designed for the Canadian trade. They had accommodation for between 400 and 500 cabin class and approximately 1,000 third class passengers, and while they did not pretend to rival the luxury of the big express liners, the cabin class public rooms on 'A' deck were spacious and comfortable. Forward of the main staircase was a winter garden lounge, and aft of the staircase was the smoking room and a gymnasium. There was also a children's nursery and a long gallery and drawing room. The third class passengers were well catered for with two-berth cabins and several recreation rooms including a lounge and smoking room. All three ships were oil fired and driven by double reduction geared turbines giving a speed of 15 knots.

The first of the trio to be launched was the *Ascania* and she took to the waters of the River Tyne at the Armstrong Whitworth shipyard on 20 December 1923. Her fitting out, however, was delayed, and it was 2 May 1925 before she ran her trials on the delivery voyage from Newcastle to Southampton. She left the latter port on Friday 22 May for a 12-day maiden voyage to Cherbourg, Queenstown, Quebec and Montreal.

The *Aurania* was also built on the Tyne, but at the shipyard of Swan Hunter & Wigham Richardson, and on the same slipway as the *Mauretania*. She was launched on 6 February 1924 and was completed on 6 September the same year, when she sailed for a trial passage round the north coast of Scotland. However, with thick fog lying between Duncansby Head

The Ascania *moving up the Thames to her berth.* (Museum in Docklands)

Above and top *Two excellent starboard-side views of the* Ascania. *(J.K. Byass and Author's collection)*

and the Orkneys, she had to anchor off Wick Harbour for almost 24 hours. She finally arrived in the Mersey on the evening of Tuesday 9 September and made her maiden voyage to New York four days later.

The last of the trio to be launched was the *Alaunia*, and she was built on the Clyde by John Brown & Co, taking to the water on Saturday 7 February 1925. Just over five months later, on 24 July, she made her maiden voyage from Liverpool to Quebec, and was not long before she

joined her two sisters on the Canadian service, although she kept Liverpool as her terminal port.

On the evening of 3 October 1934 the *Ascania* was homeward bound from Montreal and was steaming through one of the fiercest storms on the North Atlantic for some years, when, at the height of the storm, she picked up SOS messages from the 4,000 ton British cargo steamer *Millpool*, 700 miles from the Labrador coast, bound for Montreal from Danzig with a cargo of grain. The messages said that three of her 26 crew were injured and that her mainmast had fallen, stoving in cargo hatches. She was taking in water and with her engine room

The Alaunia *off Gravesend.* (Maritime Photo Library)

flooded she was sinking. The *Ascania* made for the position at full speed and during the night the signals from the *Millpool* grew fainter, until at 2 am the following day they ceased altogether.

By dawn the *Ascania* had reached the spot and together with the Canadian Pacific ship *Beaverhill* she started to search the area in an attempt to find wreckage and survivors, but with 80 mph winds, driving rain and huge seas there was no hope. The *Millpool* had foundered without any trace and even if her crew had managed to launch the lifeboat, it would not have survived long. After 12 hours the search was called off and the *Ascania* resumed her voyage, arriving in London on 8 October.

In the following month the *Ascania* was in collision with the Canadian Pacific cargo ship *Beaverbrae* at Quebec, causing damage to the starboard side of her bridge and to her starboard propeller as she fouled the *Beaverbrae*'s anchor cable. After temporary repairs the *Ascania* was able to sail for London the next day, and on her next outward voyage she went to the assistance of the *Usworth*, which was sinking in mid-Atlantic. She was able to rescue nine members of the *Usworth*'s crew, along with the help of the Belgian ship *Jean Jadot*.

In February 1936 the *Alaunia* was homeward bound from Canada when she received distress calls from a French schooner 100 miles west of the Scilly Isles. Not only did she rescue the schooner's crew, but she also assisted in the rescue of a lifeboat from the *Bellucia*, another ship which had gone to the rescue. Later that year, in October, the *Ascania* suffered some trouble to her main propulsion machinery which resulted in a delayed voyage to Montreal.

In July 1938 she was in more serious trouble, this time in the St Lawrence River off Bic Island, 150 miles below Quebec city and opposite Rimouski. She had left Quebec for London on Friday 1 July 1938 with 400 passengers and cargo which included $300,000 worth of bullion. The following day a sharp jar was felt throughout the ship as *Ascania* struck the submerged Alcide Rocks near Bic Island. She suffered damage to her port side forward, which flooded the four forward holds, and lost her port propeller. Not only was she down by the head, but she was stuck fast on the rocks. She was not refloated until Wednesday 6 July and the following day, with the assistance of tugs, she was back in Quebec. Her passengers had been taken to Rimouski in tenders and most were transferred to the CPR liner *Montclare*, with a few travelling to New York to board the *Queen Mary*. After her cargo had

The Alaunia *at sea.* (Museum in Docklands)

been discharged, the *Ascania* was drydocked at Lauzon, and it was 26 August before she was able to leave Quebec for London, She left again for Canada on 10 September that year, in the middle of the crisis over Czechoslovakia.

Twelve months later, in August 1939, all three ships were employed on the London–Montreal route, and when the *Aurania* arrived back in the Thames on 29 August 1939, she was immediately requisitioned by the Admiralty. After being converted for service as an armed merchant cruiser, the *Aurania* was commissioned into the Royal Navy on 15 October, and sent to join the Northern Patrol. She remained in this theatre until April 1940 when, after a refit, she joined the Halifax Escort Force.

At 10.50 am on 12 July 1941 HMS *Aurania* left her anchorage off Sydney, Cape Breton, as escort for a Reykjavik-bound convoy. By 8 pm the next evening there were icebergs in sight and the following morning she took up station ahead of the convoy. By 3.30 pm she was passing through a field of loose ice and thick fog banks, and an hour later she was passing large icebergs as close as six cables to her. At 7.03 pm the forecastle lookout was doubled and 16 minutes later, as *Aurania* emerged from a fogbank, a large iceberg loomed up ahead. Despite putting the

engines full-astern and the wheel hard to port, at 7.20 pm she hit the iceberg bows on.

She was in a position of 51° 49'N/55° 50'W, off the coast of Labrador, and she immediately signalled the convoy to stop. The whole convoy remained stationary until midnight before moving ahead cautiously once again. At daybreak on 15 July the remainder of the convoy continued on its original course whilst the *Aurania* made her way slowly to Halifax NS, where she anchored on the evening of the 17th. The next day she went alongside berth 39, and after disembarking the RAF personnel on board and discharging her cargo of fruit, she left Halifax NS for Newport News in the United States for repairs.

HMS *Aurania* completed her repairs on 12 September 1941, and two days later, after taking on ammunition in the Hamplin Roads, she left the USA for Halifax NS, via Bermuda. She arrived back in the Canadian port on 26 September, and 17 days later, on Monday 13 October, she sailed from Halifax for the Clyde, steaming in a convoy of HM ships which included the AMCs *Wolfe*, *Ranpura* and *Maloja*. By 2.27 am on Tuesday 21 October the convoy was in a position 50° 48'N/18° 41'W when a torpedo hit HMS *Aurania* on the port side for-

The Ascania was designed for the service between London and Canada. (A. Duncan)

The armed merchant cruiser HMS Aurania in the Atlantic Ocean, 1941. (F.T. Grover)

ward. The ship took a 25-degree list to port so her captain turned to starboard in an attempt to get away from the submarine; the listing decreased and speed was increased to 12 knots.

However, from somewhere in the ship the order 'abandon ship' was circulating when in fact the captain had only ordered 'turn out the boats'. So when lifeboat P2 was lowered with its five occupants, it was severely damaged, the ship being still under way, and the men were thrown into the sea. Fortunately most were picked up, but one man was lost, as was another crew member who fell overboard when he was preparing the ship's cutter in case it should be needed. It was not known who had ordered the ship to be abandoned, but it could have been disastrous as the engine and boiler rooms were left unattended. Fortunately the engineer officer of the watch realized that the captain intended to go on steaming, and he remained below until he

was rejoined by the others.

Although HMS *Aurania* had been badly damaged on the port side between Nos 2 and 3 holds, she was not on fire and the lighting system and pumps were working, so there was every chance of getting the ship back to the Clyde. Once daylight came, Hudson aircraft of Coastal Command kept a continual reconnaissance overhead, and at 3.45 pm on 23 October HMS *Aurania* anchored in Kames Bay off the Island of Bute. A month later, after salvage teams had cleared her holds, the *Aurania* was moved into a floating dock at Rosneath for repairs. She remained there until 12 February 1942 when she was refloated and anchored off Greenock. By this time there was an urgent need for heavy repair ships, and HMS *Aurania* was

Right The Aurania *became the heavy repair ship HMS Artifex and served with the Eastern Fleet.* (Imperial War Museum)

Below right The Ascania *as an armed merchant cruiser in the Clyde in early October 1941.* (Peter Jackson)

Below HMS Aurania *anchored in Kames Bay in October 1941 after having been torpedoed in the Atlantic Ocean. It can be seen that she is down by the head.* (Imperial War Museum)

purchased outright from Cunard and sent to Devonport for the conversion work. She arrived alongside No 5 berth at Devenport dockyard on 6 March, her days as an AMC over, and when she emerged she would have a new role and a new name.

It was May 10 1944 before she recommissioned again at Plymouth as the heavy repair ship HMS *Artifex*. After carrying out trials off the Clyde she left the UK in June for Trincomalee, sailing via Port Said, Aden and Bombay. She remained in the Far East for the remainder of her career, and in January 1946 she visited Hong Kong. By the spring of that year she was back in Ceylon, and on 3 May she left the Far East Fleet and returned to Cardiff in South Wales where the bulk of her crew went on foreign service leave. After unloading a cargo of 'food for Britain', she left the Barry Roads on 26 June 1946 bound for Gareloch and the reserve fleet. The *Artifex* never entered active service again and in early January 1961 she was sold and delivered to shipbreakers at La Spezia.

The *Ascania* was taken up for service as an AMC, and after commissioning on 16 October 1939 she joined the 3rd Battle Squadron at Halifax NS. She was employed in this role until October 1941, when she left the Clyde with a convoy bound for the Middle East via Freetown, Durban and Port Elizabeth, where she was detached from the convoy and ordered to Colombo. From there she was ordered south through the dangerous waters of the Indian Ocean via Freemantle and Melbourne to Auckland in New Zealand. She remained on this station for some months patrolling the Pacific waters to Suva with HMNZS *Monowai*. This was a very active theatre of war at that time, with the Japanese advancing southwards.

In August 1942 the *Ascania* left New Zealand for the UK, sailing via Panama, up the east coast of the USA and across the Atlantic in convoy to Southampton where she was paid off and underwent a conversion to a landing ship (infantry). The purpose of these ships was to carry the bulk of any invasion force to a beachhead where they would be transferred to assault landing craft

(carried on the LSIs) for the final run in to the beaches. During her service in this role the *Ascania* took part in the invasion of Sicily, Salerno and, in 1944, the Anzio landings.

Later in 1944 she became a troop transport and remained as such until September 1947. One of her last roles was to repatriate 115 Gibraltarians who had been evacuated to Northern Ireland during the war. Also on board at that time was Sir Kenneth Anderson, the Governor of the colony, and all of them received an enthusiastic welcome when they returned to 'the Rock'. In early September 1947 the *Ascania* was returned to Cunard and was given a partial reconditioning at Liverpool. She was the only ship of the 1925 trio to return to the company's service and three months later, on 20 December 1947, she made her first post-war voyage from Liverpool to Halifax. She now carried 250 first and 534 tourist class passengers, with the latter accommodated in dormitories for six, eight or ten. Even the first class cabins were fitted with berths for two, four or six passengers and the austere conditions were justified at the time because of the heavy demand by emigrants to Canada.

The *Ascania* continued on Cunard's Liverpool to Montreal service until September 1955, when she was transferred to Southampton, leaving the new *Saxonia* and *Ivernia* to maintain the Liverpool route. Just over a year later, in October 1956, it was announced that the *Ascania* was to be withdrawn the following month and would be disposed of soon afterwards. However, before she was sold, the Suez Crisis gave her a short reprieve when she was used for two trooping voyages between Southampton and Malta, but she was sold to the British Iron & Steel Corporation in December 1956 and allocated to J. Cashmore of Newport for demolition. The *Ascania* arrived at the Blaina Wharf in the River Usk at Newport, Monmouthshire, on 1 January 1957, and about five months later the job was completed. The hulk floated until the last day, when the remains of the engine room compartment, probably 300 tons, was removed at low tide.

The *Alaunia* arrived back in London from

Montreal on 20 October 1939, and she did not sail again for Cunard. Towards the end of that month she too was requisitioned and steamed to Gibraltar for her conversion to an AMC. Like her two sisters she was armed with five ancient six-inch guns and two single three-inch, high-angle guns. She was commissioned on 27 September 1939 and after trials off Gibraltar she returned to 40 berth at Southampton Docks where the conversion work was completed. The dockyard workmen painted the ship battleship grey and all the surplus furniture was landed. On 9 January 1940 an additional three six-inch guns were put into position and four days later she left for the 3rd Battle Squadron at Halifax NS. She remained on this station until mid-1941, mainly escorting convoys from Halifax to a rendezvous off Bermuda, then, in the autumn of 1941, she left Halifax for a major refit by John Brown & Co in the Dalmuir Basin at Clydebank.

She completed the overhaul on 15 December 1941, and was moved down the river to Greenock to embark stores and ammunition before sailing in convoy for Freetown, Durban and Kilindini Harbour at Mombasa. She then returned to Durban and remained there until March 1942, when she escorted the P&O liner Narkunda to Mombasa. Originally she was to have sailed for Bombay, but in the uncertainty following the disastrous Battle of the Java Sea, both ships were diverted to Mombasa. In early April that year, when the situation had eased, the Alaunia did escort a convoy to Bombay, and on 21 April 1942 she arrived in Colombo.

At this time the Japanese were on the offensive in the area, and earlier in the month a Japanese naval force had destroyed 92,000 tons of shipping along the east coast of India, and aircraft had bombed Trincomalee, sinking the aircraft carrier Hermes. Admiral Somerville, who had just taken command of the Eastern Fleet, was forced, in the face of overwhelmingly superior Japanese naval strength, to retire with his fleet to Kilindini. HMS Alaunia played a small part in this operation and she loaded large amounts of surplus stores and furniture for ship-

HMS Alaunia in the Indian Ocean with Force 'A', April 1942. (Imperial War Museum)

ment to East Africa. On Thursday 23 April she embarked members of the Admiral's staff, including a member of the WRNS, Mrs J. Dinwoodie, and sailed the following day with the fleet, codenamed 'Force A'. The Alaunia took up station with HM ships Warspite, Indomitable, Formidable and Newcastle, and in the following days Mrs Dinwoodie recalls watching 'Force A' exercising in the Indian Ocean. 'As you can imagine it was one of the highlights of our service to sail in the middle of this fleet, watching the manoeuvres, firing practice and air exercises taking place'. After fuelling at the Seychelles on 30 April, the fleet arrived in Kilindini at 4.25 pm on Sunday 3 May 1942, and immediately all the passengers were disembarked and the stores unloaded.

HMS Alaunia returned to Colombo in mid-May 1942 where she was immediately quarantined after a crew member was found to have smallpox. She remained there until mid-June when she left once again for patrols between Colombo and Kilindini. From November 1942 until January 1944 she was anchored off Bandar Abbas in Iran, with periodic refits at Bombay. After completing a refit in February 1944 and visiting Colombo, HMS Alaunia left for

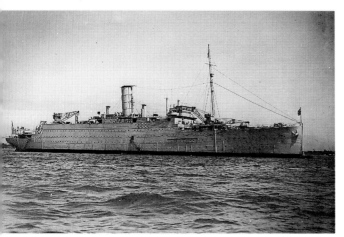

The fleet repair ship HMS Alaunia *at Devonport.*
(Wright & Logan)

England on 19 February 1944. Although AMCs still had a role to play in the Indian Ocean, mainly on convoy escort duties, it was decided that the *Alaunia* would be converted for service as a repair ship. Another factor in this decision was that she had very poor gunnery equipment, not having been modernized during her years east of Suez. She arrived in Greenock on 2 April 1944 and five days later left for Devonport where

she paid off on 17 May 1944, with most of her ship's company being drafted to Portsmouth and Chatham.

HMS *Alaunia* commissioned again at Devonport on 21 August 1945, having been converted into a large fleet repair ship. This was six days after VJ Day and the urgent need for these vessels had now eased, so she spent the remainder of her career at Devonport, mostly at No 1 buoy on the battleship trot or alongside No 5 wharf. She ended her days as a static training ship for engine room personnel under training at Plymouth before being sold for scrap in September 1957. She arrived at Blyth for breaking up on the 10th of that month.

Technical data	
Gross tonnage	13,984 (*Aurania*), 14,030 (*Alaunia*), 14,013 (*Ascania*)
Net tonnage	8,473 (*Aurania*), 8,448 (*Alaunia*), 8,437 (*Ascania*)
Length overall	520 ft (158.5m)
Breadth	65 ft (19.8m)

All three ships twin screw, powered by two sets of double reduction geared turbines; 8,500 SHP, 15 knots.

23
Carinthia, 1925

The *Carinthia* was virtually a sister ship to the *Franconia* of 1922, and like her she was designed primarily for cruising. The new ship was built by Vickers Armstrong at Barrow-in-Furness, and when the keel was laid it was intended that she should be named *Servia* after a famous Cunarder of 1881 which, in its day, was a considerable advance in technical achievement. The decision to change the name was obviously made during the time that the hull lay on the stocks, for when she was launched on Tuesday 24 February 1925 it was as the *Carinthia*.

Six months later the *Carinthia* was completed and, after running her trials in early August, she moored at Liverpool in preparation for her maiden voyage to New York. She had a gross tonnage of 20,277, and like the *Franconia* was designed to carry 330 first, 420 second and 1,500 third class passengers. She was powered by two sets of double reduction geared turbines and had a service speed of 16½ knots. She left Liverpool for New York on 22 August 1925 and remained on this route until the winter when she started the first of her world cruises from New York. This voyage lasted for 142 days, during which she travelled 40,000 miles and visited 40 ports. After this she returned to Liverpool in March 1926 and towards the end of the month made her first transatlantic voyage of the season via Queenstown to New York.

This start to her career set the pattern for the years to come, although in some summers she made short cruises from Southampton, and became particularly noted for her cruises to the Fjords and the North Cape. In early 1932 she was chartered to the Furness–Bermuda Line to fill a gap caused by a fire in their vessel *Bermuda*. Later that year, before she left New York on her world cruise, her hull was painted white to suit her mainly cruising role. Her world cruise that year took her westbound through the Panama Canal to Hawaii, New Zealand, Australia, Japan, South-East Asia, India, East Africa and Cape Town. It was whilst at the Cape that she embarked a large quantity of gifts, including two lifeboats, collected by the residents of Cape Town

The Carinthia *was virtually a sister ship to the* Franconia *of 1923.* (A. Duncan)

Above *The* Carinthia *in the Thames off King George V Dock.* (Museum in Docklands)

Right *The* Carinthia *in her white livery in New York, 1938.* (E.E. Viez)

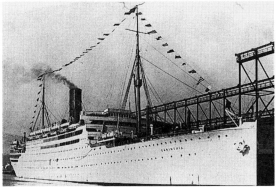

for the people of what was then known as the 'loneliest island in the empire' — Tristan da Cunha. She called at the island on Wednesday 26 April 1933 and from there she steamed to Montevideo and then returned to New York, completing what had become known as the 'millionaires cruise'.

August 1939 saw the *Carinthia* cruising out of New York, in the early days of that month to Bermuda, and in the latter part to Quebec and Newfoundland. She returned to New York at the end of August, and on 3 September 1939, the day war was declared, she sailed for Liverpool where she was immediately requisitioned for service as an AMC. During the next two months she was in dry dock undergoing conversion, and when the bulk of the work was completed on 8 December she was moved into

the Sandon Basin. She had been painted battleship grey and was armed with eight six-inch guns, two three-inch high-angle guns and two Lewis guns. Most of her furniture had been taken out and many of her second and third class cabins were removed and substituted by messdecks. Although some of her holds were packed with buoyant cargo, owing to the shortages of the day this was not fully completed, and it was to have a detrimental effect when she was torpedoed in June 1940.

After undergoing trials off Liverpool, HMS

Carinthia left for Portsmouth on 2 January 1940 and after ten days in the dockyard embarking stores she left for Greenock and the Northern Patrol. After her first patrol between Iceland and the Faroes she had a two-day break at Greenock at the end of January, and then left again for the patrol area south of Iceland, where she patrolled in company with the cruiser HMS *Manchester* and the ex-Cunarder HMS *Aurania* on what was called 'Naval Patrol 71'. At the end of March 1940 she went into No 7 drydock at Birkenhead for a refit, and when this was completed she steamed south to 'Naval Patrol 51' off the coast of Portugal. After almost two weeks on patrol she called at Casablanca at 8.30 am on 28 May for a stay of 30 hours alongside the Mole Du Commerce. After taking on water she left the following day and arrived at Gibraltar on 30 May to take on stores.

HMS *Carinthia* left Gibraltar on 3 June 1940 and steamed north once again to resume her place on the Northern Patrol. At 2.07 pm on Thursday 6 June, three days out from Gibraltar, she was in a position 55° 13′N/10° 38′W off the north-west coast of Ireland and steaming north. Her Captain, John F.B. Barrett RN, was ill in bed suffering from gastritis, and the ship was under the charge of her first lieutenant, Lt Commander F.A.E. McGlashen. Suddenly, without warning, the ship was struck on the port side by a torpedo fired by *U46*, which flooded the engine room in less than three minutes. Two officers and two ratings were killed instantly by the explosion and the vessel took a heavy list to port and swung away rapidly to starboard. Not only the engine room, but Nos 4 and 5 holds and the crew's mess on 'E' deck were also flooded, and with the pumps out of action and the water level rising there seemed little chance of saving the vessel. However, even though *Carinthia* was listing to port and starting to settle by the stern, the crew still did not give up hope and they fought hard to save their ship. Distress signals were sent out to Malin Head and to the Admiralty, and on deck the gunners opened fire on what was believed to be a submarine's periscope. Half an hour after the ship was hit, the track of another torpedo was seen to pass ahead of her, only five yards away, but fortunately no more were seen.

The next two hours were anxious ones for the *Carinthia's* crew, but at 6.15 pm aircraft from Coastal Command were sighted and an optimistic series of signals were exchanged:

Aircraft: 'Do you need help?'
Carinthia: 'Help is being sent. Am glad to see you. Last saw submarine 1430hrs.'
Aircraft: 'How long can you float?'
Carinthia: 'We hope to be towed into harbour as we are not making any more water.'

For the next five hours the aircraft kept watch over the stricken ship and at 12.30 am the following day the C-in-C Rosyth signalled that HM ships *Wren*, *Volunteer*, *Berkeley* and *Gleaner*, together with the fleet tugs *Marauder* and *Bandit*, were on their way. HMS *Volunteer* was first to arrive at 3.25 am, followed by the *Gleaner* just over an hour later. By 7 am the *Carinthia* was under tow from the *Gleaner*, but progress was slow and at just after 8 am the following signal was sent to *Gleaner* from *Carinthia*: 'Well done. Ship still aft. If this continues I want to distribute ship's company, about 300, between escort vessels. Can lower my boats but not hoist them again but I can use one cutter in addition to escort vessel's boats. I may have to do it before tug takes us in tow.'

At just after 9.30 am, with the water level within six feet of 'C' deck, most of the ship's company was transferred to the *Gleaner* and *Wren*, and this was completed an hour later. By 1 pm the tug *Marauder* had taken up the tow, and although the water was still rising aft of the engine room, it was thought that there was still chance of saving the ship. One of those who made great efforts to do so was Engineer Sub-Lieutenant S. Smith who was untiring in his work, and he visited the boiler room regularly to try to keep the water in check. At one time, in order to obtain tools from a store room, he had to break down a door with an axe and wade up to his waist in water in a dark compartment, where the water was still rising.

All day the tow continued with other ships providing an anti-submarine screen. At 4.25 pm a signal was made to the *Marauder*: 'I think the position will arise when I shall have to temporarily abandon the ship without abandoning the tow. Should the ship stand the altered conditions it may be possible to return. In any case I shall not be able to steer for many hours as the emergency engine will be giving out. I will ask you to slow down when we leave.'

Half an hour later she signalled to an accompanying trawler *British Honduras*: 'Remain fairly handy now and come alongside if "not under control" signals are dropped.' Then, at 7.25 pm as dense fog enveloped the ship, the signal was given by whistle for the trawler to close immediately and the *Carinthia* was abandoned. By now the water was lapping over 'C' deck alleyways and No 6 hold was flooding rapidly, and before Captain Barrett left he looked down the staircase on 'C' deck aft to see that the deck was awash and the stern of 'B' deck was only 6 feet above the water. It was obvious that the *Carin-thia* had very little time left afloat.

After abandoning ship, Captain Barrett made every effort to keep in sight of his doomed vessel, but this was only rarely possible due to the thick fog. The end, when it came, was quick, and at 9.40 pm on Friday 7 June 1940, in a position 55° 12'N/9° 30'W, the *Carinthia* broke up and sank by the stern in a matter of seconds in 60 fathoms of water. Her crew, and particularly the rear guard working party, had done their utmost to save their ship in the best traditions of the Royal Navy.

Technical data

Gross tonnage	20,277
Net tonnage	12,086
Length overall	624 ft (190.2m)
Breadth	73 ft 6 in (22.4m)

Twin screw, powered by two sets of double reduction geared turbines; 13,500 SHP, 16 knots.

24
Queen Mary, 1936

The building of the *Queen Mary* represented the zenith of passenger ship construction for Cunard and its role on the North Atlantic, and for 31 years she proudly carried the Cunard flag, not only on the Western Ocean but also during the war years, throughout the whole world.

The first plans for a new record-breaking liner for the company to replace the ageing *Mauretania* were put forward in 1926, but it was some four years before the ideas were realized and tenders were put out to builders. On 28 May 1930 Cunard announced that the new 1,000 foot, 81,000 gross ton liner was to be built on the Clyde by John Brown & Co and that the vessel would take three years to complete. Even in those early days Cunard had made it clear that there would be two new giant liners which would run together on the Atlantic, and politics entered the scene even before the keels were laid when attempts were made in parliament to get one ship built on the Clyde and the other on Tyneside.

The contract for the *Queen Mary* was signed on 1 December 1930, and the keel was laid on 31 January 1931. It was thought at the time that the vessel would be ready for service in 1934, and in anticipation of this the Southern Railway Company agreed to build a new graving dock at Southampton. By November 1931 the building work was proceeding well, with the launch scheduled for May 1932, and it seemed that the new Cunarder was set to enter the Atlantic trade. However, it soon became clear that all was not well, and when the order went out to paint the uncompleted hull with red lead, rumours abounded that work would soon be stopped. Then, on Friday 11 December 1931 the Cunard board decided to suspend the construction of the vessel due to 'the impact of the national crisis'. The world economic depression had hit the shipbuilding industry and soon work would be halted on some 154,000 tons of merchant shipping. All outstanding bills on the half-finished 'hull 534', as she had become known, were paid out of Cunard's liquid cash resources and, worst of all, the Clydeside workforce was laid off indefinitely. On their arrival at the ship-

A majestic aerial view of the Queen Mary. (Aerofilms Ltd/Public Archives of Canada)

yard on that grey December day, the men were met with the following statement posted on the gates: 'Notice is hereby given to all employees in Clydeside shipyard that all work in connection with contract 534 is to be stopped as from noon on Saturday. The services of all employees will therefore terminate at noon tomorrow.'

Throughout the following months, as the great hull stood deserted, the plight of 534 seemed to epitomize the effects of the economic depression in Scotland. One local MP, Mr David Kirkwood, fought to obtain Government assistance, but perhaps the situation was best summed up by the Prime Minister, Mr Ramsey MacDonald, in a letter to Mr Kirkwood: 'The trouble with this ship is not to get her built, but to get the company to believe that when she is built she can be run with some chance of paying her way.'

During the summer of 1931 Cunard had started negotiations to buy out its main British rival, the White Star Line, but when Cunard's offer to buy all White Star's ships except *Georgic* for £300,000 was rejected, the negotiations broke down. However, it was to be the merger of these two companies which was to provide a lifeline for hull 534 on the Clyde. The Government wanted to see the two great names in British shipping working together, and during 1933 there were complicated negotiations between the Cunard management, Mr Neville Chamberlain, the Chancellor of the Exchequer and the board of the Royal Mail Steam Packet Co, the ultimate owners of the White Star Line. Then, in December 1933 an agreement was announced. As a condition of the merger of the two shipping lines, the Government was to lend the new company — Cunard White Star Line Ltd — £9.5 million. Of this sum, £3 million was for the completion of hull 534, £5 million was for the building of a sister ship, and £1.5 million was an injection of working capital into the company.

It was another four months before the agreement became a reality for the Clydeside workforce, but at 7.40 am on Tuesday 3 April 1934 work re-started at the yard. Crowds began to gather outside the shipyard gates at 6 am that day and at 7.30 the 600 men who had received

notices to start work marched in led by the Dalmuir pipe band. By the end of the week the workforce had increased to 1,000, plus a night shift, and it was hoped that the vessel would be launched in the autumn of that year.

In May 1934 it was announced that the launch would be performed by Her Majesty Queen Mary and the date was set for Wednesday 26 September. When the day arrived the weather on Clydeside was atrocious, with heavy rain and strong winds. There was a brief lull in the morning but by the afternoon it was pouring once again and the spectators could only obtain a blurred impression of the royal party in the special pavilion built under the ship's bows. The ceremony started with a short speech by King George V, which ended: 'May her life among great waters spread friendship among the nations'. Queen Mary then ended the speculation about the liner's name when she announced, 'I am happy to name this ship *Queen Mary*. I wish success to her and to all who sail in her.' The Queen then cut a ribbon which shattered a bottle of Australian wine against the bow, and pressed a button to send the hull down into the Clyde where the drag chains prevented her from grounding on the opposite bank. Tugs then manoeuvred the vessel to her fitting-out berth just to the west of the slipway, where there was still 18 months' work to do before she was ready for sea.

Sadly King George V did not live to see his wife's ship completed, and it was left to his eldest son, then King Edward VIII, to visit the liner on 5 March 1936, shortly before she left the River Clyde. Nineteen days later the *Queen Mary* left the fitting-out yard and, under her own power and attended by seven tugs, made her way down the narrow river to Tail of the Bank at Greenock, 15 miles away. Despite the fact that the river had been specially dredged, there were one or two difficult moments when she grounded in the Clyde mud. However, the valiant efforts of the tugs paid off and the thousands of people lining the river banks saw her arrive safely in just under 2 hours 45 minutes, and anchor off Gourock at 2.10 pm that day.

Above *The* Queen Mary *in Southampton Water.* (E.H. Cole)

Above right *The cabin or first class restaurant of* RMS Queen Mary. (University of Liverpool)

Right *The cabin class restaurant showing the trans-atlantic map.* (Author's collection)

On the following day she steamed down the Firth as far as Arran for compass trials, and when she anchored off Greenock once again that evening with her hull floodlit, the pleasure steamers did a wonderful trade making trips round the ship. Shortly before midnight she left for Southampton and the purpose-built King George V drydock. She arrived in the Cowes Roads at 5 am on Friday 27 March, and whilst awaiting the high tide several liners passed including NDL's *Bremen*. Then, as she passed up Southampton Water every ship in the port saluted her, including the once mighty *Majestic*, which was doing duty as a stand for spectators as she awaited her sale, having been withdrawn following the fusion of Cunard and White Star.

As for the new *Queen Mary*, her underwater hull received three coats of paint, then on 15 April 1936 she steamed north once again for trials in the Firth of Clyde. Although no official figures were given for the speed trials, she successfully attained speeds of 32.84 knots. On 11 May she was handed over to her owners and the Cunard White Star houseflag was hoisted. As she steamed off Arran, the residents of the island had magnificent views of the ship, and at 9.40 pm on Saturday 18 April, after giving three long blasts on her siren, she said farewell to the Clyde and set course for Southampton once again, arriving in the Cowes Roads 24 hours later and berthing in the Ocean Dock at 10 am on Monday 20 April to prepare for her maiden voyage.

The premium accommodation on this magnificent new ship was rated as cabin, tourist and third class, which was a surprise to many, for prior to this cabin class had been equated to the second class. Perhaps it was a sign of the times for the late 1930s. The *Queen Mary* had accommodation for 740 cabin class, 760 tourist class and 579 third class passengers, which meant that the emphasis was on the first two classes and much less on the third class. There were ten passenger decks and the cabin class had access to eight of them. The top two decks, the sports and sun decks, were used exclusively by the cabin class and were set aside mainly for deck games, although aft on the sun deck was the verandah grill. This room had a panoramic view aft over the sea, and it was intended for the service of à la carte meals.

Most of the cabin class public rooms were on the promenade deck. The main foyer here served as the shopping centre and led aft to the sheltered promenade, lounge and galleries. Aft again was the ballroom and smoking room. Right forward was the observation lounge and cocktail bar, library and drawing room, whilst aft was the tourist class promenade and smoking room. Beneath the Promenade Deck was the Main Deck, with the third class garden lounge directly below the observation lounge, and aft of this was the cabin class accommodation which included special suites. At the after end were tourist public rooms, including the library and writing room, children's playroom, lounge and cocktail bar.

Beneath this deck, the remainder were lettered 'A' to 'H', and right forward on 'A' deck was the third class smoking room with cabin class accommodation amidships. Further aft were tourist class cabins and the tourist lounge. Forward on

'B' deck there was the third class lounge, with more cabin class accommodation, and aft were tourist class cabins. The dining saloons for all three classes were on 'C' deck, the third class being forward. There was seating for 412, with tables arranged for parties of four to ten persons. Amidships was the cabin class restaurant, where all the passengers in that class could dine at one sitting. Perhaps the highlight of the room was the decorative map on the forward bulkhead. This was designed by Mr Macdonald Gill and represented the North Atlantic between Europe and the USA. As well as a clock at the top, an illuminated model of the ship indicated its position on the voyage between Bishops Rock and the Nantucket lightship. Further aft was the tourist class saloon and more tourist cabins. There was a swimming pool for the cabin class on 'D' deck and a pool for the tourist class on 'F' deck aft.

The *Queen Mary* was a quadruple screw vessel, each propeller being powered by a set of single reduction geared turbines. Each set of turbines comprised one HP, one LP and two IP turbines working in series, and each turbine drove a seperate pinion which engaged the main gear wheel. The turbines which powered the outer propellers were installed in the forward engine room, and the machinery for the inner propellers was housed in the after engine room. The superheated steam was supplied at 400 psi and 700°F by 24 oil-fired boilers arranged in five boiler rooms. All the boilers were of the Yarrow water tube type, constructed by the builders under licence. In addition to these, there were three auxiliary Scotch double-ended boilers which were fitted in No 1 boiler room. In all, the main propulsion machinery developed 160,000 SHP and gave the ship a speed of over 30 knots. She was set to regain the Blue Riband for Great Britain.

On 14 May 1936 the *Queen Mary* left Southampton for a 470-mile cruise with 600 guests on board, including Mr Neville Chamberlain, the Chancellor of the Exchequer, Alfred and Lady Diana Duff-Cooper and other cabinet members. On Sunday 24 May, she was visited by her spon-

Above and above right *Two views of the* Queen Mary *at Southampton.* (A. Duncan and J.K. Byass)

sor, Her Majesty Queen Mary. She was accompanied by King Edward VIII and the Duke and Duchess of York who, with their two daughters the Princesses Elizabeth and Margaret, spent some time in the children's playroom. The royal visit lasted five hours and included luncheon and tea on board.

Finally, on 27 May 1936, 2,000 passengers embarked and at 4.30 pm the *Queen Mary* moved slowly stern first from the Ocean Dock, as she left for Cherbourg and New York. The great vessel was dressed overall and as she moved down Southampton Water the whistles of scores of small boats saluted her. Thousands of people lined the shores all round the Solent to wish *bon voyage* to the ship which they hoped would regain the Blue Riband. Cunard denied that it was trying to break speed records, and it was just as well, because with thick fog which reduced visibility to 50 yards, any hope of achieving it on this crossing was out of the question.

By 9.30 am on Monday 1 June 1936 the *Queen Mary* was off the Ambrose lightship, where she was greeted by aircraft of the 29th Observation Squadron of the USAF. She anchored at Quarantine to await the tide and then, during the afternoon, in a huge procession of boats, yachts, tugs and fireboats, she made her way up river to her pier at 50th Street. During the next few days Sir Edgar Britten, her master, and the officers and crew were fêted by the citizens of

New York. Many thousands of visitors looked over the ship during her stay, then at 10.30 am on 5 June she left Pier 90 for Cherbourg and home. Although her voyage received a great deal of publicity, another Atlantic crossing at that time was really far more significant. The German airship *Hindenberg* was making the third of its experimental trips, and crossing to New York from Germany in just under 60 hours.

The *Queen Mary* spent a short spell in drydock during July 1936, during which time the turbines were adjusted and her propellers inspected, then, her return to service at the end of the month, she made the voyage from Cherbourg breakwater to Ambrose Light in four days, eight hours, 37 minutes, thereby wresting the Blue Riband form the *Normandie*. Later that year her first master, Sir Edgar Britten, died, and Captain R.V. Peel took command of the Atlantic giant.

On 22 December *Queen Mary* went into drydock for her first winter overhaul, when heavy weather damage was repaired and bulkheads were strengthened in order to reduce vibration which developed in bad weather. The alterations proved their worth, for when she returned to service she managed over 30 knots through severe gales. On completion of her first year of service in May 1937, she had carried 56,895 passengers across the Atlantic. In August of that year new propellers were fitted, but the *Normandie* won back the record for the westbound crossing.

At the end of the year *Queen Mary collided*

with the New York pier causing considerable damage to the pier but emerging unscathed herself. Six months later, on the afternoon of Saturday 30 June 1938, whilst she was being moved from the King George V drydock to Ocean Dock after a summer overhaul, she collided with a wooden jetty. There were strong winds blowing at the time and the tugs were unable to stop her demolishing the jetty adjacent to 41 berth; fortunately the ship was not damaged.

Two months later, on 14 August 1938, *Queen Mary* regained the Blue Riband, making both the westbound and eastbound voyages faster than the *Normandie*. Later in the year, on Tuesday 18 November the *Queen Mary* docked in New York under her own steam, without the aid of tugs whose crews were on strike. Captain Robert Irving managed the operation in 34 minutes, which was no longer than it usually took. On 21 December she was laid up at Southampton for her annual overhaul and she resumed her sailings on Saturday 4 February 1939.

The next seven months of service up to the outbreak of war were successful ones for the *Queen Mary* and she made her last transatlantic commercial voyage from Southampton on 30 August 1939. She had 2,332 passengers on board, most of whom were Americans leaving Europe for home before war broke out. She arrived at Pier 90 in New York on 5 September, two days after the declaration of war, the voyage having taken her well south of her usual route to avoid U-boats. Her next voyage from Southampton, which had been scheduled for 13 September, had already been cancelled and the great liner lay at New York next to her old rival the *Normandie* for the remainder of that year. The skeleton crew who remained on board had the task of painting the ship grey, and for the time being there was no role for the *Queen Mary* in the course of the war.

On 2 March 1940, the newly completed *Queen Elizabeth* left the Clyde, and five days later she appeared in New York to berth on the opposite side of Pier 90. Also in the port at this time was the (new) *Mauretania*, and for two weeks the citizens of the city could view the three drably painted Cunarders while the *Normandie* still looked resplendent in her company colours.

Six months after her arrival, the *Queen Mary*'s master, Captain Irving, received sealed orders to proceed to sea, and on 21 March 1940, at just after 8 am, she left New York and set course south for Cape Town and Sydney. The *Mauretania* had left the previous evening, and although *Queen Mary* sailed at the peak commuter time, she received some attention but none of the usual excitement. There were all sorts of rumours as to her future role, and one of them proved accurate, that she was to be hired by the Government for use as a troopship for the Australian Imperial Force from Sydney. She arrived off Sydney Heads on 17 April and the following day she was taken over by the Cockatoo Dockyard Company for conversion to a troop transport. Most of her luxury furnishings were removed and tiers of bunks and hammock rails were fitted. The main shopping centre became the military administration offices and the bridge was given extra protection. The ship was also armed with an old four-inch gun and a number of machine-guns. Her main protection was to be her speed.

With the conversion work complete, *Queen Mary* left Sydney on 4 May 1940 with 5,000 troops of the AIF on board. The convoy she was in included the *Aquitania*, *Mauretania*, three Canadian Pacific liners and the SS *Andes*, and they were escorted by two Australian cruisers. They sailed via Cape Town and arrived in the Clyde on 16 June, the day that France surrendered. It was the vessel's first visit to the Clyde since she completed her trials. Twelve days later she left for Singapore, once again via Cape Town, carrying troops to the island in an attempt to bolster the defences in view of Japan's increasing threat in the Far East. On her arrival, in August 1940, she was drydocked in the massive graving dock which had not been long completed at the Sembawang Naval Base on the northern coast of the island.

Once the overhaul was completed on 25 September 1940, the *Queen Mary* sailed once more for Sydney and for the remainder of the year she made trooping voyages between that port and India. In February 1941 she was again drydocked at Singapore and for the rest of the year she sailed between Australian ports, Singapore, Trincomalee and Suez with Australian troops. However, in late November, with serious tensions building up between the Allies and Japan and with war in the Far East imminent, it was clear that the Indian Ocean would become as dangerous as the North Atlantic.

So, on 19 December 1941, two weeks after the outbreak of war in the Far East and Pacific, the *Queen Mary* left Trincomalee for Cape Town and proceeded via Trinidad and New York to Boston naval shipyard for overhaul, since the Singapore naval base was now out of the question with the Japanese advancing rapidly down the Malayan peninsula. In Boston, the Bethlehem Steel Corporation increased her troop capacity to 8,500 by means of standee bunks, and even the swimming pool became a dormitory. Her defensive armament was also improved and she was fitted with a six-inch gun and five three-inch guns, plus numerous anti-aircraft cannon and machineguns. However, as before, her speed would continue to be her best defence. With the Allies' priority being the defeat of Germany, the *Queen Mary*'s new role was soon to be back on the North Atlantic, but first she had to carry urgent US reinforcements to Sydney to assist General MacArthur's beleaguered Pacific Command. It was at this point that Captain R.B. Irving retired, and he was replaced by Captain James Bisset.

Queen Mary left the United States on 18 February 1942, three days after the fall of Sin-

Top right The Queen Mary *leaves New York on 21 March 1940. The stern gun of the ill-fated* Lancastria *can be seen in the foreground.* (Imperial War Museum)

Centre right The Queen Mary *in the Clyde with* HMS Hood *in June 1940.* (Imperial War Museum)

Right The Queen Mary *in the drydock at Singapore Naval Base on the north coast of the island in August 1940.* (Wrather Corporation)

A dramatic photograph of the forward section of HMS Curacoa only seconds after the Queen Mary had sliced her in two. (Wrather Corporation)

gapore, with almost 8,400 troops on board, and steamed via Key West, Rio de Janeiro, Cape Town and Fremantle to Sydney, arriving there at the end of March that year. She returned to New York by the same route, arriving back on 21 July, and in early August she made an Atlantic crossing to the Clyde carrying US troops. Altogether she had 10,755 people on board, of which 875 were civilian passengers, and she followed this with a voyage via Cape Town to Suez. After she had disembarked British troops at Suez, she returned to New York with German POWs, once again stopping at the Cape and Rio. On her arrival in the USA, even more standee bunks were fitted following a decision to transport a whole division of the US Army to Europe in one voyage, which meant over 15,000 troops.

At this point her future as a troopship was

not absolutely assured, for there were ideas put forward to convert her to an aircraft carrier. Although control of the vessel remained with the Ministry of Transport and she continued to be manned by Cunard, the vessel came under the operational command of the US Army, since from this time until the spring of 1946 she would be used mainly to transport US troops. The first of her fast eastbound voyages with 10,000–15,000 troops on board began on 2 August 1942, and it was on the third such voyage that she was involved in the worst collision of her career.

Due to her high speed she was considered to be safe from U-boat attack, and accordingly she travelled unescorted from New York to a position approximately 15°W. From that position until she reached the Clyde she was at risk from the German long-range Focke Wolf Condor bombers, so an anti-aircraft escort was arranged to meet her to escort her to the safety of the Clyde. One of these escorts was the elderly cruiser HMS *Curacoa*, a vessel first commissioned in 1916 and which had been damaged by a mine whilst blockading the Bolshevik fleet at Kronstadt in the Baltic during 1919. She had also already seen action in the Second World War, having been damaged by dive bombers during the campaign in Norway.

The *Queen Mary* left New York on 27 September 1942 with 10,398 troops on board, and five days later, at about 7 am on 2 October, she sighted her escort cruiser the *Curacoa* and accompanying destroyers. The *Queen Mary* was steaming at 28 knots on what was known as zigzag No 8, which took 40 minutes to complete and which meant that she steamed for four minutes on a mean (straight) course, then on a 25-degree course to starboard for eight minutes, a 50-degree course to port for eight minutes, and then back on to her mean course for a further four minutes. After this, the zigzag took her on these changes of course to port and starboard alternatively. As the *Curacoa*'s best speed was 26 knots, she performed a modified zigzag which kept her as close as possible to the great liner, whilst maintaining the same mean course.

With her greater speed the Cunarder would

overtake her escort, and by 2.15 pm the *Queen Mary* was on the starboard leg of her zigzag when the *Curacoa* converged on her from the starboard side and the *Queen Mary* collided with the cruiser about 112 feet from the latter's stern, slicing straight through the warship. The story is best told by Mr Allin Martin of Swindon Village, Cheltenham, a survivor from the *Curacoa*.

'I relieved the duty telegraphist in the lower bridge radio office at 2 pm. Shortly afterwards the upper bridge speaking tube clanged and my signalman "oppo" indicated that if my camera was to hand a particularly good view of the Queen Mary *was available. Unclipping the bulkhead door I stepped outside, where to my horror I saw the enormous bulk of the* Queen Mary *bearing down on our port quarter at about 50 yards range. Her huge white bow wave seemed as tall as a house and it seemed inevitable that we were within seconds of being torn apart. I dived inside for my lifebelt and whilst in the process of inflating same the impact came, hurling me against the starboard bulkhead.*

'I remember charging for the door through a mass of broken batteries, radio equipment etc, to reach the outer companionway where I encountered my signalman "oppo" racing down from the upper bridge. At this time I remember seeing the starboard oerlikon platform in seething water — this was normally about 20 feet above sea level — and it appeared that the Curacoa *had been rolled over onto her starboard side. Together we ran down to the main deck and picked our way aft to the foremost funnel where we located a wooden "paint ship" ladder which we hurled overboard.*

At this point I remember looking aft and seeing nothing beyond the after funnel. I reckoned that the stern had been sheared completely off and had already sunk. Scrambling down the sloping port side we grabbed our ladder, but so many other swimmers had the same idea that I decided to strike out and put my trust in my lifebelt. By this time the severed fuel tanks were disgorging oil so I aimed to make for clearer water. My "oppo" declined to follow and I never saw him

again. Having put some distance between the ship and myself I turned on my back to rest and survey the situation. The bow section was pointing skywards at an almost vertical angle and sliding slowly backwards into the sea. Whilst about 30 feet was still visible the foredeck appeared to explode, hurling debris skywards — upon reflection this was probably due to air being forced upwards internally by the pressure of the encroaching sea. As she finally slid beneath the waves I remember seeing a figure scrabbling over the breakwater.

'In about four or five minutes from the moment of impact all that remained was a floating mass of debris — oildrums, loose gear, woodwork, bodies and survivors, in a welter of oil. The Queen Mary *had gone, everything had happened so quickly that no boats or carley floats had been launched. Of the ensuing two and a half hours I have only fleeting recollections. I recall the group nearest me having several half-hearted attempts at community singing — I remember "Roll out the barrel". I remember an empty boot floating past, also an object about the size of a football which I firmly believed to have been a disembodied head and which, in my blind panic to avoid, caused me to swallow a considerable quantity of sea water. I distinctly remember the dwindling number of swimmers, in particular a robust able seaman who just seeemed to give up and quietly drown.'*

Eventually Mr Martin was rescued by HMS *Bramham*, but of the *Curacoa*'s 430 crew members there were only 101 survivors. Indeed, once he was aboard the *Bramham*, Mr Martin remembers seeing 'the lines of shrouded bodies being conveyed back for burial'. On board the *Queen Mary* the collision had been marked merely by a jolt, and Staff Captain H. Grattidge saw '150 feet from the bridge on the port side, almost smothered in awesome clouds of black smoke, the fore part of a vessel going down. Running to starboard I could see the after end of the same vessel, trembling to settle beneath the waves.' In fact, Mr Martin, who has very clear memories of the incident, believes that what was taken for black smoke was in fact dirt and debris being blown out the wreck of the *Curacoa*.

For the *Queen Mary* with nearly 11,000 troops on board, there was no question of stopping to assist, and the most that the troops who had witnessed the event could do was to throw life-belts over the side. Damage control parties reported that the liner's stem was badly damaged beneath the waterline. Speed was reduced to 14 knots in order to slow the entry of water, and fortunately her bulkheads held and she arrived

safely in the Clyde. The disaster was kept a closely guarded secret during the war, but then a long legal battle followed between the Admiralty and Cunard, and in the event the House of Lords eventually laid the blame equally on both vessels.

Whilst the *Queen Mary* lay at Greenock, cement was used to provide temporary repairs, and on 8 October she left for Boston naval ship-yard for more permanent rebuilding of her bows. Following this refit, in December 1942 she returned to Gourock and two days before Christmas she left for a 38,000-mile voyage to Cape Town, Suez and Sydney, carrying British troops to the Middle East and Australian troops home to Fremantle and Sydney, and returning to the Clyde again by way of the Cape. The whole voyage took four months and she arrived back off Tail of the Bank on 22 April 1943. After leaving for New York in early May, and drydock-ing in New Jersey, she then started the 'GI ferry service' which was to be her role for the rest of the war.

Left *The damage to* Queen Mary's *bow after her collision with the* Curacoa. *(Imperial War Museum)*

Below *The log of the* Queen Mary *for 2 October 1942 showing the entry relating to her collision with the* Curacoa. *(Dept of Transport)*

Date of Entry.	Entries required by Act of Parliament.	Amount of Fine or Forfeiture inflicted.
2/10/42.	At 2.12. p.m. 2nd October 1942 this vessel was in collision with H.M.S. "CURACAO" in Lat. 55° 51'N , Long. 8° 38'W	
	J. Hom. Aut. Purser. *[signature]* MASTER	
8/10/42.	F. 489. B. M. Gordan, General has this day	

There is no doubt that *Queen Mary's* role in this capacity is the one for which she is best remembered, and there must be many thousands of ex-US servicemen and women today who have memories of their voyages across the North Atlantic. The vessel was split into three sections, red, white and blue, and upon boarding the ship each person was allocated to a section to which they were restricted during the voyage. Many will remember the never-ending queues for meals in what had been the cabin class dining saloon, whilst ex-officers will recall the spartan, but more comfortable conditions, in the second class saloon. During this period she carried the Prime Minister, Mr Winton Churchill, over the Atlantic and back on three occasions, the first time in May 1943 for the Washington (Trident) Conference, the second occasion being in August 1943 for the Quadrant Conference at Quebec, and then in September 1944 for the second

Quebec Conference.

When the end of the war in Europe came in May 1945, the conflict in the Pacific and Far East was still far from over and there was an urgent need to redeploy the thousands of US combat troops in Europe. VE Day itself saw the *Queen Mary* in New York, and after a refit in New Jersey she started the long process of repatriation. On Saturday 11 August the great ship returned to Southampton after an absence of six years and she was given a terrific welcome with great

Right *US troops in the main mess hall, formerly the first class dining saloon (see the photograph on p171).* (Imperial War Museum)

Below right *The officers' lounge, formerly the first class lounge.* (Imperial War Museum)

Below *The officers' dining saloon, formerly the tourist class saloon.* (Imperial War Museum)

crowds of people lining the shore from South-sea to Netley, and the western shore of Southampton city. The move had the distinct advantage of enabling the ship to embark her complement of 15,000 passengers in two days, as opposed to three at Gourock.

In January 1946 the Queen Mary started to transport GI brides in what became known as the 'bride and baby fleet' to their new homes, then on 3 May she transferred to the Halifax service to repatriate the wives and children of Canadian servicemen. She remained on this service until her return to Southampton on 27 September 1946, when she was handed back to the Cunard Line for refurbishment and return to the company's service. During her war service she had travelled over 600,000 miles and had carried nearly 800,000 people to just about every campaign area — no mean record.

The refit at Southampton was to last for ten months, and to supplement the workforce over 1,000 employees of John Brown & Co were brought from Clydeside. They were accommodated in a disused army camp outside the city and were bussed in to their work each day. The task of collecting together all the vessel's furniture was in itself an enormous task as it had been stored in places as far apart as New York and Sydney. During the refit a new stem, which had

The Queen Mary *and the* Aquitania *in the Clyde during the war.* (Imperial War Museum)

been constructed in America after the Curacoa collision, was fitted, and an air-conditioned theatre was installed.

By 25 July 1947 the work was completed, and the Queen Mary, resplendent once more in her Cunard colours, carried out trials in the English Channel. She left Southampton on 31 August that year, with one modification in the designation of her three classes. The former cabin class now became the first class and the tourist class became cabin class, with the old third class being designated tourist class. One passenger who made it to New York only to be arrested by the police there was Martin G. Eppich, a German POW, who escaped from a camp near Reading in August and stowed away in the Queen Mary at Southampton.

As both the Queens settled down to their peacetime service together for the first time since the Queen Elizabeth left the builders' yards, their passenger lists were full for both eastbound and westbound sailings. However, befor the end of 1947 industrial troubles started to disrupt the Queen Mary's routine sailings and continued to be a problem for Cunard in the post-war years. Although air travel had not yet been taken as a serious threat to the great liners, it is interesting to see that after the Queen Mary had run aground at Cherbourg on 1 January 1949 in severe gales, while outward bound for New York, she was forced to return to Southampton for repairs, and a number of passengers left her and travelled to Northolt, which was then London's airport, to fly on to the United States. On that occasion, the Queen Mary left Southampton five days later having had cement poured into her keel as a temporary measure before permanent repairs could be made, which was not until November of that year.

In November 1951 the now middle-aged Queen Mary had a one-month overhaul, and on her return to service on 29 December she was again to carry Mr Winston Churchill to the United States. However, the ship's departure was delayed by 60 hours by a combination of bad weather and a jammed anchor, and to keep his schedule the Prime Minister was met 20 miles off New

York by a coastguard cutter. Although the great ship had made some fast crossings after the war, she was unable to compete with the new American liner *United States*, and in July 1952 the latter vessel took the Blue Riband with an average speed of 35.59 knots, a record which still stands.

But speed records at sea were rapidly becoming irrelevant as aircraft continued to make rapid progress. When the *Queen Mary* went into dock for her annual overhaul in January 1957, preliminary work was done to fit her with stabilizers, a job which was finished in March 1958 at a cost of £500,000. It was a sign of the times that, when the ship arrived at Southampton on 13 November 1961, she had only 437 passengers on board and for the first time only one boat train was required. In the following year publicity was given to her fastest passage from New York and the fact that she could stand up to competition from aircraft, but the reality was that passengers for Southampton had spent six nights on board and had taken longer to reach the port than on any other occasion. In January 1963 Sir John Brocklebank said that the old ship still had six years of useful life left, but already there was speculation as to her future. Sir Billy Butlin, the British holiday camp entrepreneur, made an offer of £1 million for the vessel, which was refused.

In December 1963, with heavy losses being suffered during the winter season, the *Queen Mary* made her first cruise, to the Canaries. In 1965 cruising became more a part of her role and she was chartered to the *News of the World* newspaper, with plans being announced for an 8,700-mile cruise to New York and the Bahamas. The end for the ship was brought about rapidly by the seamen's strike which started in May 1966 and lasted for six weeks. It cost Cunard £4 million and was predicted to be the death blow for the *Queen Mary*. In early 1967, Cunard added Cobh (formerly Queenstown) to the itinerary of the *Queens*, but by now the *Queen Mary* was losing thousands of pounds a day and it was clear that this could not go on.

Originally it had been intended to keep the *Queen Mary* in service until 1969, when the QE2 would be handed over to the company. However, on Monday 8 May 1967, the new chairman of the Cunard company, Sir Basil Smallpiece, announced that the *Queen Mary* was to be withdrawn that autumn and the *Queen Elizabeth* a year later. Meanwhile, on the same day as the public announcement, Lord Mancroft, the company's Deputy Chairman, boarded the ship at Cobh and handed a sealed envelope to Captain William Law who broke the news to the ship's company whereupon a 'great gloom descended over the ship'. It came as a surprise, but with

The Queen Mary *arriving at Southampton on an early post-war voyage.* (Maritime Photo Library)

A magnificent aerial study of the Queen Mary *in the Channel.* (Skyfotos Ltd)

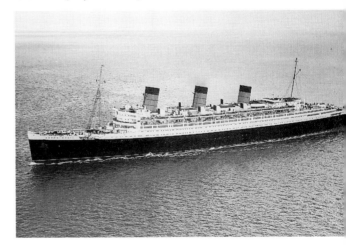

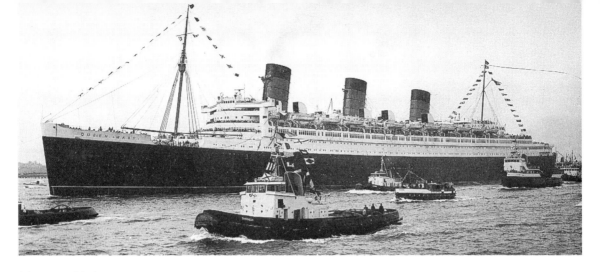

Above and below *The last farewell, 31 October 1967 — the* Queen Mary *leaves Southampton for the last time.* (F.R. Sherlock)

each ship losing £750,000 a year it was inevitable.

There then began the rumours as to the *Queen Mary*'s fate. There was speculation that she would be used to house homeless families on the Clyde, or be a transport museum in Tokyo Bay, or a tourist attraction at Long Beach, California. Tenders were invited for the old ship with the closing date set as 24 July 1967. Then, at the end of July, it was announced that Cunard had agreed to sell the liner to the town of Long Beach for £1,230,000. It was intended to moor

the vessel in a concrete basin and use her as a museum, hotel and convention centre. On 19 August formal contracts were exchanged and the purchasers paid a 10 per cent deposit, with the balance payable on delivery.

The *Queen Mary* left Southampton for her last transatlantic crossings on 16 September 1967, and six days later she bade a final farewell to New York. The city gave her a fine send off and she arrived back in Southampton on 27 September, where she was welcomed by huge crowds. One passenger, Mrs Phyllis Larkin, recalls the welcome: 'As we neared Southampton the pleasure boats began escorting us, to be joined later by smaller boats. One by one they all blew their whistles and each one was answered by three

blasts from the *Queen Mary*. The fire boats were giving their displays as the *Queen Mary* sailed majestically into Southampton at the end of an unforgettable journey.' The great ship made a cruise to the Canary Isles before the time came for her final sailing to Long Beach via Cape Horn.

Cunard had agreed to provide the crew for the delivery voyage and the new owners wanted to sell the trip as a cruise, which a travel agency organized for them; the 1,093 tickets sold helped to recoup some of the costs of the voyage, which was via Lisbon, Las Palmas, Rio de Janeiro, Calloa, Balboa and Valparaiso. The *Queen Mary* left Southampton at 9.30 am on 31 October 1967 under the command of Captain John Treasure-Jones, accompanied by hundreds of small boats and a formation of helicopters overhead. However, once at sea she had a rough passage to Lisbon, and when they reached tropical climes life became very uncomfortable for the passengers. This was aggravated by the slow speed of 20 knots to conserve fuel, and the complaints about conditions on board were numerous. The old ship passed by Cape Horn on 19 November and at 11.30 am on Saturday 9 December 1967 she arrived in Long Beach and was handed over to the city.

So ended her seagoing career, but her new role has lasted over 20 years now with varying degrees of success, and she remains at Long Beach to this day, now set in concrete and classified as a building. She remains the supreme achievement of the Atlantic ferry and a reminder of the pre-war days when Britain really did rule the waves.

The luxurious 390-room hotel Queen Mary *at Long Beach, California.* (Wrather Corporation)

Technical data	
Gross tonnage	81,235
Net tonnage	34,120
Length overall	1,019 ft 6 in (310.74m)
Breadth	112 ft 6 in (34.29m)
Quadruple screw, powered by four sets of single reduction geared turbines; 160,000 SHP, 29 knots.	

25
Mauretania, 1939

When the second *Mauretania* entered service in early 1939, the memories of the incomparable first ship of that name were still very vivid and it was clear that great things were also expected of the new vessel. Unfortunately times had changed, and the second *Mauretania*, which had never been built to be a record breaker, would fall victim to the rapid progress in air travel.

Her keel was laid on 24 May 1937, and she was the first ship to be built for the newly formed

Right *The cabin (first) class grand hall.* (Author's collection)

Below *The second* Mauretania, *almost a smaller version of the* Queen Elizabeth. (J.K. Byass)

Above *The cabin (first) class dining saloon.* (Author's collection)

Above right *The tourist class dining saloon.* (Author's collection)

Below right *The third class lounge.* (Author's collection)

Cunard White Star Line with the company providing the finance for her construction without any subsidy from the Government. The new ship was designed for the London–New York service and was to be the largest vessel ever to navigate the Thames and use the Royal Docks. It was also intended that she should be able to take over from the *Queen Mary* and the big new Cunarder which had been laid down in 1936, which was of course the *Queen Elizabeth*.

The *Mauretania* was built at Birkenhead by Cammel Laird & Co, and at 35,739 gross tons she was the largest ship ever to be constructed in an English shipyard at that time. She was launched on Thursday 28 July 1938 by Lady Bates, the wife of the Cunard chairman. All work in the yard stopped between 10.30 am and 1.30 pm that day and at 12.15 pm Lady Bates pressed the button which sent the new liner into the water from No 6 slipway. Eight tugs then towed her to the fitting-out berth next to HMS *Ark Royal*, the aircraft carrier which had preceded her on the stocks by some 15 months.

The new ship would always be regarded as a smaller version of the *Queen Elizabeth* and her profile was very similar. The main features of her hull design were her terraced bridge superstructure, cruiser stern, two masts and two funnels. The latter feature gave increased deck space for games and promenading, and more interior passenger accommodation. Like the *Queen Mary*, the new ship's first class was designated cabin class, her second class was tourist class, while the third class remained the same, and she had berths for 440, 450 and 470 passengers respectively.

There were ten passenger decks which included a sports deck and sun deck and a large number of sheltered promenades. For cabin passengers there was an observation lounge, smok-

ing room, writing room and library, a children's room, gymnasium and a verandah café. The tourist and third class facilities were both well appointed, and included a ballroom and cinema space. Much of the interior decoration was by leading British artists and perhaps one of the most striking designs was by Mr C. Baillie, who created a carving 13 feet (4m) long for the cabin class restaurant featuring the North Atlantic bridged by the two *Mauretanias*. It also depicted St Paul's Cathedral with a London silhouette and a group of New York skyscrapers dominated by the Empire State Building.

The first *Mauretania* was also recalled in the glass panels of the restaurant, where constellations of stars engraved into the glass showed the date of the old ship's launch, her maiden voyage and her final sailing from New York. The grand hall on the main deck was the centre of entertainment for the cabin class passengers and the room was dominated by a series of panels in red, black and gold lacquer work. It was designed by Mr C. Gerrad and the theme was the birth of speed, with the panels showing groups of antelope in various phases of life. In view of *Mauretania*'s proposed association with the port of London, there was also a large painting by Mr H. Davis-Richter of the Tower of London. Down below in the machinery spaces the *Mauretania* was powered conventionally by two sets of single reduction geared turbines, with the steam being provided at 465 psi by six oil-fired boilers. The whole developed 8,373 NHP and gave the ship a speed of 23 knots.

At 7 am on Sunday 14 May, in that fateful year of 1939, the *Mauretania* entered the Mersey from the fitting-out berth and an hour later was nosing her way into the Gladstone Graving Dock on the Liverpool side of the river. Once there the underwater hull was painted and her 50-ton rudder was fitted, after which she left for the Clyde and her acceptance trials on 31 May. She underwent her speed trials off Arran on 2 June and cruised off the Irish coast for other tests to be carried out. Her first master was Captain A.T. Brown, the last commander of the old *Mauretania*. After successfully completing her

trials, the new vessel returned to Liverpool on Saturday 3 June, with her trials having been described as 'highly satisfactory'.

She sailed on her maiden voyage from Liverpool to New York on Saturday 17 June 1939, but ahead of her she had only two full months of peacetime service. She arrived in New York for the first time at 8.30 am on 24 June and thousands of commuters from New Jersey had a chance to greet her. After a stay of a week in the USA, she returned to Southampton, and made her second voyage to New York on 19 July. This time her return passage to England took her first to Southampton, then on to Le Havre and London where she berthed in King George V Dock in the Thames for the first time on the evening of Sunday 6 August. *Mauretania* left the Thames on Friday 11 August for her final pre-war westbound crossing which took her to Southampton–Cobh and New York. She left for England once again just nine days before Britain declared war on Germany. She was to make one more voyage for Cunard to the United States, but this time her passengers were mainly US citizens returning home. Then, when she returned to Liverpool she was taken on hire by the Government and was defensively armed with two six-inch guns and various smaller calibre weapons. She was painted battleship grey, and at the end of December she was sent to the United States until a role could be found for her.

On her arrival in New York she tied up close to the *Queen Mary*, and for the next three months the two ships lay idle in the port. In London it was decided that the *Mauretania* and both the *Queens* would be used as troop transports, and the conversion work was to be done in Sydney, Australia. At 8 pm on Wednesday 20 March 1940, a dark stormy night, the *Mauretania* left New York Harbour. She was completely hidden at times by the driving rain and thunderstorms, but this was good for security and her departure went almost unnoticed. At the time her destination was a well-kept secret, so when she arrived at Cristobal five days later the US press speculated on her future. In fact, all assumptions were accurate, that she was bound for Australia. As she transited the Panama Canal, security was tight and fighters of the USAF patrolled the skies. After passing through the Canal, *Mauretania* steamed north to San Francisco where most of her luxury furniture was removed and put into storage. She then sailed via Honolulu to Sydney where she was taken over by the Cockatoo Dockyard Company for full conversion to a troop transport. During April of that year she remained in dockyard hands and in early May she left Sydney in company with the *Queen Mary*, *Aquitania*, *Andes* and Canadian Pacific liners, with 2,000 troops of the AIF bound for the Clyde. The convoy sailed via Cape Town, and as they crossed the Bay of Biscay the evacuation of Allied forces in France was nearing its end, and the surrender of that country only days away.

During the early years of the war the *Mauretania* transported mainly Australian troops to Suez, India and Singapore, but after the entry of the USA into the war she was employed chiefly on the North Atlantic. On 8 January 1944 she was involved in a collision with an American tanker, the *Hat Creek*, in New York Harbour. Her voyage with US troops was cancelled, but within 24 hours she had been repaired and was at sea again. After the end of the war in Europe she went to Australia via Panama and returned by the same route, calling at Cape Town and other African ports. She arrived back in Liverpool on 24 September 1945 to a warm welcome, for she had on board 4,000 servicemen together with 1,000 civilian passengers, all of whom had been abroad for a number of years.

Mauretania had been away from England for 81 days and she had steamed 28,662 miles. In the following month she left for Bombay and returned to Liverpool with 6,000 service personnel on 25 November 1945, having steamed from

Top right The Mauretania *was the largest ship ever to navigate the Thames and use the Royal Docks.* (Museum in Docklands)

Right The Mauretania *in the King George V Dock, London.* (Museum in Docklands)

Bombay in 11 days. Following this she made a number of voyages to Canada with troops returning home, before steaming east once more, this time to Singapore via Port Said and Trincomalee. She returned home to Liverpool in record time on 2 August 1946 with 5,000 service personnel, despite having to assist an Italian tug and experiencing a slow passage through the Suez Canal. Following this voyage the *Maureta-*

Left *The* Mauretania *on war work, packed with troops outward bound from the Clyde.* (Imperial War Museum)

Below *25 November 1942 — the* Mauretania *at Liverpool with 6,000 troops from the Far East.* (Imperial War Museum)

In her peacetime livery once again, a fine aerial view. (Skyfotos Ltd)

nia made only one more for the Government, and this was a further trip to Halifax NS. One of her passengers was Lord Montgomery, the Chief of the Imperial General Staff, who was visiting the USA at the personal invitation of General Eisenhower. The *Mauretania* returned to Liverpool on Monday 2 September and was released from Government service. Later that day she entered the Gladstone Dock at Liverpool for reconditioning by Cammell Laird & Co.

The work of refurbishing the *Mauretania* took seven months and it cost £1 million. More than 75 per cent of her furniture and fittings had to be returned from Australia and the USA, and 300 of her cabins were rebuilt. During this refit her after funnel was temporarily removed in order to install some air-conditioning machinery and her crew quarters were improved at the cost of 100 tourist class cabins. Her three passenger classes were redesignated as first, cabin and tourist class. On Saturday 19 April 1947 she was moved from the Gladstone Dock to the Princes Landing Stage to embark 400 guests for her trials off Arran. These were successful and she returned to Liverpool two days later, but gales kept her waiting outside the port for another three days.

Mauretania's first post-war Atlantic crossing to New York for Cunard was on 26 April 1947 from Liverpool. That port was also the starting point of her second voyage in the following month, but thereafter she was based at Southampton. Following her overhaul in December 1947 she spent the winter months cruising from New York to the West Indies and Caribbean ports on 'dollar-earning cruises' to assist the shattered British economy. On these cruises she carried only 750 passengers in one class, and she was always fully booked.

For the next ten years the *Mauretania* was employed on the Atlantic during the summer and on cruises from New York in the winter. In December 1957 she underwent her annual overhaul at Liverpool and the opportunity was taken to fit the entire 18-year-old ship with air-conditioning. This cost £500,000 and meant installing over two miles of piping, but it was considered necessary in response to the demand from US cruise passengers. Following this refit she left for New York in mid-January 1958 for a series of cruises to the West Indies.

However, after four more years the now 23 year-old liner was facing competition from much more modern ships both on the Atlantic and on her cruising programme, and by 1962 she was losing money for her owners. In October of that year she was painted in Cunard's pale green

In October 1962 the Mauretania *was painted in Cunard's pale green in an attempt to boost trade with cruises.* (E.H. Cole)

livery before she embarked on her cruising season. In the following year she started a new Mediterranean–New York service, but this was a failure and by 1964 she was employed mainly cruising from New York to the West Indies.

Mauretania's final voyage was a 56-day Mediterranean cruise, leaving New York in September 1965. Just three weeks later it was announced in Liverpool that upon her return to Southampton on 10 November, she was to be withdrawn from service and offered for sale. It was a further move to streamline the company's passenger operations, which included £1 million conversions of *Carmania* and *Franconia*, to fit them out for cruising, and the air-conditioning to the *Queen Elizabeth*.

The *Mauretania* arrived in 46 berth at

Southampton Docks on Wednesday 10 November 1965 and berthed opposite the *Queen Mary*. In fact, she had already been sold to the British Iron & Steel Corporation, and on Tuesday 23 November she arrived at Ward's shipbreaking yard in Inverkeithing, Fife. She was commanded for this final voyage by Captain John Treasure-Jones, who navigated the mud straits from the Forth without tugs, and with only a few feet to spare.

Technical data

Gross tonnage	35,739
Net tonnage	20,170
Length overall	771 ft 6 in (235.15m)
Breadth	89 ft 4 in (27.23m)

Twin screw, powered by two sets of single reduction geared turbines; 42,000 SHP, 23 knots.

26
Queen Elizabeth, 1940

It had always been Cunard's intention to build two new superliners for its express service to New York, and no sooner had the *Queen Mary* left the builder's yard than Sir Percy Bates was negotiating Government assistance for the second great ship. In a letter to Neville Chamberlain, the Chancellor of the Exchequer, dated 13 May 1936, he set out the company's case for the vessel. One of his main points was that 1940 would be the earliest date by which a big new mail ship could be put into service, and by then the *Aquitania* and *Berengaria* would be struggling to survive alongside the *Queen Mary*. Sir Percy was confident that if he could go ahead quickly with the new ship, it would not obstruct the increasing naval shipbuilding programme. As a result of the negotiations, the Treasury agreed to advance £5 million to Cunard, and tenders went out for the contract. In the event it was decided that the ship would be built by John Brown & Co on the Clyde, which was an indication of how satisfied Cunard was with the *Queen Mary*.

The formal contract for what was now known as job 535 was signed on 6 October 1936. The first of the keel plates for the 83,000 gross ton vessel was laid on the 1,000 foot slipway on which the *Queen Mary* had been built, and the launch date was set for September 1938. This time there was no secret about the name of the ship; she was to be named *Queen Elizabeth* and her sponsor was to be Her Majesty the Queen.

The new vessel, with only two funnels and with none of the clutter of ventilators on her decks, would have a much sleeker look than her older sister. Another space-saving idea was the use of only 12 boilers, as opposed to 24 in the *Queen Mary*. Like the older ship she was to be a quadruple-screw ship driven by four sets of single reduction geared turbines, each developing 40,000 SHP and giving a speed of 29 knots. As the date for the launch drew near, the political situation in Europe deteriorated, with Hitler claiming the Sudetenland area of Czechoslovakia. The dispute came to a head in September 1938 with Hitler threatening to invade the country, and it appeared that war with Germany was imminent as the British and French Governments tried to negotiate with him.

The actual date for the launch of the *Queen Elizabeth* was set for Tuesday 27 September 1938, and originally both King George VI and Queen Elizabeth were to have attended. However, with the crisis over Czechoslovakia at a very delicate stage, and with Neville Chamberlain, now the Prime Minister, about to fly to Munich to meet Hitler, the King had to cancel his attendance at the launching ceremony in order to stay close to the political leaders in London. To match the gloomy international crisis, the weather that day was wet and miserable. Her Majesty, together with her two daughters, arrived at the shipyard at 3 pm that day, and after the speeches there was a pause in the proceedings to await the high tide. This short interval was occupied by the presentation to the Queen of an album containing photographs of the vessel at various stages of construction. The pause was, however, cut short when the vessel started to move on the slipway. For a moment the Queen was taken by surprise, but she quickly recovered and released the bottle of wine which broke against the ship's stem as she said, 'I name this ship *Queen Elizabeth* and wish success to her and all who sail in her.' Then, as the vessel continued down the ways, she was greeted by the cheers of at least 250,000 spectators and the deafening noise of steam whistles from all the craft in the river.

As the *Queen Elizabeth* lay at her fitting-out berth, with her completion due in the spring of 1940, the political scene in Europe seemed to brighten and advance bookings were taken for the maiden voyage on 24 April 1940. Unfortunately the respite provided by the humiliating Munich Agreement was only brief, and on 3 September 1939 war came again to Europe. On the Clyde the *Queen Elizabeth*'s hull and funnels were resplendent in Cunard's colours, but

The Queen Elizabeth's *maiden voyage to New York in March 1940. Coastal Command watched her for the initial part of her dash across the Atlantic.* (Imperial War Museum)

within weeks she had been painted grey all over and the plans for her maiden voyage were cancelled. Over the next few months the presence of the vessel on the Clyde was both a risk and an inconvenience, the former being that German bombers might damage or destroy her, and latter arising because the fitting-out berth was required for urgent warship construction.

By the end of 1939 the engines had been tested, and she was being prepared for war service. Degaussing cables were fitted to the hull and all her ports were blacked out. Although the work was far from complete, in February 1940 Cunard was ordered to move the *Queen Elizabeth* as soon as possible, and the only totally safe ports were in the United States of America. The crew joined the ship in late February 1940, and soon after this she was moved to an anchorage off Gourock. On 27 February she was handed over to the Cunard company, and five days later she left the Clyde for a lone dash across the Atlantic to New York. She was under the command of Captain J.C. Townley, and her ship's company had no idea of their destination until they were well out to sea. The interior of the ship was still not finished with loose wiring in the alleyways, and no heating or carpets.

She arrived off Fire Island at 7 am on Thursday 7 March 1940, and press reporters were able

to get some dramatic photographs of her as they flew over in light aircraft. Although tight security had surrounded her voyage, by the time she arrived in New York's Upper Harbour later that day thousands of people had gathered at all the vantage points to see the 'grey Queen' go alongside her pier. In order to accommodate her at Pier 90, the Mauretania had been moved and, despite the exigencies of her rushed voyage, she received an enthusiastic welcome in the city and the newspapers were full of photographs of her. Strict security was in force on the pier, however, and on the nearby Westside Highway the police ensured that cars were kept moving. For the next two weeks four of the world's great liners lay tied up in New York with no real role to play in the war in Europe. Then later that month both the Mauretania and Queen Mary left for Sydney, leaving the Normandie and Queen Elizabeth behind. During her stay in New York the task of completing her fitting-out was continued.

The Queen Elizabeth remained in New York for eight months until 13 November 1940, when she sailed by way of Cape Town to Singapore. There were still 12 months of peace left before war would erupt in the Far East, and the naval base on the island would become untenable. During her refit in the graving dock in Singapore she had defensive armament fitted, her hull was painted black and her superstructure was repainted grey. Internally she was fitted out to carry troops, for by now she had been requisitioned by the Ministry of War Transport. She left Singapore on 11 February 1941, exactly a year before Japanese troops occupied the naval base, and steamed south for Fremantle and then Sydney where she arrived on 21 February. Once again thousands of people turned out to greet her, and for the next few weeks, while the Cockatoo Dockyard Company completed the fitting out of her troop accommodation, she was a source of great interest to the people of the city.

Right and above right The Queen Elizabeth refitting at Singapore in May 1941, just seven months before war broke out in the Far East. (Imperial War Museum)

There followed a trooping voyage to the Middle East in April 1941, and then she returned to the naval base on the north shore of Singapore Island for a refit in the drydock there. After this she spent five months on trooping voyages between Sydney and Suez, making the last one in October and November 1941 and returning to Sydney with German POWs.

Following the entry of the United States into the war, the *Queen Elizabeth* crossed the Pacific for docking at Esquimalt, and then she embarked US troops for Sydney, crossing a now extremely hostile Pacific Ocean once again. At about this time there was much thought within the Admiralty about the future of both the *Queens*, and there was a plan drawn up at the request of the Fifth Sea Lord to convert the *Queen Elizabeth* into an aircraft carrier. Plans of the ship in top secret report dated 25 April 1942, headed 'Monster Liners as Aircraft Carriers', show her two funnels combined into one

Embarking German POWs in the Middle East, July 1942. (Imperial War Museum)

towards the forward end of the flight deck. It was proposed that aircraft would take off forward, and that this arrangement would allow sufficient length abaft the funnel to provide a satisfactory landing on deck. The vessel would have carried between 60 and 80 aircraft and the possible functions of the converted ship were given as:

1) Bomb Japan, a/c landing in China.
2) Bomb Singapore, a/c landing in Australia.
3) Reinforce areas with large numbers of fighters/light bombers.
4) Support of combined operations.

After reading the plans it was decided that, as the *Queens* were playing such an important role in the movement of troops, they would be retained in this capacity. In September 1942 the plans were reconsidered, and this time more seriously, but in the event they were abandoned and nothing ever came of them.

The *Queen Elizabeth* finally left Sydney on 19 April 1942 and set course for Fremantle, Cape Town, Rio de Janeiro and New York, where her troop accommodation was altered to carry an additional 2,000, giving her a capacity to carry 10,000 soldiers. In June she made her first trooping voyage from New York to Gourock, before heading south for Cape Town and Suez with British regiments and returning to New York via Cape Town and Rio de Janeiro. It was whilst the vessel was at Simonstown on 2 August 1942 that two of the German prisoners, Bernhart Thickes and Willie Kalz, climbed through a port on 'B' deck and attempted to swim ashore at about 11.30 pm. The alarm was raised and the former was picked up by the ship's sea boat and brought back on board, but the latter was last seen swimming strongly for the shore before he disappeared and it was assumed that he drowned.

Following her arrival in New York at the end of August 1942, the *Queen Elizabeth* started her shuttle service between that port and Gourock in conjunction with the *Queen Mary*. Together the two ships could convey many thousands of US troops to Europe, and it is accepted that between them the two vessels shortened the war with their huge troop-carrying capacities. These

Date and Hour of the Occurrence.	Place of the Occurrence, or situation by Latitude and Longitude at Sea.	Date of Entry.	Entries required by Act of Parliament.	Amount of Fine or Forfeiture inflicted.
11: 30 pm 2nd August		4th August	At some time between eleven p.m. and midnight two German prisoners of War, named Bernhart Thicker and Willi Katz, climbed through a port on B deck and attempted to swim ashore. Bernhart Thicker was picked up by the ship's sea boat and brought back on board; but Willi Katz was last seen swimming strongly for the shore. He then disappeared, and it is assumed that he was drowned. J.V. Robinson, Sm. officer.	
11. 15 am 2nd August		4th August	For dancing with a female passenger on the	

The Queen Elizabeth's *official log showing the record of the German POWs' attempt to escape.* (Dept of Transport)

short Atlantic voyages were not without incident, and perhaps the saddest cases were amongst the wounded and invalid troops being transported home on the westbound voyages. On 13 September 1942 a mentally disturbed trooper of the 1st Armoured Canadian Regiment managed to evade his guards and jump through a window on the port side of the promenade deck. On 8 November, a captain of the Canadian Army, who was suffering from anxiety neurosis, also jumped overboard. With the ship travelling at full speed, and under orders not to stop or slow down for any reason at all, there was little anyone could to to rescue them and they were listed as 'presumed drowned'.

There was also of course the ever-present danger of submarines, and in fact on 11 November 1942 a report in the German press stated, 'In the North Atlantic a U-boat scored a torpedo hit on a British battleship of the *Queen Elizabeth* class. A violent explosion was observed.' Then the following day the initial report was ammended thus: 'The enemy vessel which was reported in yesterday's announcement as having been sunk by a U-boat attack in the North Atlantic was not a battleship of the *Queen Elizabeth* class but a passenger liner.' What had happened was that on 9 November a U-boat had fired torpedoes at the *Queen Elizabeth* when she was westbound and only a day out of Greenock. The U-boat commander had presumably heard an explosion caused by the self-destructive mechanism of a torpedo, and was convinced he had hit the *Queen Elizabeth*. On board the liner they were obviously unaware of the explosion or the U-boat, for there is no reference to it in the ship's log. The evidence to refute the press report was clear to see when the liner arrived in New York a few days later.

Another type of passengers carried when the ship was westbound were German POWs, and members of the ship's company were not allowed to fraternize with them. On one voyage one of the vessel's telephone operators was caught several times attempting to sell items from the ship's stores, and on each occasion he was fined 10s (50p), a heavy penalty in those days.

By the end of the war in Europe, the *Queen Elizabeth* and the *Queen Mary* had transported

The ship's staff on board, April 1945. (Imperial War Museum)

thousands of troops to Europe and between them they had brought over a million men to the war zone. Now it was time to start the task of repatriating those men for redeployment in the war against Japan. In fact, for this immense task some 370 vessels were needed, headed by the two *Queens*. Of course Sir John Brocklebank, the company Chairman, was eager to get his ships back onto the transatlantic service in order not to lag behind his competitors. On 20 August 1945 the *Queen Elizabeth* arrived at her home port of Southampton for the first time, and she was given an enthusiastic welcome by large crowds, as well as a civic reception. A week later she left the port with 15,000 US troops on board, most of whom were men of the 8th Air Force.

In October 1945 she returned from Halifax NS with over 1,100 repatriated British POWs, including survivors of four British merchant ships sunk by the raider *Thor* in 1942. Later that month, after negotiations between the Ministry of War Transport and the War Department in Washington, when Britain requested the return of the *Queen Elizabeth* and the *Aquitania*, they were released from US service and were allocated to the repatriation of Canadian troops. This resulted in a great deal of press publicity alleging that the move was in retaliation for the cancellation of lend-lease by the US Government. For the next few months the *Queen Elizabeth* conveyed Canadian and US troops across the Atlantic on their way home, and on 6 March 1946 she arrived in Southampton at the end of her war service; the need for troop movements had diminished, so she was released by the Government. During the war she had carried over 750,000 troops and had steamed 500,000 miles.

Her overhaul and refurbishment was to be carried out in two stages, the first part on the Clyde and the second at Southampton. However, shortly after her arrival in Southampton, at 9 am on Friday 9 March 1946, a fire was discovered in a small isolation hospital on the promenade deck. Fortunately it was spotted early and the docks and city fire brigades were able to avert a disaster, although considerable damage was caused to that compartment and to the deck plating. Only eight days previously the *Empire Waveney* had been gutted by fire, and arson was strongly suspected in the case of *Queen Elizabeth*, although it was never proved. At the end of March she left for the Clyde where, anchored off Gourock, she was painted in Cunard livery and her machinery was overhauled. On 17 June she arrived back in Southampton where the work began to replace her internal furnishings, which had been brought from storage in the USA and Australia. More than 1,000 John Brown employees travelled south to work on the ship and they were accommodated at Velmore Camp, Chandlers Ford. In early August it was announced that the *Queen Elizabeth* would make her first passenger voyage to New York on 16 October 1946, and by the beginning of that month she was ready to undergo her trials on the Clyde.

Originally it had been intended that the first class accommodation would be designated as cabin class and the second class as tourist, but in line with Cunard's post-war policy *Queen Elizabeth* had accommodation for 823 first, 670 cabin and 800 tourist class passengers. The first class section, which was mainly amidships, was

In her peacetime role at last — the Queen Elizabeth *in Cunard colours.* (R.J. Inness/Public Archives of Canada)

on the sun, sports, promenade, main, 'A', 'B', 'C' and 'D' Decks. Most of the public rooms were on the promenade deck, the focus of interest being the lounge which opened directly from the main entrance foyer where shops catered for the passengers' every need. There was also a cocktail lounge and a writing room and library. Other features were the smoking room and ballroom, and there was a verandah grill which provided an attractive setting for evening festivities. By reducing the space occupied by funnel casings, a large theatre for stage or cinema shows was able to be constructed, and section on each side of the promenade deck was arranged as a garden lounge. The cabin class passengers were provided with a lounge, smoking room, drawing room and cocktail bar and the tourist passengers had the use of a lounge, smoking room and winter garden. At the forward end of the Sports Deck was a tourist class open promenade and sun lounge, which was a new location for this class of passenger.

The *Queen Elizabeth* arrived in the Clyde for her trials on 7 October 1946, and the following day she was visited by her sponsor Her Majesty the Queen, who was accompanied by the Princesses Elizabeth and Margaret. On this occasion the two princesses donned overalls and visited the engine room. Whilst the royal party was on board, the vessel underwent speed trials and at

one stage the Queen took the wheel of the great ship. On 9 October the vessel left for Southampton to prepare for her first passenger voyage. In fact, the *Queen Elizabeth* was the first British passenger ship to inaugurate the post-war transatlantic passenger service.

At 2 pm promptly on Wednesday 16 October 1946, and dressed overall, she sailed from South-

Left *The first class lounge.* (Author's collection)

Below left *The first class lounge.* (Author's collection)

Bottom left *The first class restaurant.* (Author's collection)

Below *The first class verandah grill.* (Author's collection)

Bottom *The first class observation lounge and cocktail bar.* (Author's collection)

Above *The first class smoking room.* (Author's collection)

Above right *The cabin class smoking room.* (Author's collection)

Right *The cabin class lounge.* (Author's collection)

Below right *The tourist class lounge.* (Author's collection)

Bottom right *The tourist winter garden.* (Author's collection)

ampton for New York. She was cheered by crowds at all the vantage points, and off Ryde Pier she exchanged signals with her namesake, the battleship HMS *Queen Elizabeth*. Among her passengers was Mr Molotov, the Soviet Foreign Minister, and on her arrival in the American port she received a tremendous welcome. Over the subsequent months she was always fully booked, with many film stars and politicians among her passengers, and as a result her arrivals and departures were frequently in the news.

On 14 April 1947 she was inbound to Southampton in fog when she ran aground on the Brambles Bank. There was no impact but the ship appeared to be stuck fast and all the passengers and baggage were disembarked. Once the bulk of the fuel had been pumped out, at 8.40 pm on 15 April the ship was refloated, but because of the fog she was unable to go alongside the following day. Although no damage was done, her schedule was delayed by 24 hours and it was some weeks before this was made up. On 25 July, while she was outward bound to New York in the Solent, she passed the *Queen Mary* which had just undergone her post-war refit and trials. It was the first time the two ships had met

The Queen Elizabeth *at Southampton.* (J.K. Byass)

in peacetime and at last they were able to run together on the Atlantic, seven years after they had been schedule to do so.

In late 1948 the *Queen Elizabeth*'s sailings were disrupted by industrial troubles, although not all of these came from within the company. A strike of New York dockers delayed the ship's sailing from Southampton, and when Cunard announced her destination as Halifax NS a large proportion of her crew walked off. Cunard gave in to the strikers, but the ship was delayed for 14 days before she finally left for New York. In September 1951, the *Queen Elizabeth* made her 100th Atlantic crossing since October 1946. She had proved to be a success but she had not broken any speed records and in this respect she would always be outshone by the *Queen Mary*. In June 1952 she made a crossing at an average speed of 29.29 knots, but two months later the *United States* took the record once and for all, because ten years later it would become irrelevant.

In January 1952, during the *Queen Elizabeth*'s annual overhaul at Southampton, her fuel capacity was increased by utilizing feed water tanks, and the air-conditioning was extended to some cabin class cabins. During the refit some mysterious fires broke out in passenger cabins which,

although they did not cause serious damage, were thought to be the result of arson, although once again investigations were unable to prove this. In January 1955 the *Queen Elizabeth* was fitted with Denny Brown stabilizers, becoming the largest ship to be so fitted. However, whatever improvements were made to the passenger liners they would be unable to compete with air travel, and in the late 1950s and early 1960s there were more people crossing the Atlantic by air than by sea. Added to the falling passenger lists were problems caused by industrial trouble which led to unacceptable delays.

At 3.30 pm on Wednesday 29 July 1959, when the *Queen Elizabeth* was outward bound from New York, she was in collision with the inbound United States Lines cargo ship, *American Hunter*. Both ships were between buoys 17 and 18 in the Ambrose Channel when thick fog closed in. The closest ship on the *Queen Elizabeth*'s radar screen was four cables away and both vessels were moving slowly, then suddenly the *American Hunter* appeared out of the fog at right angles to the *Queen Elizabeth* and collided with her starboard bow. By chance all the passengers were at lifeboat drills and they remained at their stations until tugs towed the *Queen* back to her berth. Fortunately damage was confined to the

The Queen Elizabeth *in the Channel in a choppy sea.* (Skyfotos Ltd)

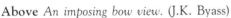

Above *An imposing bow view.* (J.K. Byass)

Right, above right and top right *Berthing at Ocean Terminal.* (Wayne Morris and J.K. Byass)

Queen Elizabeth's starboard hawse pipe and the damage to the cargo vessel was slight. Temporary repairs were quickly made and the *Queen Elizabeth* left the port the next day.

On Sunday 25 September 1960, three cabins on 'A' Deck were damaged by fire following an electrical fault in the switchboard. The vessel was in the Western Approaches bound for Southampton, and with the aid of the automatic sprinklers the crew soon put the fire out.

In May 1962, with passenger lists continually decreasing, and with her accommodation sometimes only 25 per cent full, it was announced that the *Queen Elizabeth* would cruise for the first time early the following year. This was a desperate measure, for with her heavy operating costs it was doubtful whether she could cruise economically. The cruise programme started in New York in February 1963 and consisted of three to five days to Nassau with a reduced passenger capacity of 2,200. The minimum fare was £66 and an extensive entertainment was included. During one of these cruises, when the vessel was 90 miles south-east of Cape Hatteras, a light aircraft crashed into the sea only a few hundred yards from her stern. The pilot was killed and there was little that could be done other than notify the coastguard.

In January 1965 the *Queen Elizabeth* went aground for about 40 minutes at Cherbourg, but she was freed by tugs on the rising tide and her sailings were not affected. Two months later Cunard announced that it was going to spend £1,500,000 on a major overhaul of the vessel so that she would be a worthy running mate for

the proposed new *Queen*, the so-called *Q4* when she entered service in 1968. The whole ship was to be extensively redecorated and more cabins were to be fitted with private facilities. In addition, an open-air swimming pool would be installed and it was thought that the improvements would enable her to remain in service for another ten years. The work was done at Greenock in a new drydock which had to be specially lengthened to accommodate the vessel. The refit was completed in the spring of 1966, but in May and June of that year a seamen's strike brought the British Merchant Marine to a halt for some seven weeks. The stoppage was to cause far-reaching and serious repercussions, and there is no doubt that it was partly responsible for the early demise of the *Queen Elizabeth*. During the strike the port of Southampton was a splendid sight for shiplovers, with the cream of Britain's merchant fleet laid up, including the *Queen Elizabeth* at berth 106, astern of the *Vaal*.

By this time there had been a change of management at Cunard, and Sir Basil Smallpiece was now at the helm. He was determined to take any measures, however drastic, to make the company profitable. On 8 May 1967 he announced that, not only was the *Queen Mary* going to be withdrawn that year (which was not unex-

The Queen Elizabeth *cruising at Madeira.* (M. Beckett)

pected), but that the *Queen Elizabeth* would follow in the autumn of 1968. The deciding factor had been that, despite the expensive refit, the *Queen Elizabeth* was still running at a heavy loss and there was no prospect of this changing. The seamen's strike, too, had had a major effect, for this had lost Cunard some £14 million.

Speculation as to the ship's future was rife, and when the *Queen Elizabeth* was sold to a group of Philadelphia businessmen for £3,230,000 it was thought that she would end her days in a similar manner to the *Queen Mary*. However, the plans seemed to go wrong from the start and her proposed venue was changed from the Delaware River to Fort Lauderdale in Florida. The great liner completed her final Atlantic crossing on 5 November 1968, and on the following day Her Majesty Queen Elizabeth the Queen Mother visited the ship to say goodbye. The *Queen Elizabeth* made a short farewell cruise that month, before leaving Southampton for the last time on Friday 29 November.

She opened to the public at Port Everglades in February 1969, but by the end of that year the business was in trouble. She had been closed

by the local authorities as a fire hazard and she was losing money just as she had on the Atlantic. In September 1970 her owners filed a bankruptcy petition (with Cunard amongst the creditors), and the vessel was auctioned. She was purchased for $3.2 million by the C.Y. Tung shipping group of Hong Kong and it was intended that she become a floating university. Her owning company was registered as the Island Navigation Corporation of Panama, and the *Queen Elizabeth* was renamed *Seawise University* (a play on her new owner's name, 'C.Y.'s University').

She left Port Everglades to steam to Hong Kong on 10 February 1971, looking battered and rusty with her new name painted on her bows and stern, but she left under her own steam with her last master, Commodore Geoffrey Marr, on the bridge, and it seemed that the former Atlantic giant had been given a new lease of life. However, the voyage was plagued by machinery troubles and it was not long before she was taken in tow. She finally arrived in the colony in mid-July 1971, and anchored off Tsing Yi Island near Kowloon. Work started on a £5 million refit to convert her into a university, and by January 1972 the work had almost been completed and she was waiting to start her new role.

Security on board was lax, and although some

The Seawise University *at Cape Town.* (Robert Pabst)

crewmen were making fire patrols, this was secondary to other duties. During the night of 9 January a series of fires were discovered in various parts of the ship and these soon spread to form a single conflagration. The vessel burned for more than 24 hours, and throughout the night the ship glowed red as she became a gigantic furnace. There was only one serious injury among the 500 workmen on board, and at 2.30 pm local time she rolled over into the water on her starboard side, still burning. The hulk burned and smouldered for over a week before it finally burned itself out, and it was clear that the old ship was fit only for scrap.

In July 1972 an Inquiry found that the fires had been the work of an arsonist, but the culprit was never found. In December 1973 the owners decided to scrap the hulk on the spot and work began soon afterwards. But the former Cunard liner could still cause mischief despite her destruction. On 5 November 1975, as the wreck was being broken up, it suddenly rolled from a 48-degree list to 34 degrees and at the same time disgorged several tons of fuel oil which polluted the surrounding waters and beaches. It was her last protest against all the humiliations that had been heaped upon the once proud ship.

Top *A sorry sight — the* Seawise University *still smoulders after the disastrous fire in Hong Kong Harbour in January 1972. (Hong Kong Government Information Service)*

Above *The remains of the* Seawise University *as the scrap men demolish the wreck. (James L. Shaw)*

Technical data	
Gross tonnage	83,673
Net tonnage	42,011
Length overall	1,030 ft (313.94m)
Breadth	118 ft 6 in (36.12m)
Quadruple screw, powered by four sets of single reduction geared turbines; 160,000 SHP, 29 knots.	

27
Media and Parthia, 1947-48

These two small vessels had the distinction of being the first passenger ships to enter service for Cunard in their post-war building programme. Their careers with the Cunard Line were cut short by a combination of competition from airlines and industrial trouble, but the *Media* went on to a successful period of service as a cruise ship. She was the first of the two sisters, built by John Brown & Co at Clydebank and launched on Thursday 12 December 1946 by Mrs A. Barnes, the wife of the Minister of Transport. The *Parthia* was built by Harland & Wolff at Belfast and she was launched two months later on Tuesday 25 February 1947 by Lady Brooke, the wife of Northern Ireland's Prime Minister.

Both ships had a gross tonnage of just over 13,000, and were twin screw vessels powered by two sets of double-reduction geared turbines which gave a speed of 17 knots. They were good-looking ships with clipper bows, single masts and midships superstructures topped by single funnels. They had accommodation for 250 passengers in one class, and capacity for 7,000 tons of cargo. The passengers were well catered for with six air-conditioned public rooms all situated on the Promenade Deck, and a spacious Sports Deck. Perhaps the most impressive area was the Smoking Room which was situated forward and had large windows which followed the curve of the bridge and allowed a fine view over the bows. The crew accommodation was also excellent, consisting mainly of two-berth or four-berth cabins.

The *Media* completed her trials and arrived on the Mersey on 13 August 1947, commanded by Captain Robert G. Thelwell and fully booked for her maiden voyage to New York, one week later. The *Parthia*, which was named after a Cunarder of 1870, then still in service as the *Victoria* in North America, made her maiden voyage on 10 April 1948. She too was fully booked and her cargo included 60 British cars being exported

The Media, *the first of the two 13,000 tonners to be built following the war.* (J.K. Byass)

The Parthia, *second of the two sisters.* (J.K. Byass)

to the USA. Between them, the ships provided two sailings a month between Liverpool and New York, and for those travellers not in any hurry they offered a leisurely voyage of seven days between the ports. In November 1950 the ship's bell from the *Parthia* of 1870 was installed in her new namesake, and 14 months later the *Media* was fitted with Denny-Brown stabilizers at John Brown's yard. In the following year the *Parthia* was also fitted with stabilizers during her winter overhaul, and both ships were more comfortable as a result.

On Saturday 22 January 1955 the *Parthia* was inward bound to Liverpool from New York, with only 32 passengers on board, when she was in collision with the 8,000 ton *Valparaiso* and the 5,000 ton *City of Worcester* in the Mersey Channel. The accident happened in thick fog and the ships were travelling slowly so there was little damage done. The *Parthia* was able to sail on schedule for her next voyage, this time with a full complement of passengers.

By the late 1950s the two ships were having difficulty attracting passengers and cargo, and their Cunard careers ended rather suddenly. In January 1961 the *Parthia* was undergoing her annual overhaul on the Mersey when a strike of boilermakers and ship-repairers stranded her in the Gladstone Graving Dock. Thirteen weeks

later, with the ship still lying in Liverpool, Cunard announced that it was negotiating the sale of the vessel. The two ships had been losing money for some time and the strike, which had cost the company £900,000, was the deciding factor. Soon after this it was decided that both ships would be sold, and in early July 1961 if was announced that the *Media* had been purchased by Cia Genovese d'Armamento of Genoa for £750,000. The new owners intended to use the vessel on their Mediterranean–Sydney emigrant service. As for the *Parthia*, the initial negotiations for her sale had broken down, and on 28 July that year she was bought by the New Zealand Shipping Co for the same price as that paid for her sister. It was thought at the time that New Zealand Shipping's parent company, P&O, were behind this move, in order to stop the Italian company buying both ships.

The *Media* was overhauled during the summer of 1961 and she resumed service on 12 August, making two voyages to New York before ending her career when she returned to Liverpool on 30 September. She was handed over to her new owners in the following month and was then taken to Genoa to be rebuilt and modernized. The work lasted for ten months and her passenger accommodation was extended to carry 1,224 in one class. She was renamed *Flavia* and her gross tonnage was increased to 15,465. When the vessel made her first voyage from Genoa to

Unrecognizable as the former Media, *the completely rebuilt* Flavia. (F.R. Sherlock)

The Parthia *became the New Zealand Co's* Remuera. (F.R. Sherlock)

Sydney in September 1962, she was totally unrecognizable as the former *Media*. Later that year she started sailing to Sydney from Bremerhaven, and in the following year from Rotterdam via Panama. By 1968 she was employed as a cruise ship, and in January 1969 she was sold to Costa Armatori SPA of Naples and based in Miami. On 17 January 1969, when she had just started cruising from the USA, she took part in the rescue of passengers from the Cunarder *Carmania*, which had grounded a mile off the west side of San Salvador island in the Bahamas. In 1982 she was sold to a Panamanian company and renamed *Flavian*, and soon after this she was laid up at Hong Kong.

The *Parthia* was handed over to the New Zealand Shipping Co in November 1961 and was sent to the Clydeside yard of Alexander Stephens & Son for refitting. Her superstructure was extended and her accommodation was altered to carry an additional 100 passengers. She

made her first voyage from London to Wellington on 1 June 1962 as the *Remuera*, and she remained on this route until 1964, when she was sold to the Eastern & Australian Steamship Company, another P&O subsidiary. Her new owners renamed her *Aramac*, and she was used on voyages between Australian ports and Japan. She was finally sold in 1969, and arrived in Kaohsiung for demolition on 22 November that year.

Technical data	
Gross tonnage	13,345 (*Media*), 13,362 (*Parthia*)
Net tonnage	7,480 (*Media*), 7,393 (*Parthia*)
Length overall	531 feet (161.84m)
Breadth	70 ft 4 in (21.44m)

Both ships twin screw, powered by two sets of double reduction geared turbines; 15,000 SHP, 17 knots.

28
Caronia, 1949

The second *Caronia*, whose keel was laid in February 1946, could probably be described as the world's first purpose-built cruise ship, and for 20 years after the Second World War she was extremely successful in this role. During her career with Cunard she had a pale green livery which earned her the nickname 'the green goddess' and she became renowned, particularly in the United States, for her world cruises.

The *Caronia* was built by John Brown & Co at Clydebank and at 34,183 gross tons she was the largest passenger ship under construction in the years immediately following the war. Financially she was not a success for the builders; with the fixed price quoted and sharply rising wage costs, they lost £250,000 on her. With her cruising role in mind, she had a yacht-like appearance, with a clipper bow, a tripod mast situated abaft the bridge and a single but enormous funnel amidships. She was also built with an open-air lido and swimming pool, and her decks were terraced aft to the stern.

She was launched on 30 October 1947 by HRH Princess Elizabeth, undertaking her last public engagement before her marriage, and the citizens of Clydeside gathered in force to cheer.

Above left *The* Caronia *fitting out at John Brown's Clydebank yard.* (Author's collection)

Left *Fitting out the first class lounge.* (Author's collection)

Just over a year later, the *Caronia* was completed and she steamed south for drydocking at Liverpool before returning to the Clyde for trials. Following her trials, which were completed on Saturday 18 December 1948, she left Gourock that evening for Southampton. On board there were 250 guests, including HRH The Duke of Edinburgh, and upon the vessel's arrival two days later she berthed alongside the elderly *Aquitania*. She was due to make her maiden voyage to New York on 4 January 1949, and on her second voyage take a southerly course calling at Bermuda before steaming north to New York. Fares for the voyage started at £52 for a cabin class berth and £82 in the first class.

The *Caronia* was a two class ship with accommodation for 581 first and 351 cabin class passengers, and the emphasis was on large cabins. There were ten passenger decks, from the sports deck down to 'F' deck, with the first class public rooms mainly on the promenade deck. These included an observation lounge overlooking the bows, a lounge, smoking room, library, writing room and theatre. Aft of this were the cabin class lounge and the staircase leading down to the smoking room and cocktail bar which were on the main deck. The two restaurants, named Balmoral and Sandringham, recalled the ship's royal associations. At the after end of the sports deck there was a verandah café for the first class passengers which overlooked the lido and swimming pool.

When cruising, the *Caronia* carried a maximum of 650 passengers, and to provide a shuttle service to ferry them ashore, six of the lifeboats were fitted with powerful 130hp diesel engines and deck shelters, which made them fast tenders. Externally the cruising role of the ship was apparent in the blending of four shades of green in the hull colours. Tests over 18 months were carried out before the shades, which besides being attractive would prove durable in varying weathers, were produced. Two ship's plates were painted in the approved shades and despatched on voyages. One was carried on the foredeck of a cargo ship and the other was exposed to the tropical sun of West Africa. The *Caronia* was a twin screw ship powered by geared turbines, and she had a speed of 22 knots.

In those austere days of rationing following the Second World War, the *Caronia*'s dollar-earning cruises were most important to Britain's economy and for this reason they could only be booked in the United States and had to be paid for in US dollars. Although she had been designed as a cruise ship, Cunard intended to employ her on the North Atlantic in the busy summer season. Following her two Atlantic voyages in the summer of 1949, she started on a series of cruises from New York to the West Indies and South America. Later that year she made an 18-day Christmas cruise and, following her first annual overhaul at Liverpool, she left New York on 12 January 1950 on an 80-day cruise. Her accommodation was fully booked and she visited the Caribbean, South Africa, East Africa and the Mediterranean. The voyage ended at Southampton on 22 March and she then participated in the transatlantic summer season.

In January 1951 she left New York on the first of her world cruises, which were later to become legendary. The itinerary took her to 30 ports

A splendid view of the 'green goddess' at Southampton. (F.R. Sherlock)

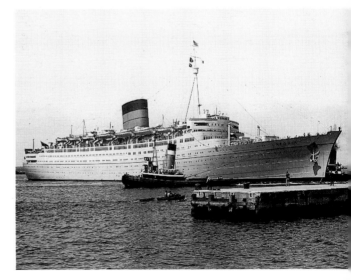

ranging from Mexico, the Pacific Islands and Australia to Malaya, India and the Mediterranean, and once again the voyage terminated at Southampton in the spring. During her transit of the Suez Canal in March, she went aground near the El Ferdan Bridge for about an hour. This caused some delay to the Canal traffic, but *Caronia* was undamaged and she completed the long cruise. Following this, during the summer of 1951, she made a 35-day cruise from New York to Europe and there is no doubt that these cruises earned much-needed dollars for the British economy.

During her annual overhaul in the Gladstone Dock in December 1952, more than 50 firemen fought a blaze in the funnel uptake. The fire was caused by soot deposits, so the clouds of thick black smoke pouring from her funnel made it look worse than it actually was. In the summer of 1953 the *Caronia* brought visitors from the USA for the Queen's Coronation ceremony and their cruise tickets included seats at vantage points on the processional route.

In June 1956, whilst *Caronia* was on a Mediterranean cruise from New York, she ran aground on a sandbank outside the port of Messina. She remained fast for almost 24 hours before tugs from Sicily managed to refloat her and she was

able to resume her voyage to Naples. During her annual overhaul at the end of 1956 a complete air-conditioning system was installed, and upon her return to New York she undertook a 180-day, 33,428-mile world cruise. She sailed out via the Atlantic and Cape Town and returned by way of Japan and the Pacific, having called at 23 ports. The following year this was repeated, but as she was leaving Tokyo Bay on 14 April she struck and demolished a light tower at the entrance to Yokohama port. She had just spent a week in Japan and was bound for Honolulu, but with underwater damage immediate repairs were necessary and the US Navy allowed her to use its Yokosuka Dockyard. There followed a lengthy legal action which resulted in Cunard paying nearly £9,000 in compensation.

In October 1959 the *Caronia* made a visit to the Soviet Union and called at Yalta on the Black Sea, recalling Cunard's association with the Yalta Conference in 1945, when the *Franconia* had visited the port. Six years later, in early November 1965, while the *Caronia* was undergoing her annual overhaul at Harland & Wolff's yard in Belfast, severe gales lashed the British Isles and during the storms the vessel broke away from her moorings and was swept to the opposite side of the channel. Fortunately she was not damaged, but when she returned to Southampton at the end of December that year she suffered a fire which caused damage to her elec-

Below and below right *Two views of the* Caronia *at Southampton.* (J.K. Byass/E.H. Cole)

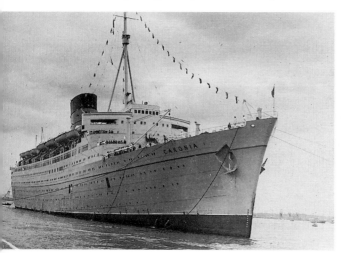

trical wiring. The incident did not, however, delay her sailing to New York a week later to start a cruise programme.

By now the *Caronia* was nearly 20 years old and alongside the new Scandinavian and Dutch cruise ships she was showing her age; this was also reflected in the falling number of passengers booking for her cruises. This problem, combined with her high overheads, meant that the *Caronia* was losing money for Cunard, and on 20 October 1967 it was announced that the *Caronia* together with the *Carinthia* and *Sylvania*, were to be withdrawn from service in early 1968. The *Caronia* actually ended her Cunard career in November 1967, sailing empty from New York on the 16th, and upon her arrival at Southampton she was laid up at 101 berth alongside the other two.

The *Caronia* was put up for sale on 4 January 1968 and two weeks later it was announced that she had been sold to a Yugoslavian company, Domus Turist of Zagreb, for £1,040,000. They intended to use the ship as a floating hotel at Dubrovnik or some other seaside resort, but it soon became clear that a suitable mooring could not be found and the transaction was never completed. Following this the vessel lay at Southampton until she was finally sold on 24 May 1968 to the American-backed Panamanian company, Star Shipping Co, for £1,250,000. She was renamed *Columbia* and left Southampton on 29 July bound for Piraeus and a refit. Whilst in Greece undergoing the overhaul, her name was changed to *Caribia* and Universal Cruise Lines, her New York sales agents, announced that a series of cruises from the port would start on 11 December of that year.

However, as the date approached it was clear that the schedule could not be kept due to a delay in the delivery of engine spares from Britain, and the cruises were rescheduled for February 1969. A further problem was encountered when the ship's boiler tubes were examined and many were found to be in need of replacement. The work was eventually completed and in January 1969 the *Caribia*, now in a white livery with gold funnel, raced across the Atlantic

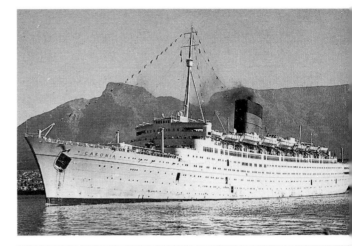

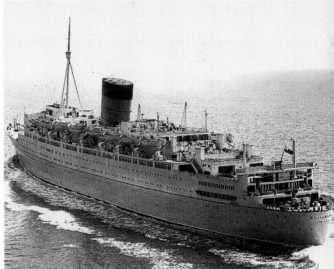

Top *The* Caronia *at Cape Town.* (A. Duncan)

Above *An aerial view of* Caronia *at sea.* (Skyfotos Ltd)

to start her cruises. However, on her arrival the ship already looked shabby; the cheap paint used was no match for the elements, and the funnel now appeared a rusty brown. Nevertheless, she left New York on 11 February on an inaugural 14-day cruise with 500 passengers on board, but upon her return to New York over 400 of the passengers signed a petition complaining of the service and conditions on board, including a foul odour which permeated the whole ship.

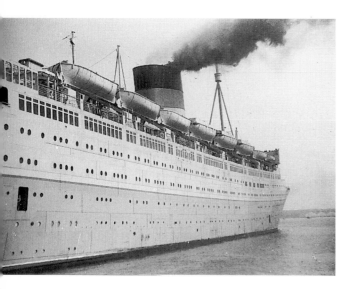

Despite this bad publicity, the *Caribia* left on a second cruise on 28 February, with 325 passengers. Five days later, shortly after she had left St Thomas, a steam pipe split spraying out superheated steam which killed one crew member and badly scalded another. The resulting fire cut all power in the ship and left the *Caribia* drifting helplessly, and according to many passengers the situation on board was chaotic. After about 20 hours, temporary repairs were made and the ship returned to St Thomas where the

Left and below *The* Colombia *(ex-Caronia) bows out — one of Southampton's best loved post-war liners, with her new funnel colours, heads down Southampton Water for the last time on 29 July 1968. (Wayne Morris)*

cruise was terminated. The remainder of her cruise programme was cancelled and the *Caribia* returned to New York where she anchored in Gravesend Bay.

Whilst the vessel lay idle, the legal claims, which included a $1.5 million writ from Cunard who held a mortgage on the ship, mounted. She was sold to a Turkish national who wanted to run the ship between New York and Nassau, but raising finance to refit her was to prove impossible. For the next five years the *Caribia* remained at New York with various legal problems over her berthing keeping her in the news. Eventually, in the spring of 1974, the vessel was sold to Taiwanese shipbreakers for over $3 million and she finally left New York on 27 April that year towed by the ocean tug *Hamburg*.

The voyage to Kaohsiung was scheduled to take 100 days, but the first problems were encountered some 1,300 miles from Honolulu when the *Caribia* took an 11-degree list. With the assistance of the US Navy this was corrected, and the tortuous journey continued. On 12 August the *Hamburg* and her charge were off Guam battling with tropical storm 'Mary'. Buffeted by winds of up to 55 knots, the *Hamburg*'s generator failed when they were only

three miles off Apra Harbour, and the tugboat's captain decided to cut the towline. As the great vessel drifted towards the breakwater, a US helicopter lifted three of the tug's crew from her decks. By early morning it seemed as if the *Caribia*, propelled by the wind and sea, was making a normal entry into Apra when she suddenly altered course and, at 9.15 am, impaled herself on the tip of the breakwater. After being subjected to a night of pounding by mountainous seas, the ship broke up on the afternoon of Wednesday 14 August, with the stern section slipping into the entrance to Guam's only seaport. It seemed that the once proud *Caronia* had decided to end all the indignities which had been heaped on her since her sale by Cunard, and make her own dramatic farewell.

Technical data	
Gross tonnage	34,274
Net tonnage	17,921
Length overall	715 feet (217.93m)
Breadth	91 ft 6 in (27.89m)
Twin screw, powered by one single and one double reduction geared turbine; 35,000 SHP, 22 knots.	

29

The 1950s Quartet

Saxonia, Ivernia, Carinthia and *Sylvania*

At the end of the Second World War, Cunard had four of the ageing vessels of the 1920s on its Canadian service, the *Franconia, Ascania, Scythia* and *Samaria*, and in 1951 it was decided to build a completely new class of ships for the Liverpool–Montreal route. Despite the fact that all the commercial indications of the day were against them, Cunard persisted in completing all four vessels, the last of which, the *Sylvania*, did not enter service until the middle of 1957. By that time in Britain, and in the USA, work was well advanced on the two jet aircraft, the Comet and the Boeing 707, and they would sound the death knell of the Atlantic ferry for Cunard and all the other shipping companies. The latter aircraft, travelling at 500 mph and carrying 130 passengers, was to be a major factor in the demise of the passenger liner.

The new ships were to be built on the Clyde by John Brown & Co. Originally it was stated that they would be 20,000 tonners, but the builder's calculations soon indicated that the figure would prove to be some 2,000 tons greater. On 25 November 1953 it was announced that the first two vessels would be called *Saxonia* and *Ivernia*, names that were welcomed by shiplovers for reviving memories of the early years of the twentieth century. In January 1954 it was announced that Lady Churchill had accepted an invitation to launch the *Saxonia* the following month, and that the *Ivernia* would be launched later in the year by Mme St Laurent, wife of the

Canadian Prime Minister.

At noon on 17 February 1954, the *Saxonia* took to the water and Lady Churchill was presented with an eighteenth-century diamond brooch as a memento. The launching went without any hitches, despite the bad weather, and *Saxonia* was then towed to the fitting-out basin. On 9 August she left the berth under her own power to be drydocked for a final inspection before she left the Clyde for Liverpool, from where she was due to sail on her maiden voyage on 2 September.

She was a handsome-looking vessel. The curved rake of her stem and the placing of the mast abaft the bridge was reminiscent of the *Caronia*, but the domed Clydebank funnel would distinguish her class from all other ships of the Cunard fleet. As they were designed for the Canadian service, it was Canadian themes which inspired much of the interior decoration. The first class Cocktail Bar was decorated with Yukon scenes, while in the first class restaurant the maple leaf appeared in murals with such symbols as the fleur des lis, the tomahawk and the bow and arrow. In the tourist Smoking Room there were designs taken from the tribal blankets of the Choctow Indians, flanked by panels of Douglas fir. Totem poles supporting a husky dog carved in perspex divided the Smoking Room from the Cocktail Bar. Other Canadian themes dominated the foyers and staircases, including a large map of the Dominion which passengers

The first of the 1950s quartet, the Saxonia. *(A. Duncan)*

could scan with specially provided opera glasses.

As the ships were being built with immigrant trade chiefly in mind, *Saxonia* had berths for 125 first class and 800 tourist passengers. It is perhaps worth mentioning that she was the first Cunard ship to be fitted with stabilizers. She undertook her trials during August 1954, and arrived in Liverpool on the 23rd of that month. She left on her maiden voyage to Quebec and Montreal ten days later, commanded by Captain Andrew McKellar and carrying a full complement of passengers. She returned to Liverpool 18 days later, on 21 September, nine hours ahead of schedule. In spite of gales she had reduced the existing record of just over five days, to four days, 23 hours, 24 minutes, an average speed of 20.74 knots. The new ship had it seemed, got off to a good start.

The second vessel of the class, the *Invernia*, was launched on Tuesday 14 December 1954 by Mrs C.D. Howe, wife of the Canadian Minister of Trade, after the original plan that she be launched by the Canadian Prime Minister's wife had been altered. Again, being winter, the weather conditions on the Clyde were bad, and there were some anxious moments as the new ship slid into the Clyde and was caught by a strong cross wind which, within minutes, slewed

her round close to the river bank; at one point her stern came within five or six feet of a store quay. It took six tugs to move her slowly but surely to the fitting-out berth.

She was due to sail on her maiden voyage from Liverpool to Quebec and Montreal on 30 June 1955, but before she could leave the first of many industrial disputes to affect the Cunard Line changed these plans. On 31 May the catering staff of the *Ascania* went on strike, and the

A magnificent view of the Ivernia, *the second of the sisters. (F.R. Sherlock)*

Top The Carinthia *was launched in December 1955.* (Maritime Photo Library)

Above The Carinthia *in the River Mersey with Princes landing stage and the Royal Liver Building in the background.* (Skyfotos Ltd)

trouble quickly spread to other Cunard ships in the Mersey. The *Saxonia* had been due to sail on 13 June but, in the event, she was some 90 crew members short. Meanwhile, 730 passengers who were waiting at the landing stage were sent home. It was another two weeks before *Saxonia* was able to sail.

On 25 June Cunard announced that the *Ivernia* would make her maiden voyage from

Greenock, and on 1 July she sailed from the Clyde with 900 passengers bound for Quebec and Montreal. So the first two ships were in service sailing to Canada, and during the winter months, when the St Lawrence became impassable, they were transferred temporarily to the Liverpool–New York route.

In December 1955 the third vessel was launched on the Clyde, as once again wind and rain swept the river. Despite the foul weather her sponsor, Princess Margaret, insisted on walking down the building berth to examine the launching mechanism. Then, to the applause of the 20,000 onlookers, she sent the *Carinthia* down the slipway to the Clyde. This time there were no problems and the ship was soon towed to the fitting-out berth. In May 1956 it was announced that Captain McKellar was to be transferred from the *Saxonia* to command *Carinthia* on her maiden voyage on 27 June. Then, at a luncheon on the new ship, Mr F.H. Dawson, the General Manager of Cunard, announced that *Saxonia* and *Ivernia* would transfer from their Liverpool base to Southampton. The *Sylvania*, yet to be launched, and the *Carinthia* would continue to be based at Liverpool.

On 23 November 1956, the last of the class was launched. It had been doubtful whether the launch would be on time as there had been serious industrial trouble at John Brown's yard. Fortunately, however, work was a month ahead of schedule, so Mrs N.A. Robertson, wife of the Canadian High Commissioner in London, was able to send the *Sylvania* down into the Clyde on time. This time the weather was much kinder than it had been on the three previous occasions. In her speech, Mrs Robertson said that she hoped 'it would not be long before Britons could visit Canada with the same ease that Canadians could visit Britain.' Happily it would not be long, but would they be travelling by sea? Some figures had been published which must have caused a certain amount of uneasiness in the Cunard boardroom.

During the years 1954 to 1956 the numbers of travellers crossing the Atlantic by sea had remained static, but the numbers of those travelling by air had been growing by at least 100,000 a year, and were poised to overtake sea travellers for the first time. The four sister ships had cost the Cunard Line £21 million, and there must have been some doubts by now as to whether it had been a wise investment.

The *Sylvania* sailed on her maiden voyage from Greenock on 5 June 1957. At last the four sisters were in service, and Cunard could proudly advertise six sailings a month to Canada. One problem encountered in the St Lawrence in the spring and autumn was ice, and in April 1959 *Carinthia* buckled one of her propellers on the ice in Montreal. A year later ice jams on Lake St Peter prevented the *Saxonia* from reaching the port. However, later in 1960, more serious problems hit the *Carinthia*. In late June there were two minor fires on board, which were easily extinguished but were obviously the work of an arsonist. Then, on 6 July a large number of her crew went on strike, and Cunard was compelled to cancel her voyage and assist the passengers on board to make other arrangements. Even a personal appeal by Captain Geoffrey Marr failed to get the men back to work. *Carinthia* was finally able to sail later that month.

Later in the year, on 20 November, it was announced that the *Sylvania* was to be transferred to the Liverpool–Cobh–New York route, to replace the last of the White Star vessels *Britannic*, which was making her final voyage. The *Sylvania* was already scheduled to run the winter route to New York via Halifax NS, and she would take over the new route in April 1961. In the meantime, the *Carinthia* was in the public eye once again. In November 1960 she had been chartered by the Canadian Government to undertake trooping voyages. These were completed on 15 December, when the last brigade of Canadian troops was disembarked at Halifax. *Carinthia* then went on the New York to embark passengers for Liverpool.

She sailed from New York on 23 December and at about 10.30 pm on Christmas Day, as a result of an incident among the crew members, the Chief Officer ordered the crew bars to be closed. As Captain Marr was trying to sort

Top *The last of the four sisters to enter service was the Sylvania of 1957.* (Maritime Photo Library)

Above *With the entry into service of the Sylvania, Cunard could proudly announce six sailings a month to Canada.* (F.R. Sherlock)

out a solution to the problem, about 40 crew members went into the tourist lounge, took seats around the dance floor and demanded to see the captain. Fortunately the Purser quickly invited the passengers to a drink in the smoke room, and Captain Marr ordered the crew out. Subsequently the ringleaders were disciplined, but this was a serious breach of regulations and it could not be excused.

The resulting publicity did nothing but harm to Cunard's reputation, and *Carinthia*'s troubles were still not over. Once she arrived in Liverpool, she went into drydock for her annual overhaul, and on 11 January 1961 the shipyard engineers went on strike. It was 18 weeks before the ship was able to sail for Montreal, but by now she had a lot of empty berths and on this voyage carried only 370 passengers. Shortly after this, on 30 August 1961, she was involved in a

Below *In 1963 the* Saxonia *was renamed* Carmania, *and was given a pale green livery for cruising.* (E.H. Cole)

Bottom *A stern view of the* Carmania *in drydock in May 1969. She had by then been given a white hull.* (Wayne Morris)

collision on the Lower St Lawrence with the 7,000 ton Canadian ship *Tadoussac*. The accident occurred in thick fog but fortunately damage to both ships was only slight.

Then, in June 1962, at a stormy meeting of shareholders, Sir John Brocklebank, Chairman of Cunard, announced company losses of £1,700,000 during the previous financial year. He assured shareholders that he was taking the best possible advice regarding the future of the fleet, and then announced that the *Saxonia* and *Ivernia* were to be reconditioned on the Clyde and fitted out for cruising. So at the end of the summer season on the North Atlantic both ships were back in the hands of John Brown on the Clyde, leaving only *Carinthia* on the Liverpool–Montreal route. Then, in September that year, it was announced that not only would the *Saxonia* and *Ivernia* be reconditioned, but they would be renamed *Carmania* and *Franconia* respectively. It was to be a fresh start for both vessels.

When the *Carmania* and *Franconia* emerged from the Clydebank yard in the spring of 1963, they looked resplendent in their distinctive cruising green livery, with the traditional Cunard funnel colours. The refit on both ships had cost the company £12 million, and most of this had been spent installing full air-conditioning and bath and toilet facilities in the tourist class cabins. The contemporary furnishings and decor gave them an appearance more of 'new ships' than just refurbished old campaigners, but perhaps the most striking feature was the large lido area aft, with its kidney-shaped swimming pool and spacious sun terrace sheltered by glass screens. Each ship could now carry 600 cruising passengers.

Sir John Brocklebank inspected the *Carmania* at Southampton on 2 April 1963, where he was 'overjoyed' to see the ship's transformation, and gave details of the new itinerary for both vessels. In the summer months they would run between Rotterdam and Montreal, and in winter would cruise from Florida to the Caribbean. So Cunard had given them new identities, but the old ideas of profit on the North Atlantic were dying hard.

Although the first few sailings from Rotterdam to Canada were well booked, the success did not last. Industrial trouble still seemed to dog the four ships, although not all of it was of their own crews' making. In October 1963 there were ugly scenes in Quebec when the *Carmania* docked there during a dock workers' strike, and a crew member received gunshot wounds during one incident. In December 1964 the dock workers in New York went on strike over the berth which *Carinthia* had been allocated, and in July 1965 a dockers' strike prevented the *Franconia* from berthing in Montreal.

In February 1967 the *Sylvania* was in the news again, although this time it was good publicity. She took part in an experiment to investigate the possibility of equipping cruise liners with hovercrafts, and an SRN-6 hovercraft was loaded on board. For three months, whilst the ship was based at Gibraltar operating fly-cruises, British Hovercraft did their best to 'sell' the machine at the ports of call by putting it through its paces.

Then, in October 1967 came a decision which shocked the shipping world. Sir Basil Smallpiece announced that three of the company's passenger ships, *Caronia* and the sisters *Carinthia* and *Sylvania*, were to be withdrawn from service. He told Cunard shareholders that the company had lost £2 million in the first six months of the year, and the two sisters were not designed for cruising. He was prepared to sell them, 'without any strings attached to the sale'. By now three of the sisters had been given white livery, while *Carinthia* retained her black hull. In December that year *Carinthia* and *Sylvania* were laid up at 101 berth in Southampton's Western Docks, and two months later, on 1 February 1968, both ships were sold to the Italian Sitmar Line, but continued to lay alongside Southampton Docks.

Meanwhile, *Franconia* and *Carmania* continued in Cunard service, and most of their time was devoted to cruising. In November 1967 *Franconia* made the last Cunard passenger voyage between Liverpool and Montreal. A month later, whilst cruising in the Mediterranean, she developed a leak in her starboard propeller gland. There was no immediate danger and her master,

Captain Phillip Reid, decided to go on to Tangier, arriving on Boxing Day. With no port facilities available, Captain Reid and an engineer, Kenneth King, dived and wrapped the propeller shaft in 13 layers of polythene and rope to make it watertight. The gland was then repacked by the ship's engineers. Later that day the two men went down again to remove the wrapping.

A year later *Carmania* was cruising from Port Everglades when problems with US fire regulations led to the cancellation of her Christmas

Below *The* Ivernia *was renamed* Franconia *and refitted for cruising.* (J.K. Byass)

Bottom *An aerial view of the* Franconia *in the Solent.* (Skyfotos Ltd)

Top The Sylvania (on the left) and Carinthia, now with a black hull and renamed Fairland, together with the Caronia, laid up at 101 berth in Southampton Docks awaiting sale. (Wayne Morris)

Above Fairland (ex-Carinthia) still alongside at Southampton Docks, but on her own. (F.R. Sherlock)

cruise. Modifications were made and she sailed for her next cruise on 11 January 1969. It was to be a 12-day voyage to the Caribbean with her first port of call at St Thomas in the US Virgin Islands. However, on the afternoon of Sunday

12 January, at high tide, she was cruising parallel to the shore when she ran aground on a sandbank a mile off the west side of San Salvador Island in the Bahamas. It was five days before she was refloated, and by then the rest of the cruise had to be cancelled, and her passengers were transferred to the Italian liner Flavia (ex-Media of 1947), for the voyage back to Miami.

After an inspection by divers, Carmania went to Newport News, Virginia, for repairs, and she was out of service until 8 February 1969. At an enquiry in Southampton it was found that there was a fault in the Admiralty chart of the area. Three months later, on 11 May, the Carmania was in collision with the Russian ship Frunze, but damage to both ships was slight and it made little difference to her cruising programme.

In early 1970 the two Cunard ships changed their port of registry from Liverpool to Southampton, but the company still had financial problems. Fuel and staffing costs were extremely high and even with a full passenger list it was still possible for them to lose money. In 1971 it was clear that both ships would require a refit and modernization, and once again it was going to be costly. Several British shipyards were approached for estimates, and Cunard even considered asking the Greek line Chandris to undertake the work. This would have involved selling the ships to them, with Cunard acting as managers. None of these plans came to anything, and later in the year it was decided to lay up both ships and offer them for sale.

In October 1971, when crossing from Florida for the last time under the Cunard houseflag, Franconia went to the aid of the Norwegian bulk carrier Anatina. The Norwegian ship was on fire and Franconia's launch took off eight of her crew members. In December that year both Franconia and Carmania were laid up at Southampton, and four months later it was reported that a deal was imminent with Tokyo Yusen of Japan, but this came to nothing. Then there were rumours that C.Y. Tung, the Hong Kong shipping magnate, was interested, but it soon became clear that there was in fact no immediate purchaser, and on 14 May 1972 the ships were removed to the River Fal for further lay-up.

Meanwhile, Sitmar had renamed the *Carinthia* and *Sylvania*, *Fairland* and *Fairwind* respectively but, apart from changing the funnel colours, they did little else. Finally, in January 1970, they found that the Trieste yard of Arsenale Triestino–San Marco was willing to refurbish both vessels simultaneously, so that same month they sailed for Italy and a refit which would change them beyond recognition. *Fairland* was for some reason renamed *Fairsea*, and entered service for Sitmar in November 1971. She was followed in July 1972 by *Fairwind*. Both ships now had a gross tonnage of 25,000, and were registered in Liberia. They could now carry 925 passengers in one class, and had a mixed Portuguese and Italian crew numbering 450 for each vessel. They had been completely rebuilt from the lower machinery spaces up, and were to be based in North America. They boasted 11 passenger decks, and facilities included a 330-seat theatre, five nightclubs and lounges, two restaurants, three swimming pools and many other facilities now taken for granted by cruising passengers.

The *Fairwind* was based at Fort Lauderdale, Florida, and she offered cruises of seven, ten and eleven days through the Panama Canal to Mexico and Puerto Rico. During the summer months she operated from San Francisco on 14-day cruises to Canada and Alaska. Both ships operated profitably for their owners and in 1988 they passed into British ownership once again when P&O purchased the Sitmar Line.

Carmania and *Franconia* had lain at Falmouth for 15 months when, in August 1973, they were sold to a Panamanian company, Nikreis Maritime Corporation, which was acting as agents for the Russian Black Sea Shipping Company. It was a strange transaction which could almost be described as furtive, as if the participants were ashamed to be involved. Then, as the deal was concluded, it was announced that both vessels would fly the red flag of the Soviet Union and that the *Carmania* would be renamed *Leonid Sobinov* and *Franconia* was to become *Fedor Shalyapin*. Shortly afterwards, CTC Lines, which

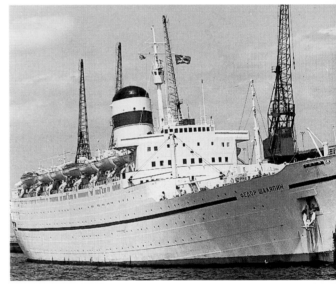

Top *The* Leonid Sobinov, *formerly the* Saxonia/ Carmania. (F.R. Sherlock)

Above *The* Fedor Shalyapin, *formerly the* Ivernia/ Saxonia. (F.R. Sherlock)

was to market the vessels, announced that both vessels were to sail for Australia after they had been refitted on the Tyne.

The two ships were overhauled by Swan Hunters at South Shields and, on 20 November 1973, *Fedor Shalyapin* sailed from Southampton for Australia where she was to be based. She was followed in February 1974 by *Leonid Sobinov*. During the summer months she would be used by her new owners for cruising and for voyages between the UK and Australia. In May 1976 Shaw Savill Cruises of Australia chartered *Fedor Shalyapin* for six months, and it was towards the end of this period that a rather intriguing incident occurred. During a crossing of the Tasman Sea between Auckland and Sydney, the ship came to a sudden halt in the early hours of the morning, and all lights were extinguished. Those passengers still about heard clanking and the ship's cranes start up, and upon scanning the gloom they witnessed a submarine coming alongside. According to witnesses, goods and personnel were transferred to the submarine and vice versa. Upon the return to Sydney both the Russian Embassy and Shaw Savill denied the incident (but would Shaw Savill have known about it anyway?). A letter to the Australian press was signed by over 200 passengers, who could not all have been mistaken.

In December 1979, when Soviet troops invaded Afghanistan, the Australian Government banned Russian passenger ships from operating from that country and they were given until February 1980 to leave. *Leonid Sobinov* was first to go, followed a week or so later by *Fedor Shalya-pin*. From there it is believed that they went initially to Vladivostock and Nahodka on Russia's Pacific coast. This is the base of the Russian Far East Shipping Company, and a large military area. In the summer of 1980 it is believed that both vessels were being used by the Cuban Government to transport troops to Angola.

Fedor Shalyapin called at Southampton on 23 June 1984 while on a cruise to Genoa and the Far East. Whatever her present role it is certainly one which could never have been envisaged all those years ago when Lady Churchill named the first of the four ships.

Technical data

Gross tonnage	22,592 (*Saxonia*), 22,637 (*Ivernia*), 21,947 (*Carinthia*), 22,017 (*Sylvania*)
Net tonnage	11,721, (*Saxonia, Ivernia*), 11,630 (*Carinthia*), 11,679 (*Sylvania*)
Length overall	608 ft (185.32m)
Breadth	80 ft 3 in (24.46m)

All ships twin screw, powered by two sets of double reduction geared turbines; 24,500 SHP, 20 knots.

30
Queen Elizabeth 2, 1969

The QE2 is the last of the great Cunarders which was built for service on the North Atlantic, although that role was to be a very minor one because essentially she is a cruise ship. It was back in December 1958 that the question of a replacement for the *Queen Mary* and the *Queen Elizabeth* first arose, and in April the following year Cunard began talks with John Brown & Co and Government representatives from the Ministry of Transport. Originally Cunard planned to replace both the *Queens* and it was intended that the new liners should by 80,000 tonners. It was clear, however, that to build ships of this size the company would need a Government subsidy of some sort, and the company's main arguments in favour of this was the national prestige attached to such ships. However, even in the later 1950s there were doubts as to whether two ships of that size would be able to pay their way, and a committee under Lord Chandos was set up to report on the whole question of a replacement for the *Queens*. The committee finally came up with a recommendation that the Government provide a grant of £18 million to build a vessel of 75,000 gross tons to replace the *Queen Mary*, the total cost of which was to be £30 million and the ship was to be ready for service by 1966.

In March 1961 Cunard invited tenders for its new ship, whilst in Parliament the North Atlantic Shipping Bill was debated. Although the stage appeared to be set for the building of

another vessel, there were some disturbing statistics which spoke for themselves. In 1948 240,000 people crossed the Atlantic by air and 637,000 by sea, whilst ten years later in 1958, 1,193,000 people crossed the Atlantic by air and 958,000 crossed by sea. The trends were clear for everyone to see.

The main opposition to Cunard's plan came from an unexpected quarter, a group of shareholders who described the plan as 'a floating groundnut scheme'. In August 1961, when it seemed almost certain that the contract for the Q3, as the new ship had been code-named, would go to John Brown & Co, Mr Raymond Gregory, a Cunard shareholder, led a fierce opposition to the plan. Two months later it appeared that his opposition was paying off, for in October 1961 Sir John Brocklebank announced that the Q3 was to be postponed while the company re-assessed its future. At last Cunard was facing the fact that first class passengers were tending to cross the Atlantic by air, and that the steeply rising operating costs for the big liners could not be offset by fare increases. By June 1962, with the company losses running at £1,700,000 and no dividend being paid to its shareholders, it seemed that Cunard could not replace the *Queens*.

However, Cunard decided to re-plan the venture, and in early 1963 the idea was formed for a ship of 55,000 to 65,000 gross tons which was suitable for cruising and could traverse both the

Panama and Suez Canals. At this stage the company still had in mind a three-class vessel, but it was early days and this would eventually be altered. In July that year the plans for *Q4*, as the vessel was now known, received a setback when the Government refused to provide a special loan, which they had been willing to do with *Q3*. However, Cunard was advised to apply for a loan under the Government's new shipbuilding credit scheme. This time, with Mr Gregory and the shareholders in favour of the scheme, the company promptly applied for assistance and a loan of £17,600,000 at 4½ per cent over ten years from the delivery date was agreed. The best tender was received from John Brown & Co at Clydebank and the order went to them. The total cost of the ship was to be £25,427,000, with the balance of £7,800,000 coming from the company's own resources and from investment allowances, in equal quantities. The keel-laying ceremony took place on Friday 2 July 1965, but this was marred slightly by a 180-ton section of welded double bottom which refused to budge. However, this problem was overcome and on Monday 5 July the section was placed into position. By coincidence this took place during the 125th anniversary celebrations of Samuel Cunard's first obtaining the contract for the transatlantic mail service.

The building of *Q4* was surrounded by publicity, most of it detrimental. The delivery date for the vessel had been given as May 1968, and it was becoming clear that this would not be met. The labour troubles in the builder's yard were a source of continual comment, and there were rumours that Cunard would have liked to cancel the contract, but it was considered that it had gone past the point of no return. One piece of good news was that the ship was to carry two and not three classes of passenger. In January 1967 it was announced that Her Majesty the Queen would launch the vessel on 20 September that year, and that work would be completed in November 1968.

Despite the royal patronage, there were continual petty industrial disputes at the yard and at one time a strike on launching day was threat-

The QE2 fitting out on the Clyde. (J.K. Byass)

ened. There was much speculation about the vessel's name and, following the withdrawal of the second ship of the name, *Mauretania* appears to have been the media's favourite. In the week of the launching ceremony it was learned that the cost of the ship was to be £28½ million, some £3 million more than the contract price. For Cunard help came in the form of an additional Government loan, but for John Brown & Co (which was now part of Upper Clyde Shipbuilders), it meant a heavy financial loss, with worse to come.

Wednesday 20 September 1967 was fine and dry on the Clyde, and Her Majesty the Queen, accompanied by the Duke of Edinburgh and Princess Margaret, arrived shortly after noon. There were some 30,000 spectators in the shipyard and thousands more on the river bank opposite, for no one doubted that this was the last in a long line of big Cunarders to be launched at the yard. At 2.30 pm Her Majesty Queen Elizabeth II named the ship *Queen Elizabeth the Second* and the new ship was sent thundering stern first into the Clyde. The vessel's name was styled *Queen Elizabeth 2* by Cunard, and it was hailed by all but a few in Scotland who did not recognize the first Queen Elizabeth.

In July 1968 it was announced that the ship would have four maiden voyages, preceded by a dress rehearsal charity cruise over Christmas 1968. The voyages were scheduled as follows:

23-27 December 1968 Rehearsal cruise — ship being chartered to a charity who would sell the tickets.

10 January 1969 Four-day mini-cruise from Southampton; the vessel would head for the best weather within 750 miles of the port.

17 January 1969 A 13-day voyage to New York, via the Canaries and the West Indies.

1 February 1969 Maiden cruise from New York to the West Indies, followed by two more.

11 March 1969 Maiden westbound voyage from New York to Southampton, via the West Indies and the Canaries.

She would then start a regular transatlantic service with fares from £102 tourist and £185 first class (compared with £88 tourist and £179 first class on the *Queen Elizabeth*). The charity cruise was organized by the Duchess of Roxburghe and the ship was to be chartered by the Society for Cancer Relief.

The *QE2's* first master was Captain Eldon Warwick, who had started his career with Cunard in 1937 as third officer of the *Lancastria*. On Tuesday 19 November 1968, with HRH The Prince of Wales on board, the *QE2* made her first move from the builder's yard to the Scott Lithgow drydock at Greenock to prepare for her trials and maiden voyage. A week later

A 'cut-away' plan of the QE2 issued by Cunard. (Cunard)

she started her trials, some 48 hours behind schedule due to high winds, and then came the first of her technical problems. The valve in a fuel oil heat exchanger had leaked and furnace fuel oil had found its way into the boiler feed water system. This meant docking the vessel for repairs which entailed flushing the feed water system. Consequently the Christmas charity cruise was cancelled, but it was still thought that she would be ready for 10 January 1969. The trials were resumed on 17 December and on the following day on her full power trials she achieved just over 32 knots.

On 23 December the *QE2* left Greenock for her final acceptance trails with 500 Cunard employees and their families on board to test the vessel's services. Also on board were over 200 Clyde shipworkers who were finishing the fitting-out work in readiness for the new hand-over date, which was set for 1 January 1969. The trial voyage was routed south to the Canary Islands and back to Southampton where she would be accepted. However, on Christmas Eve, as she steamed south, trouble was experienced with both the ship's turbines. It started with vibration and then serious overheating. Sir Basil Smallpiece and the chairman of UCS flew out to Las Palmas, and because of the engine trouble, together with the uncompleted accommodation, it was announced that Cunard was refusing to accept delivery of the vessel.

The *QE2* steamed home to Southampton at 14 knots and arrived at the port at 1.30 pm on 2 January 1969 with no ceremony and only a few hundred spectators. When the turbine

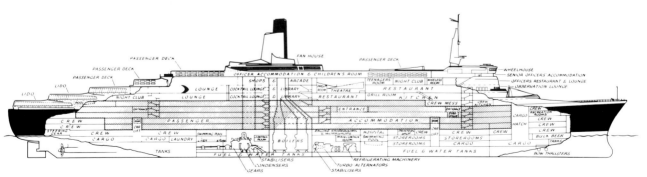

A starboard view of the QE2 at anchor in the Solent.
(Maritime Photo Library)

covers were lifted it was found that blades had been stripped on both rotors, and tests revealed that the blades were not in fact thick enough, a design fault on the part of Pametrada (the company which designed the *QE2*'s turbines, an acronym from Parsons Marine Engine & Turbine Research & Development Association). All the *QE2*'s maiden voyages were cancelled as it was obviously going to take some weeks to resolve the problem. Finally, on 23 March 1969, static tests on new rotors which had been fitted were carried out in dock, and on the following day the vessel sailed for engine tests in the Chan-

The Queen's Room. (Cunard)

nel. These were successful, as were her acceptance trials which consisted of a voyage as far south as Dakar and back.

The *QE2* is a twin screw ship, each propeller originally being driven by a set of double reduction steam turbines, which comprised an HP and a double-flow LP turbine. The steam was supplied by three Foster–Wheeler high pressure water tube boilers at 1,000°F and 850 psi. She was the largest twin screw passenger liner ever built at that time, and the 110,000 SHP for which her steam turbines were designed gave her a service speed of 28½ knots. She was originally designed to carry 564 first, and 1,979 tourist class passengers when on the North Atlantic, and 1,400 passengers in one class when cruising. Ten of her 13 decks are devoted to the passengers, with ten lounges, two libraries, 11 bars, two nightclubs, a shopping arcade, a theatre and two outdoor and two indoor swimming pools. With her raked bow, heavy single mast abaft the bridge, tall slender funnel placed amidships and terraced decks aft, the *QE2* was very different from any of her predecessors, but she could still be recognized as a Cunarder.

On 1 May 1969, on the eve of her maiden departure for New York, the *QE2* was visited by Her Majesty the Queen. On the following day, which was grey and wet, the great liner sailed from Southampton and thousands of well-wishers cheered her off. Five days later, in New York, she received a tumultuous welcome as she steamed majestically into the harbour. At last she was in service and her teething troubles were over, and with good bookings for the summer season the future looked good for the new ship. The *QE2*'s first summer was indeed successful, and on each voyage she carried over 1,500 passengers. For Cunard too the financial position was much improved, and by October 1969 the company had repaid £2½ million of the Government loans with the remaining £12 million to be repaid over the following 12 years.

QE2's first dramatic incident happened on Friday 8 January 1971 when she was cruising in the Caribbean. At 5.30 pm that evening she was anchored off Castries in St Lucia when she received an SOS call from the French liner *Antilles* which had run aground half a mile north of Mustique on a voyage from San Juan to Le Havre, and escaping fuel oil had caught fire inside the ship. At just before 8 pm, the *QE2* weighed anchor and by 10.30 pm had reached the *Antilles*, which was by then a blazing inferno. The passengers had already been taken ashore to Mustique in the vessel's lifeboats and the *QE2*, together with the French ships *Suffren* and *Point Allegre* took them all on board during the night.

As it happened, the *QE2* only had 850 passengers on board for the cruise, so there was plenty of room for the 500 extra guests. The following day the *Antilles* capsized and broke in two; her master had paid heavily for taking his ship so close in to the island to gain a view of the sunset. Most of those rescued by the *QE2* were disembarked at Bridgetown in Barbados. It is significant that during this incident the *QE2*'s passenger figures were only 850, and throughout 1970 she had just been breaking even, but fortunately in 1971 the situation improved and the revenue earned by the vessel was up by 13 per cent.

In the summer of that year, 131 years after the founding of the company, the Cunard Steamship Company was taken over by Trafalgar House Investments Ltd and soon afterwards Mr Victor Matthews became Cunard's Chairman. On 23 April 1972, the *QE2* arrived in Southampton from New York 36 hours late. She had steamed through a hurricane in mid-Atlantic which had lasted three days, and the ship had been lashed by 100mph winds and 50 feet waves. During the storm three crew members suffered broken bones and £2,500 worth of crockery and glass was broken. At the end of the voyage, the 1,000 passengers were all presented with a cer-

Top right *The tables of the World Restaurant.* (Cunard)

Above right *The Double Lounge.* (Cunard)

Right *At sea in the Channel.* (Skyfotos Ltd)

tificate, and the 600 ladies on board each received a bouquet of flowers.

The following month, on the evening of Wednesday 17 May, the vessel was two days out of New York heading for Southampton with over 1,500 passengers on board, when Captain William Law received a message from the company's New York office to the effect that there was a bomb on board the liner which was timed to go off during the voyage. A search on board by crew members proved fruitless, but in London the Ministry of Defence decided to take every precaution and to fly bomb disposal experts to the ship.

The QE2 was about 750 miles east of Cape Race, at just after 6 pm on 18 May, when an RAF Hercules parachuted four army bomb disposal officers and their equipment into the sea close to the ship, and soon a full-scale search of the liner was under way. As it turned out, the whole incident was a hoax, but it had been treated efficiently and professionally by all those involved, as well as by the FBI who arrested the culprit who was subsequently sentenced to 20 years in prison. All the bomb disposal experts were awarded the Queen's Commendation for Brave Conduct.

By April 1974 the QE2 was earning good profits for the company; the cruising business was expanding world wide, and everything

Docking at Southampton. (J.K. Byass)

looked satisfactory for the vessel. Then suddenly calamity struck. On 1 April the QE2 was on a cruise from New York to San Juan, and in the early hours of that morning she was about 200 miles SW of Bermuda when, as a result of a fractured pipe in a heat exchanger, oil contamination in the feed water system caused the main propulsion machinery to be shut down. The ship's engineers were unable to make repairs quickly and Cunard requested help from the Oslo-based Flagship Cruises. They dispatched their vessel *Sea Venture* (now P&O's *Pacific Princess*) from Bermuda to the helpless QE2, leaving most of her own passengers in Bermuda. It was the early hours of 3 April before *Sea Venture* arrived and the transfer of the 1,654 passengers from the QE2 began, taking just over seven hours to complete. As the *Sea Venture* returned to Bermuda with her passengers, two tugs were chartered to tow the immobilized QE2 back to Bermuda where temporary repairs could be effected. One ten-day cruise over Easter was cancelled, but by 16 April permanent repairs had been carried out in New York and the QE2 could sail for Southampton on her scheduled Atlantic crossing.

Over the next few years the QE2 successfully steamed on cruises from both the USA and Southampton, now making fewer and fewer transatlantic voyages. She took part in a number of rescues at sea and by 1975 she was the only liner still employed, albeit on a part-time basis, on the North Atlantic. Everywhere she went the vessel was always worthy of attention by the world's press. By the early 1980s her world cruise had become a regular annual event.

In early December 1981, after her annual overhaul in Southampton, the QE2 left for a US cruise programme and her world cruise from New York. During her New Year Caribbean cruise she went aground for about an hour at the entrance to San Juan Harbour, but no damage was done and she continued her voyage. She sailed on her world cruise from New York on 17 January 1982, and apart from a minor fire in the engine room whilst *en route* for Pusan in South Korea, the voyage was uneventful. How-

Above and above right *Two views of the* QE2 *at Ocean Terminal, Southampton.* (Neil McCart)

ever, world events had been far from uneventful and on 2 April 1982 the Argentinians invaded the Falkland Islands.

For the first few weeks this did not affect the *QE2*. She arrived back from the USA on 16 April and four days later left on an Atlantic crossing to Philadelphia with 1,400 passengers for the city's tricentennial celebrations, and it seemed that the South Atlantic war had passed her by. However, as she neared Southampton on the return voyage on 3 May, she was requisitioned by the Government for service as a troop transport. The order for the requisitioning was released early in London and it came as a surprise to Captain Alex Hutchison and his crew.

As soon as the ship was alongside at Southampton moves began to start the conversion work. Helicopter flight decks were built forward and aft and a modern communications system was installed. After embarking troops of the 5th Infantry Brigade, which comprised men of the Scots and Welsh Guards and the Gurkha Rifles, she left Southampton's 38/39 berth for South Georgia at 4 pm on 12 May, commanded by Captain Peter Jackson. She arrived at the lonely little South Atlantic island on 27 May where she rendezvoused with the P&O liner *Canberra*

in Cumberland Bay on the east coast. By the afternoon of 29 May the transfer of troops and stores was completed and the *QE2* took on board survivors from HMS *Ardent* for passage to the UK. It had also become clear that the Argentinians were using a Boeing 707 aircraft to search the South Atlantic for the Cunard liner, and it was obvious that the ship was very vulnerable at South Georgia. She left Cumberland Bay later that afternoon and during the night she steamed slowly north through a large field of icebergs.

QE2 in pale grey livery after her service in the South Atlantic. (A. Duncan)

The *QE2* arrived back in Southampton on Friday 11 June to a tumultuous welcome, which included a message from Her Majesty the Queen. Since leaving Southampton on 12 May she had steamed 14,967 miles, and of course she had been a vulnerable and prestigious target for

Left *The last of the QE2's new diesel engines being lifted into the ship during her major refit in 1986-87.* (Ralf Witthohn)

Below left *The QE's new funnel.* (Caroline McCart)

Below *The final stage of the major refit, with the new funnel in place.* (Ralf Witthohn)

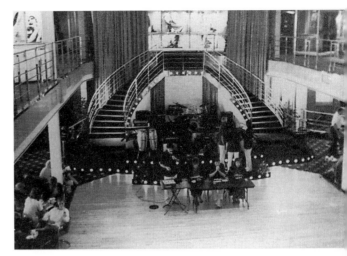

Top left *The Magradome lido deck.* (Cunard)

Top right *The Grand Lounge now has a horseshoe-shaped staircase.* (Ted Scull)

Above *The QE2 at Southampton showing her new profile.* (F.R. Sherlock)

the Argentinian Air Force. Work to restore her to her peacetime condition started the following day and lasted for nine weeks. When she emerged she had been given a light grey hull livery which, although it improved her looks, was difficult to maintain and she reverted to her traditional Cunard colours in June 1983.

In November 1983 the QE2 was sent for her annual overhaul to Bremerhaven, which caused a stir in the British media, and during the refit a magradome was fitted over the lido swimming pool on the quarter deck. Following her return to service in mid-December there were problems with the ship's boilers, which caused the cancellation of a cruise and more coverage in the press, but the ship soon settled down again. In April 1984 she suffered minor damage after colliding with a breakwater at Piraeus, and repairs were made when the ship called at Lisbon a few days later. In October that year the vessel was homeward bound from New York when an electrical fire caused a complete loss of power on board for a number of hours. The damage was

repaired by the ship's engineers, but she was two days late arriving in Southampton. It was thus no real surprise when in the following month, Sir Nigel Broackes, the Chairman of Trafalgar House, announced that serious consideration was being given to replacing the *QE2*'s steam propulsion machinery with diesel engines.

The contract went to the Lloyd Werfte yard at Bremerhaven, which again provoked reaction in the British press and led to questions being asked in Parliament. The steam turbine machinery in *QE2* had never given total satisfaction to her owners and the re-engining of the ship was designed to reduce fuel costs by £12 million a year and to extend the vessel's life by 20 years. It had been decided to replace the steam turbines by nine MAN B&W L58/64 diesel-electric engines, which would provide 1110,000 SHP and give a service speed of 28½ knots. They were to be complemented by waste heat equipment which would utilize heat expelled from the engines to provide hot water for the passengers' use. Her two six-bladed propellers were also to be replaced by two five-bladed controllable pitch propellers. There were also many improvements to the ship's passenger facilities, perhaps the most apparent of which was to remodel the double lounge to provide two curving staircases on each side of a retractable stage. New terraced seating was provided to offer comfortable viewing for the entertainments provided.

Altogether the work cost £100 million and kept the *QE2* out of service from 1 November 1986 to 29 April 1987, when she underwent trials in the North Sea. The most obvious external sign of the changes to the vessel was the new chunkier funnel which had been fitted and which enhanced the ship's good looks more than anything else which could have been done. Since the refit there have been a few teething troubles which, as usual, received more than their fair share of publicity in the press. However, regardless of this the transformation of the vessel from the 'SS' to the 'MV' *Queen Elizabeth 2* has been a success, and it should take the last of the great Cunarders into the twenty-first century.

Above far left *The QE2.*

Far left *The QE2 on her trials in the North Sea following her refit.* (Financial Times)

Left and above left *The QE2 at Southampton, summer 1987.* (Caroline McCart)

Technical data

Gross tonnage	65,863
Net tonnage	38,244
Length overall	963 feet (293.52m)
Breadth	105 feet (32m)

Twin screw, originally powered by two sets of double reduction geared turbines; 110,000 SHP, 28.5 knots. 1987 — Nine MAN B&W 9 L58/64 diesel-electric engines; 110,000 SHP, 28.5 knots.

Bibliography

The Big Blockade, E. Keble Chatterton (Hurst & Blackett 1923).

British Vessels Lost at Sea, 1914–18 (HMSO/ Patrick Stephens Ltd 1980).

British Vessels Lost at Sea, 1939–45 (HMSO/ Patrick Stephens Ltd 1980).

Warships of World War One, H.M. Le Fleming (Ian Allan Ltd).

Seven Days to Disaster, Des Hickey & Gus Smith (William Collins Ltd 1981).

Lusitania, Colin Simpson (Penguin Books 1983).

Gray Ghost — The RMS Queen Mary at War, Steve Harding (Pictorial Histories Publishing Company 1982).

Merchant Fleets in Profile (Vol 2), Duncan Haws (Patrick Stephens Ltd 1979).

Great Passenger Ships of the World (Volumes 1–6), Arnold Kludas (Patrick Stephens Ltd 1980–86).

Transatlantic Liners 1945-80, William H. Miller (David & Charles 1981).

Shipping Wonders of the World (Volumes 1 & 2) (Clarence Winchester 1925).

Ocean Liners of the Past — The Cunard Quadruple Screw Atlantic Liner Aquitania (The Shipbuilder/Patrick Stephens Ltd 1971).

Ocean Liners of the Past — The Cunard Express Liners Lusitania & Mauretania (Shipping World & Shipbuilder/Patrick Stephens Ltd 1979).

Hospital Ships & Ambulance Trains, Lt Colonel John H. Plumridge OBE RA (Seeley Service & Co Ltd 1975).

Troopships and their History, Colonel H.C.B. Rogers OBE (Seeley Service & Co Ltd 1973).

The Blue Riband of the Atlantic, Tom Hughes (Patrick Stephens Ltd 1973).

Armed Merchant Cruisers — Their Epic Story, Kenneth Poolman (Secker & Warburg 1985).

Lancastria, Geoffrey Bond (Oldbourne Press 1959).

Merchant Fleets (Vol 12 — Cunard Line), Duncan Haws (TCL Publications 1987).

The Blockaders, A. Cecil Hampshire (William Kimber & Co Ltd 1980).

The Only Way To Cross, John Maxtone Graham (Patrick Stephens Ltd 1983).

Liners to the Sun, John Maxtone Graham (Macmillan Publishing Co 1985).

Gallipoli Memories, Compton Mackenzie (Cassell & Co Ltd 1929).

Famous Rescues at Sea, Richard Garrett (Arthur Barker Ltd 1977).

Leviathan (Vol 1), Frank O. Braynard (South Street Seaport Museum 1972).

RMS Queen Mary — 50 Years of Splendour, David F. Hutchings (Kingfisher Railway Productions 1986).

American Passenger Ships 1873–1983, Frederick E. Emmons (University of Delaware Press 1985).

A Night to Remember, Walter Lord (Penguin Books 1978).

Titanic — Destination Disaster: The Legends and the Reality, John P. Eaton & Charles Haas

(Patrick Stephens Ltd 1987).

Titanic — Triumph and Tragedy: A chronicle in words and pictures, John P. Eaton & Charles Haas (Patrick Stephens Ltd 1987).

The Titanic — End of a Dream, Wyn Craig Wade (Futura Publications Ltd 1980).

The Story of the Titanic — As Told by its Survivors, Jack Winocour (Dover Publications Inc 1960).

Coronel & The Falklands, Geoffrey Bennett (B.T. Batsford Ltd 1962).

The Ship That Hunted Itself, Colin Simpson (Weidenfeld & Nicolson 1977).

QE2, Ronald Warwick & William Flayhart (W.W. Norton & Co 1985).

The Cunard Story, Howard Johnson (Whitlet Books Ltd 1987).

Queen Elizabeth At War — His Majesty's Transport 1939-1946, Chris Konings (Patrick Stephens Ltd 1985).

Majesty At Sea — The Four Stackers, John H. Shaum & William Flayhart (Patrick Stephens Ltd 1981).

The Cunard Turbine Driven Quadruple Screw Atlantic Liner Lusitania, ed Mark D. Warren (Engineering/Patrick Stephens Ltd 1986).

The Cunard Turbine Driven Quadruple Screw Atlantic Liner Mauretania, ed Mark D. Warren (Engineering/Patrick Stephens Ltd 1987).

Wings Over The Sea — A History of Naval Aviation, David Wragg (David & Charles 1979).

Wings Across the World — A History of British Airways, Harold Penrose (Cassell Ltd 1980).

The Sway of the Grand Saloon, John Malcolm Brinnin (Arlington Books (Publishers) Ltd 1986).

Unpublished Sources

Admiralty Records held by the Ministry of Defence.

Admiralty Records held by the Public Record Office.

Department of Trade/Department of Transport Records held by the Public Record Office.

Department of Transport Records held by the General Register of Shipping & Seamen held at Cardiff.

Cunard Records held by the University of Liverpool.

Newspapers

The Times, London.
Daily Telegraph.
New York Times.
New York Tribune.
South China Morning Post.
Cork Examiner.

Index

Abraham Rydberg, 84
Admiral Scheer, 149
Ainderby, 145, 146
Alaunia 1913, 87, 93-96
Alaunia 1925, 119, 157-164
Alaunia HMS, 163
Albania 1911, 86-88, 93
Albania 1921, 123-124
Alcantara, 154
Alcock, Mr John, 79
Alexander Stephens & Co, shipbuilders, 207
American Banker, 54
American Expeditionary Force, 103
American Hunter, 200
American Merchant Lines, 54
American Ocean S N Co, 12
Anatina, 220
Anchor Line, 27, 138
Andania 1913, 87, 93-96
Andania 1922, 144-151
Anderson, Sir Kenneth, 162
Andes, 174, 187
Andrew Jackson, 19
Annamite, 136
Antilles, 227
Antonia, 144-151
Aquitania 1914, 13, 97-109, 130, 174, 187, 191, 196, 209
Arabia, 12
Aramac, 207
Arctic, 12
Ardent HMS, 229
Ark Royal HMS, 27
Ark Royal HMS (1937), 185
Armistice Commission, 136
Armstrong Whitworth, Sir W.G. & Co, shipbuilders, 104, 117, 120, 144, 157
Artifex HMS, 149, 162
Ascania, 1911, 86-88
Ascania 1925, 157-164, 214, 215
Asia, 63

Audacious, 35
Audra, Madame Ruth, 143
Aurania 1913, 93-96
Aurania 1925, 149, 157-164
Aurania HMS, 160, 161, 167
Ausonia 1911, 86-88
Ausonia 1922, 144-151
Ausonia HMS, 144, 148-151

Badger, W. & Co, 150
Baillie, Mr C., 186
Bain, Captain D.K., 147
Bain, Mr James, 56
Baker, Mr C.J., 149
Baldebutte, 54
Ballin, Albert, 40, 62, 110, 111, 114
Bandit, 167
Bank Line, 86
Barnes, Mrs A., 205
Barr, Captain J.C., 43, 49, 50
Barrett, Captain John F.B. RN, 167, 168
Batavia 1870, 14
Batavia 1899, 40
Bates, Lady, 185
Battenburg, Princess, 86
Battenburg, Vice Admiral Louis, 86
Beardmore, Lady, 138
Beardmore, Sir William, 138
Beaverbrae, 159
Beaverhill, 159
Beazley, Mrs J.H., 129
Bell, Mr Thomas, 71
Bellucia, 159
Ben-My-Chree HMS, 27
Berengaria 1920, 12, 13, 54, 104, 110-122, 126, 191
Berkeley HMS, 167
Berlin, 51
Bermuda, 153
Bernard, Captain Vivian H.G. RN, 64
Bethlehem Steel Corporation, 175
Bismarck, 110
Bisset, Captain Sir James, 175

Black Cock, 21
Black Sea Shipping Co, 221
Bluebell HMS, 68
Blytheswood, Lady, 48
Bode, Baron de, 76
Bohemia, 17, 18
Boot, Mr Charles, 84
Booth, Sir Alfred, 79
Bramham HMS, 177
Bremen, 13, 82, 171
Brio, 145
Britannia, 11
Britannic, 103, 145
British Honduras, 168
British India Line, 38, 39
British Iron & Steel Corporation, 107, 128, 131, 132, 156, 162, 190
British North American SP Co, 12
British Statesman, 146
Britten, Captain Sir Edgar, 102, 119, 173
Broakes, Sir Nigel, 233
Brocklebank, Sir John, 181, 196, 218, 223
Brooke, Lady, 205
Brown, Captain A.T., 85, 186
Brown, Captain F.G., 123
Brown, Mr Arthur W., 79
Brown, Mr Ernest G.F., 45
Burfitt, CPO John, 51
Burns, Lady G.A., 23, 31
Burns, Sir G.A., 23, 55
Butlin, Sir Billy, 181

Cairnrona, 86
Cairns, Mr Russel, 86
Cairns Noble & Co, 86
Caledonia, 131
California, 124
Cameronia, 138
Cammel Laird & Co, shipbuilders, 129, 134, 146, 185, 189
Campania 1893, 12, 21-30, 55
Canada, 16

Canadian, 102
Canadian Expeditionary Force, 78
Canadian Northern SS Co, 49
Canberra, 229
Capellini, 136
Cap Trafalgar, 50, 51
Caribia, 211, 213
Carinthia 1925, 165-168
Carinthia 1956, 211, 214-222
Carlisle, Mr A.M., 76
Carmania 1905, 46-54, 64
Carmania 1954, 190, 206, 218-222
Caronia 1905, 46-54, 63, 102, 126
Caronia 1949, 208-213
Carpathia 1903, 42-45, 50, 63
Cashmore, J., shipbreakers, 162
Cedric, 126
Chamberlain, Mr Neville, 13, 170, 172,
    191
Chandos, Lord, 223
Chatterton, Lt Keble, 68
Cherbourg, 63
Children Overseas Reception Board, 126
Choate, Mr, US Ambassador, 46
Choate, Mrs J., 46
Churchill, Lady, 214
Churchill, Sir Winston, 143, 179, 180
Cia Genovese d'Armamento, 206
City of New York, 22
City of Paris, 16, 22, 23
City of Worcester, 206
Coke, Admiral, 35
Collins Line, 12
Columbia, 211-214
Columbian, 90
Consuelo, 86
Cook, Captain Theodore, 15
Cook, Thomas, travel agents, 130
Costa Armatori SPA, 206
Cotes, Miss, 26
Cottam, Harold, 44, 45
Cotterell, Mr E.C., 104
Cove, Captain G.E., 107
CTC Lines, 221
Cunard, Mr E.H., 62
Cunard, Henry, 11
Cunard, Joseph, 11
Cunard, Sir Samuel, 11, 12, 224
Curacoa HMS, 176-178, 180
Currie, Mr, 75

Davis-Richter, Mr H., 186
Dawson, Mr F.H., 216
Denby, Mr A.J., 140
Derby, Countess of, 97
Deutschland, 62
Dinwoodie, Mrs J., 163
Dobson, Able Seaman H.E., 137
Dolphin, Captain G.R., 140
Domus Turist, 211
Donitz, Grand Admiral Karl, 133
Dovic Shipyard, 155
Dow, Captain David, 66

Dreadnought HMS, 69, 70
Dresden, 77
Duck, Captain, 17
Duff-Cooper, Alfred, 172
Duff-Cooper, Lady Diana, 172

Eastern & Australian SS Co, 207
Edinburgh Castle, 108
Edinburgh, HRH Duke of, 209, 224
Edward VIII, HRH King, 170, 173
Edward B. Winslow, 52
Egerton, Countess of, 23
Eisenhower, General Dwight D., 189
Elbe, 20
Elizabeth, HRH Queen, 191, 197
Elizabeth II, HRH Queen, 173, 197, 224,
    226, 230
Elizabeth, HRH Princess, 173, 197, 208,
    224
Embleton, 25
Empire Waveney, 197
Empire Windrush, 108
Empress HMS, 27
Empress of Australia, 120, 154
Empress of Britain, 105, 130
Empress of Ireland, 99, 100
Empress of Scotland, 129
Engadine HMS, 27
Eppich, Mr Martin G., 180
Eskimo HMS, 130
Etruria 1884, 14-21
Europa, 1930, 13, 82
Europa (Imperator), 110
Eversley, Lord, 101

Fairey Campania, 27, 28
Fairfield Shipbuilding Co, 22
Fairland, 221, 222
Fairwind, 221, 222
Fedor Shalyapin, 221, 222
Ferguson, Captain, 17, 18
Fitzgerald, Vice Admiral, 16
Flavia, 206, 220
Flavian, 206
Formidable HMS, 163
Forwood, Lady, 89
Fowler, Captain Cole C. RN, 64, 77
Franconia 1911, 89-92
Franconia 1923, 152-156, 165, 214
Franconia 1955, 190, 218-222
Freyburg, Captain G. CBE RN, 149
Freyburg, Major General Bernard VC,
    149
Frunze, 220
Furious HMS, 29, 105, 130
Furness Bermuda Line, 153
Furness, Sir Christopher, 38
Furness Withy, 153

Galileo, 16, 17
Gallia, 17, 18
George Balfour, 131

George III, HRH King, 98
George V, HRH King, 76, 170
George VI, HRH King, 191
George, HRH Prince, Duke of Kent, 105
Georgic, 145
Gerona, 87
Gerrad, Mr C., 186
Gibbons, Captain George, 121
Gill, Mr Macdonald, 172
Gladstone, William Ewart, 101
Gleaner HMS, 167
Gloene, 136
Glorious HMS, 29
Gobrcht, Mr Hans, 144
Golden Effort HMS, 68
Goliath HMS, 52
Grant, Captain Noel RN, 50, 52
Grattidge, Captain H., 177
Great Eastern, 14, 22
Great Western Railway Co, 76
Gregory, Mr Raymond, 223, 224
Gunderson, Captain, 17
Gurkha Rifles, 229

Hamburg, 212
Hamburg-Amerika Line, 40, 62, 110, 114
Hamburg-South Amerika Line, 50
Hampton & Sons, Auctioneers, 107
Hankinson, Mr Thomas W., 45
Harker, Dr J.A., 95
Harland, Sir Edward, 23
Harland & Wolff, shipbuilders, 23, 102,
    103, 149, 205, 210
Harper, Mr Henry J., 17, 18
Hartenstein, Lt Commander, 136
Hat Creek, 187
Havelock HMS, 142
Haverford, 62
Hawthorne Leslie & Co, shipbuilders,
    144
Hay, Miss Elizabeth, 92
Hay, Mrs Mary, 92
Hellespont, 35
Hennesey, Mr George, 77
Hermes HMS, 163
Hindenberg, airship, 173
Hitler, Adolf, 191
Holgate, Mr J.J., 95
Hoover, President Herbert, 118
Hope, Hon Mrs, 14
House, Colonel Edward, 66
Howe, Mrs C.D., 215
Hughes-Bolckow & Co, shipbuilders, 54
Hughes, Mr Evan H., 45
Hunter, Mr G.B., 69
Hunter, Mr H., 70
Hutchison, Captain Alex, 229
Hylan, Mayor, 36

Imperator, 12, 104, 110-117
Indomitable HMS, 163
Inglis, Mr John, 23
Inman Line, 12, 16

International Mercantile Marine (IMM), 55
International Refugee Organization, 127
Inverclyde, Lady Mary, 56, 61, 71
Inverclyde, Second Baron, 55, 56
Iredale & Porter, 25
Irvine, Captain W.R.D., 92
Irving, Captain Robert B., 174, 175
Ismay, Mr Bruce, 23
Ivernia 1900, 31-37, 63, 89
Ivernia 1955, 162, 214-222

Jackson, Captain Peter, 229
Jarvis, Sir John MP, 120, 122
Jean Jadot, 159
Jellicoe, Admiral Sir John, 28
Jervis Bay HMS, 149
John Brown & Co, shipbuilders, 31, 38, 46, 56, 57, 97, 128, 152, 155, 158, 163, 169, 180, 191, 205, 208, 214, 218, 223, 224
John Elder & Co, shipbuilders, 14
Johnstone, Mr Alexander B., 45
Jones, Captain, 18
Jutland, Battle of, 28

Kaiserin Augusta Victoria, 129
Kaiser Wilhelm II, 49
Kaiser Wilhelm der Grosse, 12, 25, 55
Kalz, Mr Willie, 194
Kelvin, Lord, 23
Kerr, Lady Anne Emily Innes, 69
King, Mr Kenneth, 219
Kirkwood, Mr David MP, 170

Laconia 1911, 89-92, 102
Laconia 1922, 130, 133-137
Laing, Sir James & Sons, 38
Lancastria 1922, 135, 138-143, 225
Large, Able Seaman A.V. BEM, 136
Larkin, Mrs Phyllis, 182
Lauder, Mr Harry, 78
Law, Captain William, 181, 228
Leonid Sobinov, 221, 222
Leuyel, Dr, 45
Leviathan HMS, 115
Lewis, Mrs Jane, 66, 67
Libia, 153
Litchfield, Captain RN, 50
Lloyds Triestino, 124
Lloyd Werfte, 223
London City & Midland Bank, 116
Loring, Captain E.K. RN, 101
Lucania 1893, 12, 21, 22-27, 30, 48, 55, 61, 62
Lusitania 1907, 12, 20, 26, 27, 31, 46, 55-68, 69, 74, 77, 89, 97, 98, 110, 112

McGee, Dr, 45
McGlasken, Lt Commander F.A.E. RN, 167
McKellar, Captain Andrew, 215, 216

McLaren, Sir Charles, 57, 61
McLean, Captain Donald M., 128, 156
McMicken, Captain, 16
McNeil, Captain, 82
MacArthur, General A., 175
MacDonald, Miss Isabel, 118
MacDonald, Mr Ramsey, 118, 170
Mackenzie, Compton, 91
M'Kay, Captain, 16, 17, 18
Macedonia HMS, 51
Magdalena, 16
Magersfontein, Battle of, 19
Majestic 1889, 22, 23
Majestic 1922, 171
Majestic HMS, 52
Maloja HMS, 160
Manchester HMS, 167
Mancroft, Lord, 181
Manhanset, 17
Manxman HMS, 27
Marauder, 167
Margaret, HRH Princess, 173, 197, 216, 224
Mariston, 52
Marr, Commodore Geoffrey, 203, 217
Martin, Mr Allin, 177
Martin, Mr Walter, 84
Mary, HRH Queen, 170, 173
Maryland, 53
Matthews, Mr Victor, 227
Mauretania 1907, 12, 13, 20, 26, 27, 31, 46, 54, 56, 57, 63, 64, 69-85, 89, 97, 102, 104, 110, 112, 157, 169
Mauretania 1939, 106, 174, 184-190, 193, 224
Maxwell, Mrs S., 125
Media 1947, 205-207, 220
Maduana, 133
Metal Industries (Salvage) Ltd, 84, 109
Meteor, 69, 70
Millpool, 158, 159
Minneapolis, 50
Minnewaska, 52
Molotov, Mr, 199
Monrovian, 17
Montclare, 159
Monowai HMNZS, 162
Montgomery, Lord, 189
Moran Towing Co, 17
Morro Castle, 84
Morton, Able Seaman Leslie N., 68
Murphy, Quartermaster, 142
Musketeer, Operation, 156

Nairana HMS, 27
Narkunda, 163
Nash, Mr Charles, 35, 67
National Steamship Co, 16
Nelson HMS, 134
Nelson, Lord, 98
Newcastle, HMS, 163
New Zealand Shipping Co, 206, 207
Nicholas II, Tsar, 154

Nicholls, Mr W.J., 95
Nigara, 101
Nikreis Maritime Corporation, 221
Nilssen, Captain, 25
Niobe HMS, 52
Noble, Admiral Sir Percy, 134
Noordam, 50
Nordeutscher Lloyd, 12, 62, 82
Normandie, 173, 174, 193

Oceanic, 20
Oceanic SN Co, 12
Odessa, 50
Olympic, 102, 110
Oram, Rear Admiral, 56
Oregan, 1883, 16
Oronsay, 141, 142

Pamir, 52
Pannonia 1903, 38-41, 42
Pan Royal, 133
Paris, 23, 24
Parry, Able Seaman Joseph, 68
Parsons, Hon C.A., 55, 61
Parthia 1870, 14
Parthia 1948, 205-207
Pearce, Sir William G. MP, 23
Peel, Captain R.V., 173
Pegasus HMS, 27
Persia, 12
Peskett, Mr L., 152
Point Allegre, 227
Potter, Captain Thomas, 34, 35
Prince of Wales, HRH, 225
Prinzess Irene, 40
Pritchard, Captain John T., 74, 75, 76

Q3, 13, 223
Q4, 202, 224
Quebec & Halifax SN Co, 11
Queen Elizabeth 1940, 13, 105, 120, 185, 191-204, 223, 225
Queen Elizabeth 2 1969, 13, 223-233
Queen Elizabeth HMS, 199
Queen Mary 1936, 13, 84, 106, 110, 159, 169-183, 185, 186, 191, 193, 202, 203, 223

Radziwill, Prince Albert, 76
Radziwill, Princess, 76
Raleigh HMS, 138
Ramillies HMS, 29
Ranger, 41
Ranpura HMS, 150, 151, 160
Ravensworth, Countess of, 13
Reid, Captain Phillip, 219
Remuera, 207
Renown HMS, 134
Revenge HMS, 29
Rifleman HMS, 36
Riley, Able Seaman E.A., 137
Risicati, Dr, 45
Riviera HMS, 27

Robertson, Mrs N.A., 216
Robinson, Captain J.H. USN, 115
Roosevelt, President Franklin D., 69, 118
Rostron, Captain Sir Arthur, 43, 44, 45,
    50, 79, 81, 84
Roxburgh, Duchess of, 69
Roxburgh, Second Duchess of, 225
Royal Dublin Fusiliers, 94
Royal Inniskilling Fusiliers, 94
Royal Mail SP Co, 170
Royal Oak HMS, 29
Royal Sovereign Lightship, 94
Royal William, 11
Royden, Lady, 152
Royden, Sir Thomas, 80, 152

Sagafjord, 13
Sagaing, 149
Samaria 1922, 105, 129-132, 133, 152, 214
Savannah, 11
Saxilby, 118, 119
Saxonia 1900, 31-37, 89
Saxonia 1954, 162, 214-222
Scham, Captain RN, 27
Scheldestadt, 140
Schwab, Mr Gustave, 63
Scots Guards, 229
Scotts Shipbuilding & Engineering Co,
    93
Scythia 1921, 125-128, 129, 133, 152, 214
Seaforth Highlanders, 19
Sea Venture, 228
Seawise University, 203
Servia 1881, 12
Servia (Carinthia 1925), 165
Sharp, Captain Rudolph CBE RD*
    RNR, 135, 137, 141-143
Shaw Savill Cruises, 222
Sims, Admiral USN, 29
Sitmar LIne 221
Skallagrinur, 147
Sklenar, Mr L., 150
Slavonia 1903, 38-41, 42
Smallpiece, Sir Basil, 181, 202, 219, 225
Smith, Captain C.A. CBE RD* RNR,
    102, 115
Smith, Captain Edward J., 44
Smith-Park, Colonel J., 138
Smith, Sub Lt S. RN, 167
Snowdrop HMS, 45
Somerville, Admiral Sir James RN, 163
Southern Railway Co, 169
St Laurent, Mme, 214
St Wistan HMS, 136

Star Shipping Co, 211
Straits Maru, 14
Suffolk HMS, 52
Suffren, 227
Surrey Scheme, 120
Swan Hunter, shipbuilders, 31, 42, 69,
    87, 89, 94, 97, 133, 157
Sylvania 1957, 211, 214-222

Tadoussac, 218
Taiseiyo Maru, 54
Teutonic, 22, 23
Thelwell, Captain Robert G., 205
Thickes, Bernhart, 194
Thomson Line, 86, 93
Thor, 196
Thorneycrofts, 80, 117
Tirpitz, Grand Admiral von, 111
Titanic, 19, 42, 43, 44
Todd Shipyard, 83
Tokyo Yusen, 220
Tomlinson, Mr, 17
Torch, Operation, 126
Tortona, 86, 87
Townley, Captain J.C., 192
Townshend, Mr A.H.E., 134
Trafalgar House Investments Ltd, 227,
    233
Treasure-Jones, Captain John, 182, 190
Triumph HMS, 52
Tung, C.Y., 203, 220
Turbinia, 56
Turner, Captain William, 36, 63, 66, 67,
    76, 98
Tweedmouth, Lord, 69
Tyrrhenia 1922, 138, 139

U46, 167
U55, 45,
U156, 135, 136
U506, 136
U507, 136
UB47, 36, 92
UB67, 96
Umbria 1884, 14-21, 63
Unicorn, 11
United States (Danish), 52
United States 1952, 181, 200
Upper Clyde Shipbuilders, 224, 225
Uranian SS Co, 49
Usworth, 159

Vaal, 202
Valparaiso, 206

Vanguard HMS, 29
Vaterland, 110, 115
Vedra, 19
Vickers Armstrong, shipbuilders, 54,
    125, 144, 165
Victoria, HRH Queen, 22, 48, 56, 69
Viking, 126
Vindex HMS, 27
Vines, Acting Leading Seaman H.J.
    BEM, 136
Vistafjord, 13
Volturno, 49, 50
Volunteer HMS, 167
Vulkan Werft, shipbuilders, 110, 114

Wabana, 128
Walker, Captain, 25
Walker, Mr J.H., 136, 137
Wallsend Slipway & Eng Co, 71
Ward, Thomas W., shipbreakers, 21, 27,
    128, 156, 190
Warr, Commodore R.C., 21, 48
Warrener, Vice Admiral Sir George, 28
Warspite HMS, 163
Warwick, Captain Eldon, 225
Warwickshire, Derbyshire & Durham
    Militia, 19
Washington, 12
Watson, Mr William, 61
Watt, Captain James B., 62, 63
Wayland HMS, 147, 148
Welsh Guards, 229
White, Sir William, 42, 70
White Star, 63
White Star Line, 12, 55, 145, 170
Wilhelm II, Kaiser, 111, 113
William Beardmore & Co, shipbuilders,
    138
William Cliff, 19, 20
William Henry, Prince, 98
Wills, Captain C.S., 90
Wilson, President Woodrow, 66
Wirth, Captain Julius, 50
Wizey, Captain D. RN, 148
Wolfe HMS, 160
Woollatt, Captain R.B.G., 108
Wren HMS, 167

Yamuna, 38, 39
York, HRH Duchess of, 173
York, HRH Duke of, 173

Ziegenbaum, Captain, 82
Zinnia HMS, 88